Children and
Anthropological
Research

Children and Anthropological Research

Edited by

Barbara Butler

University of Wisconsin—Madison
Madison, Wisconsin

and

Diane Michalski Turner

Michigan State University
East Lansing, Michigan

PLENUM PRESS • NEW YORK AND LONDON

Library of Congress Cataloging in Publication Data

Children and anthropological research.

"Based on a conference on Children in Anthropological Research, held May 1,
1982, at Michigan State University, East Lansing, Michigan"—T.p. verso.
   Includes bibliographies and indexes.
   1. Ethnology—Field work—Congresses. 2. Anthropologists—Family relationships—
Congresses. 3. Children of Anthropologists—Congresses. I. Butler, Barbara (Barbara
H.) II. Turner, Diane Michalski. III. Conference on Children in Anthropological Research
(1982: Michigan State University)
GN346.C48   1987   306′.072   86-30517
ISBN 0-306-42499-1

Based on a conference on Children in Anthropological Research,
held May 1, 1982, at Michigan State University, East Lansing, Michigan

© 1987 Plenum Press, New York
A Division of Plenum Publishing Corporation
233 Spring Street, New York, N.Y. 10013

Printed in the United States of America

PREFACE

The first time that we, the editors of this volume, met, a chance remark by one of us, newly returned from fieldwork in Fiji, quickly led to an animated discussion of our experiences doing anthropological research with children. Following that occasion, we began to seek each other out in order to continue such conversations, because we had found no other opportunity to discuss these significant events. We knew our experiences were rich sources of cross-cultural data and stimuli to rethinking anthropological theory and methods. A cursory review of the literature on fieldwork revealed, to our surprise, that fieldworker's experiences with children were rarely and only briefly mentioned (Hostetler and Huntington, 1970, are an early exception). In order to learn more about research that included the ethnographers' children, we organized a conference on the topic at Michigan State University on May 1, 1982. This volume includes papers from that conference, as well as insights and ideas from the formal and informal discussions among the conference participants and audience.

This volume, like the conference which preceded it, is intended to be an exploration of the effects of accompanying children on anthropological field research and on the effects of fieldwork on the children themselves. Additionally, we see this book as part of an anthropological inquiry into research as a cultural process, by which is meant the effects of the researchers' cultural identity--class, gender, age, ethnicity, and other characteristics--on fieldwork. For this reason we discuss the shared expectations, values and class affiliation of the contributors. More generally we reflect on the influence of the fieldworkers' gender on ethnography as well as the cultural meanings attached to professionalism, social science methodology, and the cultural division of human activities into domestic and public domains.

As part of this exploration into the wide range of issues associated with taking families into the field, each contributor focuses on a special topic in a different culture. Each article's focus emerges from the contexts in which the ethnographers found themselves and their families, and from their professional interests and personal backgrounds. Some of the insights provided by the contributors include the following: Butler, who did research among Quichua-speaking Indians in Ecuador, suggests that much of what passes for a concern with a child's well-being and proper development is in fact a concern that the child become a proper member of

v

a cultural group. In effect the model of child development is analogous to a model of ethnic affiliation. Huntington reveals how much children can teach their ethnographer-parents in the field, based on her experiences among the Hutterites, but also cautions that the interests of her children, and the hosts as well, should not be sacrificed for the research. Jacobson's report on research in India focuses on how the public and domestic domains are merged during fieldwork although professional publications in anthropology maintain the separation. Kleis's fieldwork in Nigeria with his children deepens his understanding of the costs of ethnic pluralism on families and on the transmission of cultural values and ethnic identity among his African neighbors and in his family. Research in the Fiji Islands produced Turner's observation that when the hosts treat the ethnographer as a child, her own identities as adult and member of a culture are called into question and her childhood can be vividly recalled. The Whitefords' paper recapitulates their two decades' worth of fieldtrips in several Latin American countries and Spain, and includes suggestions for maximizing the entire family's experience. They conclude that cross-cultural experiences need not produce long-term deleterious effects on the researchers' children.

There are two equally important reasons for publishing this material on how professional and familial concerns affect each other. The first addresses the needs of individuals who are parents and anthropologists. These personal accounts and the introduction provide useful information for those anthropologists and other researchers who are considering, planning, in the midst of, or reflecting upon research as a family. The second reason is to contribute to discussions on anthropological theory and methodology. The consideration of family research units can provide new information on the process of participant-observation, the traditional hallmark of anthropological methodology.

A question we have frequently been asked addresses the first issue of how field research affects families. The question we are asked is, given the stressfulness of parenting in the field, do we think it is a good or bad idea to take children along for anthropological research. As the reader may anticipate, evaluating the costs and benefits to every member of a family involved in cross-cultural research is a very complex issue. Furthermore, each field situation is different. While public opinion in general greatly exaggerates the dangers of temporarily taking children out of their familiar cultural milieu, particularly to the rural Third World, the few published discussions of the subject by anthropologists frequently err in the opposite direction. In what is most likely an attempt to counteract overly negative public opinion of such an enterprise, anthropologists usually avoid or trivialize the negative effects of doing research with their children. Because we felt inadequately prepared for the rigors of our own fieldwork with children, we make a special effort to describe the negative as well as positive aspects of our own experiences. Nonetheless, our general position is that, like any other all-involving commitment, such as marriage, professional career or parenthood itself, field research with children frequently results in a tenuous balance between the problems and the rewards. However, it is a personally and professionally enriching experience that can also contribute to the development of anthropology.

Publishing this material contributes to the anthropological imperative, as expressed by Agar (1980), to remove the "mystique" from participant-observation. Demystification involves learning how this process is conducted in order to better assess the reports it generates. As long as qualitative methodology is a part of anthropology, the intersubjective, introspective, and reflexive (Ruby, 1980) components of data gathering and analysis must be analyzed publically. It is necessary to understand these elements of the ethnographic endeavor because the ethnographer is like an actor who seeks permission to join an improvisation where the other actors share a language, training, a repertoire of characters, story lines and dialogues, and a dramatic intent different from the ethnographer's own. Nevertheless, based upon the particulars of that improvisational collaboration, the anthropologist plans to publish generalizations about the social patterns and cultural models of his or her fellow actors' dramatic world over time, usually with little or no reference to the ethnographer's own participation. Only by knowing as much as possible about both the events of the particular drama enacted (the "text" in Dumont's (1978) terms), and about the prior social and cultural models (Dumont's "context," ibid.), which the ethnographer has had available to "interpret experience and generate behavior" (Spradley and McCurdy, 1975) during the improvisation, can we trust the methodology and its application, or fully interpret the published results.

Although three recent volumes have made major and fascinating contributions to the goals of elucidating the ethnographer's perceptions and sentiments (Rabinow, 1977; Dumont, 1978; and Cesara, 1980), the distinctive experiences of fieldworkers with families are missing. The roles of parent-researchers and of researchers' children must be made a part of a full description of the social, cultural, and psychological text and context of fieldwork. Parenting is always an intellectually and emotionally involving activity, and the changes occasioned by a move to a foreign culture increase the challenge. Such a significant part of the ethnographer's life cannot fail to affect the processes of data gathering and analysis. Furthermore, an anthropologist's children themselves may become passive or even active researchers, as illustrated in several of the papers here. They are not merely adjuncts of the researcher's persona among the research population, but interacting persons with roles, however involved or truncated, of their own. Their unique contributions to anthropological fieldwork need to be recognized.

What, in brief, makes the experience of doing participant-observation with one's children different from doing it without them? Although individuals are subject to the influences of their native culture whether they are alone or in a family group, a researcher's family is a functioning social system, however small. Although a family may be separated from its usual socio-cultural context and may feel prepared for cross-cultural adventure, it will nevertheless perpetuate patterns of interaction adaptive to the society from which it comes, both by force of habit and in order to ensure continued communication among the family's members. A research team may similarly continue previously learned social styles. However, neither is it usually a unit before fieldwork, nor does it carry the functional and symbolic importance of the family in the culture as a whole. Part of the special significance of the family is the responsibility parents have to socialize their children. This partially unconscious mandate to teach children specific values and behaviors instead of others contrasts with the equally powerful responsibility of ethnographers to suspend their own cultural values, to the best of their ability, in order to better understand the culture under study. In sum then, the most important difference between the tasks of lone ethnographers and fieldworkers with children is the extent to which parent-researchers must contend with conflicting norms and complex interactions. These culture conflicts and complexities are a source of both added stress and additional data and insight.

We have had the opportunity to discuss and to publish on some of the phenomena associated with taking children along on fieldwork because of several fortunate events: Professor Bernard Gallin, Chair of the Department of Anthropology at Michigan State University, encouraged, facilitated and participated in the conference that led to this volume. The College of Social Science at Michigan State University, under the leadership of Dean Gwen Andrew, provided funds for the conference and the transportation for out-of-town participants. One of the conference discussants, Dr. Hiram Fitzgerald, suggested that Plenum Press publish the conference proceedings. For their belief in our endeavor and their various forms of support, we extend our heartfelt thanks to them.

Dr. Fitzgerald and Dr. Marjorie Kostelnik offered us sage advice and patiently allowed us to find and to hone our editorial skills. We are very grateful to have worked with such understanding mentors.

We owe an immeasurable thanks to the contributors who have shared their research experiences and their personal lives with us. The overall conclusions of this volume emerged only from the exploration of the issue that was done by all the contributors.

Discussions at the conference of the papers and of others' experiences sparked many insights about anthropological research with children. Those who participated in the conference, but who regrettably could not provide chapters for this volume, were Drs. Peter Gladhart, Iwao Ishino, Patricia Whittier, and Ruth Useem. The support, encouragement and editorial assistance of Dr. Ann Millard for both the conference and this volume also deserve mention.

For typing the manuscripts and for making them into camera-ready copy, we thank Carrie DeMyers and Margaret A. Burritt.

Throughout the process of preparing for the conference and working on this book, we have had the benefit of the professional opinions, the suggestions, and the help of our husbands, Dr. P. Sudevan and Dr. Jim Turner. We are very grateful for their assistance.

To our daughters, Marisa and Megan, who joined us in some of the most exciting, exhausting, trying, yet enlightening days of our lives, we give our love and gratitude.

Lastly, on behalf of all the volume's contributors, we thank all our hosts for graciously allowing us to know about their lives and to reside among them.

Barbara Butler
Diane Michalski Turner
1986

CONTENTS

CHILDREN AND ANTHROPOLOGICAL RESEARCH

CHILDREN AND ANTHROPOLOGICAL RESEARCH: AN OVERVIEW

Barbara Butler

Department of Sociology and Anthropology
University of Wisconsin at Stevens Point
Stevens Point, Wisconsin

and

Diane Michalski Turner

Department of Anthropology
Michigan State University
East Lansing, Michigan

REVIEW OF LITERATURE

In the fieldwork literature of the past twenty-five years there are approximately two dozen published references to children accompanying their researcher parents. Several generalizations can be made from these often quite brief accounts. Over time these accounts have become somewhat less apologetic about discussing the personal aspects of field-work, as the authors increasingly scrutinize the use of participant-observation as a research tool. All but one of the accounts conclude that the experience was a positive one on balance, and many claim it to have been overwhelmingly so. Nonetheless, over the years more candor about the negative aspects of fieldwork with children, such as limitations on time for research and concern about the children's well-being, become evident. What deserves note is that almost all parent-anthropologists mention, however briefly, at least one major crisis of physical health for their child due to the field situation. That they have successfully weathered the crisis signifies that the parent-anthropologist has demonstrated substantial prowess in this important professional *rite de passage*. It is significant that the only account which gives no such positive evaluation of the experience of fieldwork with children (nor a negative one) is written by someone whose child died in the field. The most negative evaluation is given, however, by Margaret Mead, who never took her daughter along for research --"...children of any age add tremendous hazards to field work" (1970, p.254). We will return to this question of why the experiences are judged in retrospect to have been positive after reviewing the accounts themselves.

3

The earliest published account we have discovered is a richly illustrated article in the *National Geographic Magazine* in 1961. Entitled "Blue-Eyed Indian: A City Boy's Sojourn with Primitive Tribesmen in Central Brazil," it relates the adventures of Alexander Teemaree, the eight-year-old son of Harald Schultz, then Assistant Ethnologist and Chief of Expeditions at the Sao Paulo State Museum, during one summer of field research. Written in the entertaining style appropriate for the popular magazine, the article gives the impression that, despite a number of incidents that would give pause to the squeamish, such as the boy's near-miss with a piranha, living in the jungle was wholesome and fun. On his return to school in Sao Paulo, the boy's teachers remarked that the formerly excellent student was unable to pay attention or follow instructions. Schultz responds by saying that his son's greater strength, health and gaiety were adequate compensations for what he considered this temporary academic difficulty.

The second published account of fieldwork with a child, also concerns Central Brazil. It is David Maybury-Lewis' *The Savage and the Innocent* (1965), which he claims is "not an essay in anthropology" (p. 9), but an account of "our impressions, our personal reactions, and above all, our feelings about the day to day business which is mysteriously known as 'doing fieldwork'" (p. 9). After two years studying in Sao Paulo and one previous fieldtrip of eight months' duration with his wife in Sherente territory, Maybury-Lewis returned to the field with his wife and baby son to spend about nine months among the Shavante, a different tribe of the Amazonian basin. He reports that it was difficult to decide which action would be more harmful for the baby--to take him along or to leave him for the extended period of research. Maybury-Lewis' wife worried more than he did about the baby's well-being. Before entering the field they stocked up on medicine, advice on tropical diseases and a radio and transmitter as "insurance against mishap" (p. 154), but felt "obliged to present a front of experienced confidence to our friends and relatives. These tended to be either jocular or lugubrious about the responsibility we had towards the child" (p. 153). Upon reaching the Shavante, Maybury-Lewis was glad to have his expectation confirmed that the baby would help him develop rapport with their hosts. Although avoiding the breezy tone of an adventure story that Schultz had adopted, Maybury-Lewis continues here with the same confident reserve that he and his wife maintained before friends and relatives, even when he describes the near-death of his son from dysentery and dehydration. Maybury-Lewis only briefly mentions that his son spent several weeks in a Sao Paulo hospital and that his own research schedule was therefore upset.

May Diaz's 1966 ethnography, *Tonala: Conservatism, Responsibility and Authority in a Mexican Town*, includes a brief but positive account of the fieldwork with her two sons and her husband. Hers is the first report to state what becomes a familiar theme in the published literature, namely that bringing a family along enables the ethnographer to collect more and better data about people in different age and sex cohorts. She, her husband

and children were "sometimes a team" (p. 6), and her sons' activities "revealed nuances and flavors of town life that adult observers might miss" (p. 8). Although her sons reported a vast amount of information on the life of the village children when unobserved by adults during the first months of fieldwork, as they "became Tonaltecan, rather than Berkeley, children" (p. 7), the flow of information dwindled. Nonetheless, the Diaz house in Tonala was a favorite playground for the neighborhood and Diaz could therefore observe the children as she followed her daily routine, which she says was much the same as other Tonaltecan housewives.

Powdermaker's book of the same year, *Stranger and Friend* (1966), is the first to take seriously the task of explicating the interface between the personal and the scientific in fieldwork. Although she did fieldwork alone and never had children, her book does touch on some issues of interest here. Powdermaker claims that whereas the initial fieldwork pattern had been the lone ethnographer, the family and the team were becoming increasingly common research units (p. 144). Reflecting on her own experience, Powdermaker suggests that a spouse and children may reduce the loneliness in fieldwork; that they may help gain data from their own age and sex groups; and that children may be an asset to the study of family life (p. 144). However, she cautions that the social integration of such a large group may be difficult for the hosts.

Several books on fieldwork were published in 1970, partly because of an increase in interest in anthropology. Anthropology departments in the United States were experiencing a decade of rapid expansion as a result of the "baby boom," which meant a surge in the number of students and of the growing national economy with an accompanying emphasis on and funds for higher education. This economic and demographic growth favored a liberal re-evaluation of social institutions, presumably as a means to ensure a more equitable distribution of resources. Interest in anthropology grew among students and intellectuals because of this questioning of social institutions. Within the discipline itself, a similar process of critical review was also taking place (e.g., Hymes, 1969), which included questioning the limits of objectivity and the benefits of subjectivity in social science research.

Three collections of essays published in 1970 contain references to children accompanying their researcher-parents. These are found in Morris Freilich's *Marginal Natives: Anthropologists at Work* (1970); Peggy Golde's *Women in the Field: Anthropological Experiences* (1970); and George Spindler's *Being an Anthropologist: Fieldwork in Eleven Cultures* (1970). All three describe anthropologists' personal adaptations to the field for the purpose of aiding students to understand fieldwork and to better interpret ethnographies. The accounts of research with children refer to fieldwork that occurred between 1944 (Honigman, 1970) and the late 1960's (Yengoyan, 1970; Spindler and Spindler, 1970). At least two of these publications (Fischer 1970; Spindler and Spindler, 1970) describe such experiences that spanned more than a decade. The majority of the fieldtrips described in these volumes took place during the 1960's.

Six of the nine contributors to Freilich's *Marginal Natives* mention that their children accompanied them. In his introduction, Freilich states that the authors "wish to share their experiences so that life-in-the-field will lose some of its mystery and apprehension" (p. ix). This introduction continues Powdermaker's laudable effort to examine closely the personal and the scientific aspects of fieldwork. The articles, however, typically present brief and general accounts of fieldwork. Schwab, in "Comparative Field Techniques in Urban Research in Africa" (1970), reports that his wife was a major research aide during his first fieldtrip to Nigeria, but, during their second research stint, she was too occupied with their children, who had been born in the interim, to participate in the research. Due to the Rhodesian administration's policies on racially-segregated housing, the Schwabs lived in comparative comfort with a nursemaid and European neighbor-playmates for the children. Gulick, in "Village and City Field-work in Lebanon" (1970), speaks of his unbearable loneliness during an early fieldtrip to a rural area of Lebanon without his family. On two subsequent research trips to the Middle East, his wife and children stayed with him in Beirut. Since his third study focussed on Tripoli, he commuted from Beirut so that his children would have adequate schooling. In "Open Networks and Native Formalism: The Mandaya and Pitjandara Cases" (1970), Yengoyan describes how he lived with his wife and baby daughter in a tiny trailer in Alice Springes, Australia. He, like the other male contributors to *Marginal Natives* considered here, was accompanied by a wife whose main responsibility was to care for the children.

Honigman's "Fieldwork in Two North Canadian Communities" (1970) is remarkable in that it discusses the earliest fieldtrip with children that we have found described in the literature--between 1944 and 1945. Although unusual for that period, it is probably not unique. The unbearable longing he felt for his family on a trip without them in 1943 and the fact that his wife, Irma Honigman, was also an anthropologist, possibly explain his willingness to take his family to live among the Kaska Indians and to endure the severe winter weather and the relative social isolation that this entailed. While he does not directly say that they suffered from the rigors of the trip, the fact that he lists personal comfort as a major factor in a later decision to do research in Austria suggests that they did. Honigman too says that his wife, "preoccupied with the care of two small children (a boy and an infant girl), had relatively little time to help me in my research" (p. 40).

Perlman stayed several months with his wife and 20-month-old daughter in a rural Ugandan village, as he discusses briefly in "Intensive Fieldwork and Scope Sampling: Methods for Studying the Same Problem at Different Levels" (1970). Like Maybury-Lewis, Perlman catalogues some of the measures taken to ensure his child's health, such as a house right near the road to the medical dispensary, an inflatable bathtub, and socks and shoes to protect against chiggers. Even so, his daughter developed a mild case of malaria. Perlman also points out the special role in developing rapport that children may play in a social situation of marked social inequality.

> No white family had ever lived among them in
> their village, and few had ever seen a white
> child, much less one who played happily with
> their own children. This attracted visitors and
> neighbors and helped to break down barriers of
> communication, alleviate suspicion, and gain
> rapport. My daughter occasionally served as
> my visiting card; when she wandered into
> someone's house or backyard, I was not far
> behind (p. 306).

Although Perlman states that "having a small child in the field was not as
much of a problem as one might assume" (p. 304), as he continued
comparative studies in Uganda and his family grew to include two more
children, his wife and children remained in Kampala. Having several
children with him was apparently more of a problem than he was willing to
endure.

In "Cakchiqueles and Caribs: The Social Context of Fieldwork"
(1970), Nancie Gonzalez reports that she designed her 1962 field study so
that she could live in Guatemala City with her two young sons while doing
research in a rural Guatemalan village. This intermittent fieldwork was
possible since she had previously resided there as a fieldworker. The four
to nine hours per day and three to four days per week schedule of her
second fieldtrip was sufficient to successfully complete her project. The
other effect that Gonzalez's children had on her research was to give her a
"new and higher adult status...which aided my investigation of childbearing
and childrearing, which were the topics I concentrated on..." (p. 163). "It
was not until my return...by then the mother of two, that I was able to
elicit data from a few women concerning sexual activities and childbirth"
(p. 162). This observation that the ethnographers' parenthood affects their
ability to gather certain information is a recurring theme.

Peggy Golde's *Women in the Field* (1970) probes the question of
whether women's experiences as anthropological researchers are different
from men's. The volume contributors consider the effects on the researcher as subject; the female researcher's methods; the effect of sex
roles on research; and cross-cultural attitudes about women. However,
only one contributor, Ann Fischer, did fieldwork with children. In
"Fieldwork in Five Cultures" (1970), Fischer describes her varied fieldwork
experiences with her husband and two daughters between the early 1960's
and 1979. She claims that her experiences were atypical of the times,
since women fieldworkers were usually single and those few mothers who
went to the field with their children were, as we have seen, usually
anthropologists' wives. Fischer cites two problems for women fieldworkers
who are simultaneously mothers. She suggests that anthropology as an
academic profession is not set up to accept or facilitate the dual focus on a
family and a profession (p. 270). Secondly, she notes that women
fieldworkers are likely to receive far more criticism than their male

counterparts from both informants and members of their own society because they fail to carry out the roles of wife and mother in a traditional fashion (pp. 279-280). While criticism is not necessarily disabling, it certainly creates more stress. Perhaps since a male fieldworker who is also a parent is usually accompanied by a wife, his dual roles challenge fewer preconceptions at home and in most host societies. Turner's contribution to this volume elaborates on this point (see Chapter 5).

Mead wrote extensively about fieldwork and makes a number of points relevant to the current discussion about women and family field-workers in "Fieldwork in the Pacific Islands, 1925-67" (1970a), which, like Fischer's article, appeared in *Women in the Field*. Although she claims that "Ideally a three-generation family, including children highly trained to understand what they experience, would be the way to study a culture" (p. 321), Mead goes on to say that such a method is impractical since it would create too great a strain on both the field team and the host society. In addition, women have a number of special problems as fieldworkers, ranging from greater culture shock than men to special pressure put upon them by their male professors, according to Mead. Having babies and, presumably, deferring to their husbands, frequently keeps those whom Mead describes as "feminine" women from doing fieldwork. In addition, women fieldworkers worry so much about the fates of, and their relation-ships with, those relatives, friends and lovers left at home that their research is impaired and sometimes even abandoned. Mead claims that married men may be ideal fieldworkers because their maturity and rootedness reassures their hosts that they do not intend to compete for such valued resources as women and wealth. Married male ethnographers also enjoy the relief from domestic concerns that fieldwork makes possible (p. 325). Although Mead admits that married women fieldworkers with children can be productive, they must do so by "entering the world of women and children, identifying with the women who are mothers" (p. 328). The fact that Margaret Mead left her daughter behind with friends when she went into the field is a standard bit of anthropologists' folk knowledge that is brought up when having children in the research setting is mentioned. However, what is not said is that after her return from Bali in 1939, the year Mary Catherine was born, Mead did not go back to the field until 1953, when her daughter was already a teenager.

The third volume published in 1970 considers a wider range of issues than Golde's. Spindler's *Being an Anthropologist* (1970) was meant pri-marily to help students understand anthropology and anthropologists, and secondly, to fill a gap in the methodological literature (p. vi). But, as Spindler acknowledges, the relationships among personal experience, obser-vations and interpretations in these deliberately personalized accounts are examined in a somewhat limited way, with only "tantalizing hints of.... deeper levels of awareness and influence" (p. vi). Among the contributions are two essays, one by Hostetler and Huntington and one by Boissevain, which contain the most detailed analyses so far recorded in this literature of the relationships between the anthropologists' children and their parents' field research; four others, by Hitchcock, Beals, Norbeck and Spindler and Spindler, mention their children more briefly. Several remarks by researchers who were not accompanied by children, bear an indirect relationship to the topic. Hart, who did research among the aboriginal Tiwi of Australia between 1928 and 1929 says that his experience, which he claims is probably universal for research among "simpler peoples," was that fieldwork "was not difficult provided that the fieldworker was young, healthy, undemanding of personal comfort and unmarried" (p. 145). During fieldwork among the Semai of Malaya, Robert Dentan's wife was known by a nickname, which Dentan says was not pejorative, that means "sterile woman" (p. 111). Finally, Norma Diamond discusses her anomalous position as a single woman, who, by accepted Taiwanese standards, should already have been married five or six years and had several children (p. 126).

"The Hutterites: Fieldwork in a North American Communal Society," by John Hostetler and Gertrude Huntington describes the roles Huntington's family, which included her three children, her husband and her mother, played during research. Since Hutterite society is both strictly sex-segregated and divided into clear age grades, and because the study focussed on socialization, it was important to have members of the researcher's family in each age grade and of both genders participate in the fieldwork. As the researchers recognized, the Huntington family approximated this ideal situation. Although Huntington sees her children's participation in her field research as generally positive, she warns against using either families or hosts as mere "tools to further an abstraction" (p. 213) without regard for the possible harm any of them may incur in the process. In her contribution to the present volume, Huntington explores more deeply the reciprocal effects of her research on her children and of her children on her research.

Boissevain's "Fieldwork in Malta" discusses his year in a small village in Malta with his two daughters, aged four and six and his wife who was pregnant. Like Huntington, Boissevain gives attention to both the difficulties and the benefits of doing fieldwork with children. The problems he singles out are mainly related to the time constraints on satisfying one's own expectations for an adequate performance of the parent and researcher roles, even while accompanied by a full-time parent/spouse. He suggests, but does not elaborate upon, the possibility that the two roles are themselves incompatible in ways that go beyond the limits on one's time (p. 70), a point also made well by Fischer (1970). Most of the advantages to taking children along for research that he lists have been encountered before in this literature review. Like Huntington, Boissevain concludes that the benefits outweigh the disadvantages.

Hitchcock's contribution to *Being an Anthropologist*, "Fieldwork in Gurkha Country" devotes much less attention to the subject of taking a family into the field, but it is notable because the Hitchcocks' experience, like Margaret Mead's, have become part of the anthropological folk knowledge about taking children along for research. In 1960 Hitchcock's

18-month-old son died near the beginning of research in rural Nepal. Soon afterward, Hitchcock and his wife enrolled their two older daughters, aged eight and ten, in a boarding school in Kathmandu until the year and a half of research was concluded. Hitchcock briefly mentions his son's death in the article, although that section, indeed the whole paper, is suffused with strong, if carefully controlled, emotion. In the introduction to the paper, the author says that he is both documenting the antecedents of a question which recurred frequently during his fieldwork--"why go on?"--and attempting to reveal through "story or symbol" and "beyond...reason" where he found the answer. Undoubtedly an extremely difficult article to write, it raises many questions about the effects of his family on his research and vice versa, but provides very little of either Hitchcock's conclusions or data that would help readers make their own generalizations.

The three other articles in Spindler's volume that mention accompanying children are "Gopalpur, 1958-60" by Alan R. Beals; "Changing Japan: Field Reserach" by Edward Norbeck; and "Fieldwork among the Menomini" by George and Louise Spindler. Shortly after fieldwork was begun in rural India, Beals' wife unexpectedly became pregnant. Their daughter, born in an urban hospital, spent the first year of her life in this small South Indian village. Despite their remembered annoyance over the strength and persistence of villagers' demands that they follow native customs regarding their daughter, Beals and his wife report that their strongest reaction to fieldwork with their daughter occurred upon leaving India. From the moment they entered the U.S.-bound plane, they realized, with some shock, that the care and attention their child had received from their Indian hosts far exceeded anything they could expect at home. This theme is echoed in the papers by Turner and Jacobson in this volume.

Norbeck's wife, like Beals', became pregnant during their first field trip to rural Japan. However, they deliberately returned home in time for the baby to be born in the United States. In subsequent research in urban Japan, the Norbecks were accompanied by their two school-aged children, whom their mother taught at home. There is no mention made of the children having affected the research or having been affected by it.

The Spindlers apparently spent many summers camping and doing research among the Menomini Indians of Wisconsin accompanied by their one daughter. The most informative statement that they make about their daughter's presence is that she provided a distraction for the Menomini children, keeping them from continually bothering the ethnographers.

The next published reference to taking children into the field that we found was Carol Stack's *All Our Children* (1974). Stack's son, who was born shortly after she began research among poor urban blacks in the United States, provided companionship for her during fieldwork; gave her an area of shared interest with her female hosts; and convinced them of her goodwill and trust because she, unlike most middle class whites, allowed his active participation in their lives.

Foster and Kemper's *Anthropologists in Cities,* which also appeared in 1974 contains four articles that mention accompanying children. Bernard and Rita Gallin's "The Rural to Urban Migration of an Anthropologist in Taiwan" candidly describes the interaction of family concerns and professional goals in their decisions about fieldwork, beginning with their choice of a research topic. When Bernard was doing his pre-doctoral research in 1957 and 1958, the couple spent sixteen months in a rural Taiwanese village. But their subsequent trips to Taiwan in 1965-1966 and 1969-1970 were to the city of Taipei, because of their concerns about their two children. The research topic shifted to rural-urban migration. The urban location was necessary because they wanted to ensure that their eldest son, nearly six on their first return visit, attended an English-language school, where he would "learn to read at the 'proper age'" (p. 224). The Gallins do not argue for or against taking children into the field, nor do they point out how the children contributed directly to the research. Nevertheless, they indicate a number of indirect consequences of their sons' presence in Taiwan. For example, during their first urban field project, the house that they thought met their *family* needs perfectly, turned out to isolate them from their informants.

In "The City of Gentlemen: Santiago de los Caballeros," Nancie Gonzalez, who discussed fieldwork in Guatemala with her two sons, aged two and four, in Freilich's *Marginal Natives* (1970), here turns to a trip to the Dominican Republic five years later in 1967. While a graduate student couple carried out the rural portion of the research, Gonzalez remained in the city where she could have the amenities she thought essential for the children, such as electric lights, running water, telephones, and public transportation (p. 23). She describes in detail the difficulties associated with her doing research as a single parent of two children. For example, she was once forced to refuse what turned out to be the only invitation that she would receive for dinner at the University President's home because she had no babysitter. On another occasion she handled badly an initial meeting with university officials, partly because she "....had to bring along..(her)..frightened and exhausted children, one of whom promptly spilled Coca Cola on the rug of the President's Office" (p. 23). In contrast she also portrays their presence as an "emotional lifesaver and a professional advantage" (p. 25). Her boys' experiences and social ties among their middle and upper class schoolmates at a Catholic boys' school, and among their lower class neighborhood friends provided more than one important insight for the research that focussed on class and ethnic divisions in Dominican society. However, the strains of shifting between different classes and ethnic groups, and of being a researcher and a single parent made Gonzalez reach "a point of exhaustion more often than was good for me, my family, or my research" (p. 32). Although both children seemed to escape culture shock, her older son was forced to leave early because of increasing severe bouts of asthma, that Gonzalez suggests could have had a psychological dimension (p. 33). This account most closely mirrors those in this volume in both its revelation of the difficulties she faced and in its affirmation of the additions to data she received because of her children's

Two other articles in Foster and Kemper contain relevant observations. Andre Simic in "The Best of Two Worlds: Serbian Peasants in the City" described taking his wife and two children to the country of his ancestry. There, the time-consuming and mundane activities necessitated by the presence of his family nevertheless "yielded further insights into the functioning of Yugoslav urban society" (p. 184). In "Barrio Tulcan: Fieldwork in a Colombian City," Michael Whiteford reflects on his early experience in Popayan as a child, which his parents describe in this volume (see Chapter 6). "In many ways this was an excellent prelude to becoming a fieldworker myself; I learned Spanish at an early age and experienced a different culture without really being conscious of it" (p. 43).

In "Fieldwork as a 'Single Parent': To Be or Not To Be Accompanied by a Child" (1975), Charlotte Frisbie carries on the trend toward greater candor in discussing the interrelations of the anthropologist's personal life, methodology and research results. She highlights many of the same themes about single parenting in the field as does Gonzalez (1970, 1974), although she was only temporarily a single parent. In addition, Frisbie attempts to identify the "differential compatibility of the child with three particular ethnographic methods: participant-observation, interviewing and ethnohistorical archival research" (p. 98). In her case, participant-observation among the Navajo was aided by her three and one-half year old daughter's presence, interviewing with her daughter was mixed in difficulty depending on the distance from their home base, and ethnohistorical, archival research was close to impossible without additional childcare.

Frisbie reviews the many advantages to the presence of an anthropologist's children that we have discovered in our review of the published reports. From her own experiences she adds that single parenting in the field may be a good deal more trying than fieldwork in a family with two or more adults. She concludes her article with a list of suggestions for parents planning field research without a spouse. They include being prepared to work at a slower pace, to take frequent breaks, to cultivate friends from the child's own culture, to monitor and record the child's reaction to the new culture and to exercise unusual flexibility in all research arrangements (pp. 110-111). Frisbie warns that only with considerable foresight and continuous "reflective consideration throughout the course of fieldwork....may it (fieldwork with children) realize its potential as a positive and valuable experience for the children, the hosts and collaborators, and the anthropologist" (p. 113).

A few years later in 1978, Betty Lou Valentine published remarks about her fieldwork among Black Americans with her anthropologist husband, Charles, and their one-year-old son in *Hustling and Other Hard Work: Life Styles in the Ghetto*. As in more distant field sites, Valentine's son's health was once jeopardized because of "incompetence and irresponsibility" (p. 158) in a hospital emergency room; the night he was taken there, two other babies died unnecessarily. In addition, her son was a novel source of information and also helped build rapport with their hosts, in part because of the special significance attending the participation of a researcher's child when the hosts are members of a subordinate ethnic minority (cf. Perlman, 1970; Stack, 1974; and Butler this volume). Like other researchers, Valentine's assessment of the situation is positive-- "...we feel strongly that a female/male/child team is an ideal ethnographic group" (p. 154).

The most recent contribution discovered is a 1981 article by Carolyn Fluehr-Lobban, entitled "Josina's Observations of Sudanese Culture," detailing her two-and-a-half year old daughter's experiences in Khartoum, Sudan. Whereas earlier researchers report with surprise the ease with which their young children acculturate to a field setting, Fluehr-Lobban emphasizes that, despite her young age, Josina was already an "American culture-bearer" (p. 227), revelling in hamburgers, swimming pools and Western-style toilets when she encountered them in the American Club of Khartoum. Nevertheless, Josina's ability to selectively learn Sudanese culture with the most minimal exposure and her determined play-acting of what she had seen also amazed her parents. In contrast to Frisbie, Fluehr-Lobban wrote this article to counteract the persistent warnings of relatives and friends, and the nagging fears of parents themselves about taking children into the field. Despite Josina's bouts with malaria and pneumonia, Fluehr-Lobban claims that the experience was overwhelmingly positive for both Josina and her anthropologist-parents.

Despite the almost universal judgment that doing research with children was a positive experience, the observations offered are as frequently negative as positive (see Table 1). Of particular note is the anthropologist-parents' worry over the child's well-being, including a nearly inevitable description of a deadly health threat. In most cases the risks to a child's health and safety *are* increased in the field situation. However, since a majority of the illnesses reported result in recovery, those anthropologist-parents are free to make a retrospective judgment that the experience was beneficial on balance. Nonetheless, odds are that a small number of the children anthropologists increasingly bring with them to the field will suffer permanent injury. Their parents will be unable to claim with much conviction that the benefits outweighed the costs. Far from a reticence to discuss such matters, what is needed is increased knowledge about the risks and how to prevent or alleviate them.

Although children in the field have been credited with increasing their parents' knowledge of children's culture, sex roles, age grades, socialization and childcare, not enough attention had been paid to the ways in which their presence can negatively affect the data gathered and its subsequent analysis. What happens to a researcher's cultural relativity or objectivity when the host culture or physical environment is perceived as harmful to his or her child? Only Gonzalez spoke of the threats to rapport with informants when children were present in a setting that was inappropriate, or when they were more disruptive than what is locally acceptable. What happens if a child's culture shock is particularly severe? In general, how does the researcher's physical or emotional state, which can be affected by the behavior and experiences of his or her children, modify the course and outcome of the research itself?

TABLE 1

POSITIVE AND NEGATIVE CONSEQUENCES OF DOING FIELDWORK WITH CHILDREN AS REPORTED IN THE LITERATURE

POSITIVE	NEGATIVE
1. Increase Rapport	1. Decrease Rapport
2. Attract Visitors	2. Disrupt meetings, ethnohistorical research and note-taking
3. Distract other Children	3. Take time from research; make pace slow
4. Increase access to some information: a. age groups b. gender groups c. family life d. childbearing and rearing	4. Demand more amenities: a. better housing b. urban location c. good schooling d. water, electricity, etc. e. available medical care
5. Provide emotional support to parents: a. Reduce parents' loneliness b. Provide a refuge c. Reduce worry parents would suffer if the children were left at home	5. Increase parents' worry about health risks
6. Increase the children's health, strength, and gaiety	6. Frequently keep professionals who are mothers from research
7. Give the researcher a higher adult status	7. Own kin's worry about children results in stress
8. Help maintain objectivity (by providing more points of view)	8. Decreases objectivity because stress is increased and cultural relativity is questioned
9. Provide a shared interest with the parents among the hosts	9. Increase criticism of researchers by family, friends, mentors, and hosts (particularly for women ethnographers)

10. Children learn quickly and
     a. can teach parents
     b. can acquire skills
        effortlessly

10. Children may not learn aca-
     demic or social skills appro-
     priate to age group at home

11. Large groups are difficult
     for hosts to absorb

12. Require increased flexibility
     in research execution and
     frequent changes in plans

THE SEPARATION OF THE PROFESSIONAL AND DOMESTIC DOMAINS

The inclusion of children in fieldwork, as this cursory review of the literature reveals, is such a complex issue and one that has so many repercussions on anthropology as a discipline that it is curious that so little has been written about it. The dearth of discussion on this topic is greatly owed to anthropologists' hesitance to share their research experience. They are unwilling to see the field mystique perforated. Our colleagues' reactions to our proposed conference on taking children into the field were mixed. Not only were we suggesting that ethnographers discuss their fieldwork in a public forum, but that they break the discipline's tabu on discussing their family life, thereby mixing the "sacredness" of their professional, public lives with the "profaneness" of their domestic ones. In advising us about the possible repercussions of our professional indiscretions, a well-meaning colleague suggested that we would be stigmatized as unprofessional and not serious scholars by revealing our fieldwork experiences as mothers. Anthropologists risk losing their scholarly reputations, as our colleague cautioned and others confirm (e.g., Hill, 1974, p. 411), when they fail to observe these injunctions. We responded as anthropologists to this advice by examining the basic assumptions and meanings that support this ideology of the separation of professional and domestic domains.

The taboo on blending the professional and domestic spheres is not unique to anthropology. Most American academic and other professional institutions maintain these conceptually distinct domains and sanction those individual members who attempt to combine them. As Jacobson notes in this volume (Chapter 2), in Western culture there is a general orientation toward creating bounded categories out of the flow of human events. We maintain also that the categories established by distinguishing professional and public activities and concerns from domestic and private ones are related to a ranking of the genders identified with each. The public domain associated with men is more valued than the private sphere of women.

The separation of these domains and the identification of female and male roles with each is associated with the industrial revolution that divided the "homeplace from the workplace" (Chafe, 1979, p. 22). Industrial capitalism transformed an economy in which "production and family life were intertwined and the household was the center around which resources, labor, and consumption were balanced" (Tilly and Scott, 1978, p. 12). Compartmentalization of activities, places and people was a perceived requirement for manufacturing, because of the relative untidyness of production in domestic settings where personal interests and ties influence production and consumption. The newly created domains were differentially valued. The public sphere was rated above the domestic because of the former's connection to the acquisition of money. Most men came to rely on selling their labor in the market in order to support their dependents, and were rewarded with prestige and with an "unchallenged rule" at home.

During the last three centuries in America "one of the remarkable themes of women's history has been the constancy of prescriptive attitudes toward women's 'place' in the home" (Chafe, 1979, p. 15). When production was moved from the home, women were retained there and kept from the new economic sphere because of a system of gender stratification, i.e., "the hierarchical distribution by gender of economic and social resources in a society" (Anderson, 1983, p. 77). At all stages of the industrial period, women have engaged in economic activities within and outside the home. Notwithstanding these productive efforts, the culture's ideology of gender has maintained that they are not a proper part of women's roles.

Even in the pre-industrial period, women occupied economic positions, but a predominant ideology did not accept these as proper elements of feminine roles. For example, during the American Revolution, the war effort required women to fulfill men's usual economic and social roles as well as their own. Women's maintenance of families augmented political priorities--the need to bear and rear "liberty-loving sons" (Clinton, 1984, p. 17). Women's successes in previously masculine pursuits were acceptable to men during wartime but alarming to them when they returned to civilian life. After the war, sensing that their newfound freedom would be restricted and their expertise challenged if they pressed for the rights men claimed, women focused on improving their domestic position. Changes in female education were sought on the grounds that better educated women were finer mothers, who, by definition, were the first teachers of the nation's young. A very clear parallel to women's movement from the public to the domestic sphere after the revolution can be found in women's experiences after World War II.

In the century following the Revolutionary War, ideas about women's social roles were remarkably similar. For example, in 1889, Harland's *House and Home: The Complete Housewives' Guide* included this determination of the sexes' economic and social roles:

> Our boys are, in another score of years, to
> make the laws, heal the soul and bodies,
> formulate the science, and control the com-
> merce of their generation. Fathers who,

recognizing this great truth, do not prepare their sons to do their part toward accomplishing this work, are despised, and justly, by the community in which they live. Our girls are, in another score of years, to make the homes which are to make laws, heal souls and bodies, formulate science, and control and commerce of their generation (p. 202).

Today women are still associated with family and household concerns. "The plain fact...is that women must bear the children. And even in an age of 'equality' within the home it is clear that women still assume most of the domestic chores" (Cunniff, 1985, p. 9). Rather than simply announce as before that women's proper "place" is in the home, the current formulation attempts to explain why this is so. "The market recognizes that women cannot give the same intensity to the commerical workplace as men can, and it works this knowledge into pay scales. Or so goes the argument" (Cunniff, ibid.).

The separation between the domestic/feminine and public/masculine domains is made more acute for professionals. A professional is a person who earns most of his income from a full-time job for which he has been educated; joins others like himself in the occupation's organizations; enjoys a sense of occupational autonomy; views his work as providing a service to his clients; and, most significantly, he treats his occupation as a "calling" with an "enduring set of normative and behavioral expectations" (Moore, 1970) to which he is committed. The use of the masculine pronoun here is not a convention of speech, but a frequent assumption in sociological literature on the subject (e.g., Vollmer and Mills, 1966). A professional woman is granted an honorary masculine status and must abide by its restrictions.

The professional work role supersedes all other roles and statuses that an individual may have. A man can be many things, depending upon how you look at him...Basic to all of these roles, however, is the fact that a man is a worker...To understand men and their relations with one another, we must seek to understand their work" (Vollmer and Mills, 1966, p. v.).

Professionalism places the person almost entirely in the public domain and dedicates him to work and the company of his professional fellows as a means of succeeding in his career. The professional is expected to have no time for familial, private matters that are women's province. A professional should also guard against any lessening of his or her status by not discussing family matters with colleagues.

The onus of unprofessional behavior can fall especially heavily upon women professionals. For women to acknowledge their domestic concerns in the professional domain is to call into question their professionalism and their honorary 'maleness'. This is a problem affecting nearly all women professionals (e.g., Colombotos, 1963).

Anthropologists are professionals. We too seek rewards by separating our work, which our culture assigns to a masculine and worthy sphere, from our familial relationships, which are associated with a feminine and less prestigious domain. However, as our review of the literature and the following contributions indicate, the nature of anthropological values and practices makes the separation of work from family life extremely difficult, even undesirable, during fieldwork. Our work, fortunately or unfortunately, involves us in relationships with people who muddle the divisions we seek to maintain. The people with whom we ethnographers live and whom we observe may not categorize their world as we do, and when they do, we may find that their professed sectioning of private and public lives is incomplete. Indeed, in our own society the public/private distinction is implemented selectively, for instance, a diplomat's or President's wife is expected to play an important public role because of her domestic status. The blurring of domains that occurs when we take our children with us into the field and carry on our professional labors with, around, and through them is to be expected.

OBJECTIVITY AND SUBJECTIVITY

The canons of professionalism prevent anthropologists from mentioning their personal lives in field reports, and the standards of objectivity in social sciences reinforce that prohibition. Anthropology's concern about objectivity stems partly from its wish to represent factually the societies it studies and partly from its desire to be accepted as a science rather than as a branch of the humanities.

> A fundamental feature of science is its idea of objectivity, an ideal that subjects all scientific statements to the test of independent and impartial criteria, recognizing no authority or persons in the realm of cognition (Scheffler, 1967, p. 1).

Anthropologists maintain that they should be able to achieve observational fidelity during fieldwork by overcoming their biases, sentiments, personal histories, and the ramifications of their social relationships, among other things. Thus they attempt to eliminate

> ....the perceiving subject, i.e., [the field-workers] as participant-observers, from their reports [in] an attempt at both a more factual objectivity than that of their predecessors and

a stronger grasp of social and cultural realities
(Dumont, 1978, p. 7).

To maximize their chances of being objective, ethnographers report observable actions, confine their interpretations of these to the standards of logical reasoning, and abide by the precept of cultural relativity. The concept of cultural relativity maintains that each culture is essentially equal to every other culture and that it should be understood in terms of its own underlying logic. This tenet should prevent anthropologists from prejudice and bias in the research process and in subsequent analysis of their data.

Because of the ways in which these concepts are generally interpreted in the discipline, fieldworkers often believe that they have failed to be objective and relativistic. Negative reactions to their hosts' cultures, comparisons between their hosts' and their own cultures that yield different tallies of the relative worth of the cultures on various occasions, and reports that acknowledge their own active participation all contribute to anthropologists' perception of their failure to be objective and passive observers. But are such responses and actions indicative of subjectivity? Do they signal a violation of the principle of cultural relativity? As the following discussion of the situations that hinder the unreserved adherence to the tenet of cultural relativity will show, the research process is not a unitary phenomenon. Therefore, we should analyze the research process and decide which parts are best judged against the standards of objectivity and cultural relativity. In addition, the means for applying these standards should be more carefully defined.

Ethnographic research provides fieldworkers numerous opportunities for comparing their own cultures with those of their hosts. As noted earlier and as will be shown in the contributions to follow, fieldworkers sometimes find that they like some aspects of both cultures and dislike others. If it is their first experience of fieldwork, anthropologists are likely to become aware for the first time of their own cultural assumptions. They may be satisfied or chagrined by this new perspective on their own culture. If ethnographers vacillate in terms of acceptance of and affiliation to their own and their hosts' culture, this marginality may be disquieting. And if they notice that they and their hosts are accommodating culturally to each other, they may doubt their own presumptions of the integrity of each culture. When any or all of these things happen to ethnographers, they are faced with the subjectivity that is an inherent part of the ethnographic process. They find that the extent to which cultural relativity can be experienced is itself relative, not absolute. But are they allowed to say this?

A negative emotional reaction to the hosts' culture is frequently the first occasion when researchers question their compliance with the concept of cultural relativity. At such times they not only castigate themselves for their infidelity to the tenet but also label themselves subjective because of their emotional response. It is the negative response that bothers researchers, for they rarely question their objectivity if they have positive feelings for the host culture. Fieldworkers see themselves as subjective for other reasons as well. For example, if they find themselves appraising a cultural tenet in terms of its general worth, as opposed to trying to see how it obeys the internal logic of the specific cultural whole of which it is a part, they doubt their objectivity. Are researchers' *in situ* beliefs and sentiments sufficient to make their later reports subjective? Can they not overcome them in subsequent analyses of their hosts' culture?

We think that anthropologists should reflect on their early reactions to the fieldwork process and their hosts' cultures and understand how these have influenced their perceptions. They should realize that the participant-observation part of the research is quite different in form and requirements from the phases of reporting and analysis. Indeed, the proof of their objectivity should come from whether they overcome their affective responses during fieldwork and go on to consider why these occurred. It serves no useful purpose to categorize ethnographers as nonobjective because of what they felt.

Likewise, to label fieldworkers and their findings subjective merely because they mention their personal involvement in the fieldwork process is specious and counterproductive to the goal of improving anthropological methodology and theory. All research is biased by the researcher's background, gender, class, and other similar characteristics, as well as by the peculiarity of the milieu. In the special case of participant observation, bias is additionally the result of the dialectic relations of the hosts and ethnographer and their respective values, interaction styles, and so on. If so, then why should silence about the research milieu on the part of some ethnographers make them objective, but make those who do report about it subjective?

A better way to deal with the effects of researchers' personal characteristics and the relationships between hosts and ethnographers is to acknowledge them and to analyze their significance in the fieldwork process. When anthropologists do so, the idiosyncratic aspects of the research process become part of the research data and provide the context necessary for readers to grasp the import of actions and critically assess researchers' interpretations of them. Data on the fieldwork process that is included in a research report becomes a standard by which to judge the report's veracity and analytic worth. This is a prudent and productive course, but is a difficult one to undertake when the discipline discourages revelation of the ethnographers' feelings about their research and the way their particular histories color it. When the personal burdens imposed by cross-cultural fieldwork cannot be expressed, analyzed and incorporated into the processes of data reporting and interpretation because of the discipline's usual operationalization of the concepts of objectivity and cultural relativity, researchers may respond with feelings of professional and personal incompetence. Or they may completely repress the personal aspects in order to assure themselves of their own unusually rigorous objectivity, however spurious (or laudable) in actuality.

There is another reason for including personal factors in research reports--they yield sociological and cultural data. For example, the ways in which a society responds to the incorporation of a representative from the modern Western world may provide insights into their social relationships with that outside world and how they manage change stemming from these relationships. Similarly, women ethnographers' writings about these parts of their fieldwork have illuminated cultural expectations about gender.

Women have consistently addressed these personal aspects of fieldwork more often than their male counterparts. Indeed, the very first book-length treatment of the interrelationship of personal factors and the fieldwork experience was written by Hortense Powdermaker (1966). There are several possible explanations for this: perhaps it is more acceptable for women to address personal issues because they have lower status in the field than men and have less to lose by doing so, because women have different kinds of research experiences than do men, or because women are culturally associated with the domestic-familial domain where personal history and emotions can be revealed. Women's experiences doing fieldwork have also undoubtedly provoked their interest in the personal aspects of research. For example, contributors to *Women in the Field* (Golde, 1970) describe their hosts' various responses to the fact that they are women and their hosts' expectations of them. These fieldworkers also give their readers insights into how they perceive their professional positions were affected by their gender. Thus, not only do women write more about the domestic domain and their gender and how these impinge on their professional tasks, but they are presumably more influenced by these things. Professional women have always had to struggle against the stigma of being female and domestic while also trying to be 'male' and professional. To them has been given the dilemma of simultaneously meeting their families' needs and the demands of their jobs, while keeping these separate from each other. Margaret Mead claimed that these role conflicts make fieldwork more arduous for women and negatively affect their reports. Where they exist, such problems for female ethnographers may, however, also produce keener insights into the dialectic nature of the research process by making these anthropologists aware of how much of their data collection and analysis, and their hosts' actions, are inspired by personal and situational factors.

OVERVIEW OF THE CONTRIBUTIONS

Anthropologists' relationships with their children during fieldwork can test even more strenuously their interpretations of the concepts of objectivity and cultural relativity. When ethnographers disagree with their hosts' values and how the implementation of these may affect their children, they perceive that they may have some difficulties with these concepts. Kleis and Turner refer to this in their papers. However, as emphasized above, objectivity cannot be equated with a complete separation of the observer and host as persons. Knowledge of a culture comes from understanding the many, and presumably related, facts of others' lives, including here the ethnographers' and their children's effects on the milieu that they have all contributed to during the research period (cf. Kimball, 1972; Tedlock, 1982).

Even when the fieldworkers can insulate their professional standards from those forming their parental concern, the research situation hampers a real demarcation between the anthropologists' interactions with their families and relationships to their hosts. Anthropologists' children enmesh their parents in many ways in the host community, thus complicating the social and psychological webbing from which the parents as ethnographers want to be free. The blurring of the ethnographers' domestic and professional domains is due to the fundamental research methods of participant-observation, which rely on at least a superficial agreement to behave as do the anthropologists' hosts.

Immersing the fieldworkers' families in their hosts' lives may produce the kind of worries that Jacobson had about her children learning religious and caste prejudice or Huntington's and Turner's distress that their children's personalities may be affected by their fieldwork experiences. Parental responsibilities can also be felt for the hosts' children and can result in the type of solicitude that Kleis reports. Yet contributors to this volume do not say that they see their culture as better than those of their hosts, even though they find a few aspects of their hosts' cultures that they do not wish to have imparted to their children.

In addition to such negative observations, these anthropologists have found they prefer certain other elements of the host culture over their own. For example, Jacobson reminisces about how much better it would have been had she been in India when she broke her leg and required nursing and childcare assistance. In India the spatial and social closeness of kin would have assured her all the help she needed, while her American relatives, who did not live near her, could not provide it. Neither the positive nor the negative evaluations of the host culture, especially as it affected the ethnographers' children, preclude objectivity and cultural relativity in these anthropologists' articles.

In the papers composing this volume, various cultural meanings assigned to children and their development emerge. First among them is the fact that children are universally significant as new members of cultural systems. Once properly socialized, they will carry on the traditions of those who have enculturated them. For this reason the anthropologists' children can become the focus of a contest between the hosts and the parents for the children's cultural loyalty. This is particularly true if the hosts consider their own culture to be superior to other cultures or if the hosts know that outsiders think that their culture is inferior and they wish to prove otherwise. The children's cultural identities can be used to gauge the respective worth of the ethnographers' or hosts' culture and can be employed in the casting of politico-social relationships between hosts and researchers. Jacobson, for example, relates how her hosts, concerned about their caste purity, kept her daughter from joining a wedding party. Turner describes how her relationship with her 'housegirl' reflected her competition with her hosts over socializing her daughter.

A model of childhood socialization can be seen as analogous to a model of ethnicity. To the extent that children are enculturated in any society, they share the culture of a particular ethnic group. It is partly because enculturation produces ethnic identity that the researcher's children's adoption of the hosts' culture is so important for the hosts and researchers alike. There is also the fact that the hosts, as do people everywhere, socialize children in order to preserve the values they cherish. Since children learn such important cultural items as language faster than their parents, the hosts may claim an anthropologist's children as 'one of us'. The researchers' responses to their children's adoption of the hosts' culture and to the hosts' readiness to claim the children's allegiance may vary considerably, as the papers here demonstrate. Such responses may be looked upon as illustrations of cultural phenomena themselves.

Some anthropologists' interests in their children's socialization in the field and after their return to their home culture are complicated by the fact that they and their children have some kind of more permanent tie to the hosts. For example, when the fieldworker is not merely a visiting researcher but has affinal or consanguineal ties to the hosts' culture area or nation, the hosts are even more eager to transmit their culture to the researchers' children. This was the case for Butler, whose husband was Ecuadorian, and for Kleis, whose wife is a native of Cameroon. In her paper, Butler focuses on the zeal of several ethnic groups to enculturate her daughter as one of their members. This interethnic rivalry became an important source of additional understanding for her research on inter-ethnic relations, the transmission of ethnic identity and change in ethnic group membership.

These fieldworkers' children's socialization is also important to them because, as ethnographers, they are engaged in an acculturative process as they learn about and become participants in the hosts' culture. Indeed, the ethnographer-parents and their children are often equated by the hosts as initiates in their culture. Making parents and children similar in this way can pose problems for the parents who wish to fulfill parental roles. Turner addresses this issue in her paper. The hosts can also teach the anthropologists how to socialize their children and in this way acculturate the anthropologists. And, as Huntington suggests, when the hosts instruct the fieldworkers, the hosts reiterate for themselves how they should enculturate their children. The child socialization process recapitulates for adult instructors the culture's ideals and strengthens their commitment to these ideals.

The cultural meanings of socialization take on additional significance when we realize that there are perceived connections between it and the child development process. For instance, Butler was told by American medical and educational specialists that her child's learning disabilities were attributable to her child's intercultural experiences, which they viewed as disruptive to normal psychological development. In 1984 the diagnosis of psychogenic disorder was discarded when a congenital one was found. This interpretation of the etiology of Butler's child's developmental difficulties is related to a theme found, to some degree, in each contributor's paper, that the child development process unfolds in stages that must not be radically disrupted sequentially or in content, because such disruptions have deleterious and permanent repercussions. This orientation to the child development process, which can be dated at least to the 1928 publication of Watson's *Psychological Care of Infant and Child,* stresses the temporal dimension of the process "...once a child's character has been spoiled by bad handling which can be done in a few days, who can say that the damage is ever repaired?" (Beekman, 1977, p. 147).

Each anthropologist-parent writing here expresses similar views about the child development process and their statements articulate several cultural assumptions. Included among these assumptions are the perceived need for scheduling children's time and structuring their living areas; the need for preservation and encouragement of the children's self-confidence, autonomy, and creativity; and the need for the availability of certain educational and intellectual stimuli for the children's proper growth and preparation for life. These assumptions appear to be linked to certain American middle-class values regarding desirable personality traits, personal freedom and dignity, orderliness, and more egalitarian social relationships. And thus we read that Kleis and Turner worried that their children would not have proper academic preparation outside of the American milieu and would fall behind their peers upon their return home. Sharing this sentiment, the Whitefords recount how Marian Whiteford tutored their children using a large amount of educational materials that they carried along on their fieldtrips. Anxieties about the children's social-psychological development also existed during fieldwork: Huntington, Jacobson, and Turner say that they were disquieted by some of the social interactions that their children had and the possibility that these would have lasting effects on them. The idea that there is a certain inevitability in the child development process and that exposing the child to particular stimuli at critical phases is essential to its proper course may have increased these parents' concerns to continue their children's American socialization while in the field. Their children's eventual success in middle class American society these authors indicate, requires that they be taught specific values, behavior, attitudes, skills and language.

As these fieldworkers found, it is sometimes difficult to transmit their culture to their children in a foreign environment. Some of these ethnographers also found that socializing their children posed problems because they were unsure of what in a culture they wanted to transmit.

Parents who were bi-cultural or whose spouses belonged to other cultures describe the most difficulty in deciding what to impart to their children. These anthropologists' dilemma about cultural values appears to have been magnified during the research period when they experienced and tried to understand a new culture. For example, Turner was brought up in a Polish-American neighborhood where Polish was frequently spoken. Her desire to share a system of meanings with her child reminded her of the cultural stability and continuity that she forfeited when she affiliated with a more mainstream middle class American culture, and made her more aware of what her immigrant grandparents had endured in terms of their accommodation to American culture and the socialization of their children. Her daughter's enculturation in the Fijian village where she did her fieldwork further increased the stress Turner felt about her competing cultural loyalties.

Likewise in the papers by Butler and Kleis, the general concern for cultural continuity is made more complex by their interethnic and international marriages, and the resulting opportunity to choose between the parents' cultures or to select the best of both to transmit to their children. Applying the anthropological principle of cultural relativity while doing fieldwork can make this parental mandate to enculturate their children even more difficult. Parents in the field may feel that they vacillate between being indecisive and ineffectual in giving cultural instruction to their children and being judgmental and not culturally relative in their attitudes toward their hosts' culture.

While these contributors describe their feelings and beliefs regarding their children's socialization and of the child development process per se, they also provide us with examples of how cultures variously conceive the attributes of childhood, the circumstances that best nurture it, and the way socialization practices are associated with other institutions. For example, Kleis contrasts the American and African definitions of childhood. Unlike the ways Americans define childhood, for Africans childhood is not a state differentiated from adulthood by its own rules, rights, and developmental processes. Kleis interprets his African hosts as believing that contact with the world of adults, rather than isolation from it, best prepares children for eventual adulthood.

Whatever the differences between cultures' definitions of childhood, there is one element that they nonetheless share--children secure an important part of their parents' adult status. This can be particularly important for fieldworkers, since other markers of adulthood recognized in the host society, such as competence in certain skills, may be lacking. For this reason, fieldworkers' children may be instrumental in integrating their parents into local adult social life. For example, Jacobson found that in contrast to an earlier fieldtrip without children, research with her children established her personal reputation and made certain types of social interaction more accessible to her. She was no longer seen as a barren woman who could threaten the Indian women's fecundity and the well-being of their children, which are their primary concerns. The Whitefords wrote that their children facilitated Andrew Whiteford's research by broadening his interests in his hosts' kinship network. As the younger generation in his own and his hosts' families matured, new perspectives were gained on family life, and new research topics were suggested for Whiteford.

The accounts of American anthropologists' fieldtrips with their children in this volume suggest many commonalities in the researchers' values, such as individual worth, self-direction, assertive discipline, privacy, order and stability. The last three are most clearly expressed in the Whitefords' paper. They tell us that a stable home base and the integration of children into family and community structures gives children a sense of security that is vital for their growth and optimistic orientation towards life. Butler also reflects on how a specific type of domestic setting was suggested for her child by her visiting parents. The satisfactions of maintaining a routine for children is also noted in both papers. What is deemed necessary for the proper socialization of these children is based on assumptions that not all people share. For example, nomads must organize time and space in a different manner than we do. Butler's Quichua-speaking informants found regular naps, mealtimes and bedtimes for children ludicrous; in their experience children eat when they are hungry and sleep when they are tired. But even our efforts to structure time and space for children pale in comparison to those of the Hutterites, who, as Huntington reports, have comprehensive rules governing the allocation of space, time and activities.

Variations between fieldworkers' and their hosts' utilizations of time and space are not only associated with the cultures that underlie these arrangements but with the transmission of these cultures. The transmission of a culture is facilitated when its environment, both social and physical, reinforces it. During cross-cultural research, the fieldworkers' parental values may not be reiterated and enhanced by other institutions, neighbors, friends, and kin. Kleis reports how the lack of complementarity between the values of his hosts and his family result in childcare and disciplinary problems. This problem is shared with his African neighbors in the multi-ethnic city in which he works. The lack of articulation between home and community values poses problems for transmitting ethnic identities to children, as he and his neighbors have found.

The anthropologists' children who have been the objects of these various socializations have responded differently to their shuttling between cultures. Most cases were like Kleis's daughter, who tried very hard to adopt her Nigerian classmates' language and culture, as well as that of her parents, and who knew two variations of English and used them appropriately. However, one of the Whitefords' daughters suppressed all knowledge of Spanish when she returned to her American midwestern community where only local interests were socially approved. When one of Huntington's sons rebelled against the Hutterites' strictness and use of physical punishment, she arranged to keep this son with her, rather than with his own age groups and its adult supervisors. Jacobson's discussion of her daughter's relationships with her Indian hosts at different times shows that children may respond variously to fieldwork, depending on their ages and other variables.

It is apparent from this overview of the volume's papers that our children's presence during fieldwork has opened avenues to new data and awareness for us. Indeed, the oldest children, those of Huntington and the Whitefords, actually contributed information to their respective parents' research. This is partly the case because no one participant-observer is able to obtain as much data on a culture as a team of researchers. But some information is uniquely accessible to children. For example, Huntington's daughter's description of the Hutterite girls' playhouse, which prefaces her paper, contains many things surprising to an outside observer of Hutterite culture. This description is exceptional because no adults are near when the children occupy the playhouse. In addition, the fieldworkers' children may adopt their hosts' culture and become their parents' teachers; e.g., Huntington's daughter sometimes reprimanded her mother for such infractions as laughing in front of men or wearing the wrong type of clothes. The local children, too, may teach the researchers things that their parents may not be able to or want to do for numerous reasons. These children ingenuously may instruct the fieldworkers or somehow be given the task by their elders.

CONCLUSION

While these papers illustrate the themes found in the earlier literature on fieldwork accompanied by one's children, they also consider topics either hinted at in these works or not noted at all. In our quest to find material for an anthropological analysis of the effects of children on their parents' research, we note, among other things, the contributors' cultural assumptions; the meanings attached to children and to their socialization in a cross-cultural situation; the burdens imposed by ethnographers' commitment to their children's socialization and its symbolic content on their adherence to the concepts of cultural relativity and objectivity; and to the similarity in the position of parents and their children in the cross-cultural research situation. More generally, we have explored objectivity, cultural relativity, the professional versus the domestic parts of life, and the dialectic nature of fieldwork. Significantly, these topics and the volume's purposes articulate with trends and concerns affecting anthropology, and other disciplines as well (Sass, 1986). They are at the heart of a relatively new issue in anthropology--the doubt among many anthropologists that

> ...conventional anthropological methods can do justice to the kaleidoscopic nature of social reality, and....that so-called value-free observations do not take into account wider political realities and moral ambiguities (Sass, 1986, p. 50).

The influence of the reflexive process on these anthropologists appears in this volume, as it has in many recent works. What differentiates this volume from others is the intensity and pervasiveness of this process because of the role of the researchers' children during fieldwork. The children's presence necessitates that more attention be paid to the governing disciplinary precepts and to the dialectic nature of field research.

REFERENCES

Agar, M. H. (1980). *The Professional Stranger: An Informal Introduction to Ethnography.* New York: Academic Press.

Andersen, M. L. (1983). *Thinking About Women: Sociological and Feminine Perspective.* New York: Macmillan Publishing Co.

Beals, A. R. (1970). Gopalpur, 1958-60. In G. D. Spindler (Ed.), *Being an Anthropologist,* (pp. 32-57). New York: Holt, Rinehart and Winston.

Beekman, D. (1977). *The Mechanical Baby.* New American Library.

Boissevain, J. F. (1970). Fieldwork in Malta. In G. D. Spindler (Ed.), *Being an Anthropologist,* (pp. 58-84). New York: Holt, Rinehart and Winston.

Cesara, M. (1982). *Reflections of a Woman Anthropologist: No Hiding Place.* London: Academic Press.

Chafe, W. H. (1979). *Women and Equality: Changing Patterns in American Culture.* New York: Oxford University Press.

Clinton, C. (1984). *The Other Civil War: American Women in the Nineteenth Century.* New York: Hill and Wang.

Colombotos, J. (1963). Sex Role and Professionalism: A Study of High School Teachers. *The School Review,* No. 1;27-40.

Cunniff, J. (1985). Comparability Could be Costly to Women. In *The Free Lance-- Star.* Fredericksburg, VA: Thursday, June 13, 1985.

Dentan, R. (1970). Living and Working with the Semai. In G. D. Spindler (Ed.), *Being an Anthropologist,* (pp. 85-112). New York: Holt, Rinehart and Winston.

Diamond, N. (1970). Fieldwork in a Complex Society. In G. D. Spindler (Ed.), *Being an Anthropologist,* (pp. 113-141). New York: Holt, Rinehart and Winston.

Diaz, M. N. (1966). *Tonala: Conservatism, Responsibility and Authority in a Mexican Town.* Berkeley, CA: University of California Press.

Dumont, J-P. (1978). *The Headman and I: Ambiguity and Ambivalence in the Fieldworking Experience.* Austin, TX: University of Texas Press.

Fischer, A. (1970). Fieldwork in Five Cultures. In P. Golde (Ed.), *Women in the Field,* (pp. 265-289). Chicago: Aldine Publishing Co.

Fluehr-Lobban, C. (1981). Josina's Observations of Sudanese Culture. In *Human Organization* 40:277-279, Fall.

Foster, G. M. and Kemper, R. V. (Eds.) (1974). *Anthropologists in Cities.* Boston, MA: Little, Brown, and Co.

Freilich, M. (1970). *Marginal Natives: Anthropologists at Work.* New York: Harper and Row Publishers.

Frisbie, C. J. (1975). Fieldwork as a "Single Parent": To Be or Not to Be Accompanied by a Child. In T. Frisbie (Ed.), *Collected Papers of Florence Hawley Ellis*, (pp. 98-119). Archeological Society of New Mexico.

Gallin, B. and Gallin, R. (1974). The Rural to Urban Migration of an Anthropologist in Taiwan. In G. M. Foster and R. V. Kemper (Eds.) *Anthropologists in Cities*, (pp. 223-248). Boston, MA: Little, Brown and Co.

Golde, P. (Ed.) (1970). *Women in the Field*. Chicago: Aldine Publishing Co.

Gonzalez, N. L. (1970). Cakchiqueles and Caribs: The Social Context of Fieldwork. In M. Freilich (Ed.), *Marginal Natives*, (pp. 153-184). New York: Harper and Row Publishers.

Gonzalez, N. L. (1974). The City of Gentlemen: Santiago de los Aballeros. In G. M. Foster and R. Kemper (Eds.), *Anthropologists in Cities*, (pp. 19-40). Boston, MA: Little, Brown and Co.

Gulick, J. (1974). Village and City Fieldwork in Lebanon. In M. Freilich (Ed.), *Marginal Natives*, (pp. 123-152). New York: Harper and Row Publishers.

Harland, M. (1889). *House and Home: The Complete Housewives' Guide*. Philadelphia, PA: Clawson.

Hart, C. W. M. (1970). Fieldwork among the Tiwi, 1928-29. In G. D. Spindler (Ed.), *Being an Anthropologist*, (pp. 142-163). New York: Holt, Rinehart and Winston.

Hill, C. E. (1974). Graduate Education in Anthropology: Conflicting Role Identity in Fieldwork. In *Human Organization* 33(4):408-412.

Hitchcock, J. T. (1970). Fieldwork in Ghurka Country. In G. D. Spindler (Ed.), *Being an Anthropologist*, (pp. 164-193). New York: Holt, Rinehart and Winston.

Honigmann, J. J. (1970). Fieldwork in Two North Canadian Communities. In M. Freilich (Ed.), *Marginal Natives*, (pp. 39-72). New York: Harper and Row Publishers.

Hostetler, J. A. and Huntington, G. E. (1970). The Hutterites: Fieldwork in a North American Communal Society. In G. D. Spindler (Ed.), *Being an Anthropologist* (pp. 194-219). New York: Holt, Rinehart and Winston.

Hymes, D. (1969). *Reinventing Anthropology*. New York: Random House.

Kimball, S. T. (1972). Learning a New Culture. In S. Kimball and J. B. Watson (Eds.), *Crossing Cultural Boundaries: The Anthropological Experience*, (pp. 182-192). San Francisco, CA: Chandler Publishing Co.

Maybury-Lewis, D. (1965). *The Savage and the Innocent*. Cleveland and New York: The World Publishing Co.

Mead, M. (1970). The Art and Technology of Fieldwork. In R. Naroll and R. Cohen (Eds.), *A Handbook of Method in Cultural Anthropology*, (pp. 246-265). Garden City, NY: The Natural History Press.

Mead, M. (1970a). Fieldwork in the Pacific Islands, 1925-67. In P. Golde (Ed.), *Women in the Field*, (pp. 291-331). Chicago: Aldine Publishing Co.

Moore, W. E. (1970). *The Professions: Roles and Rules.* New York: Russell Sage Foundation.

Norbeck, E. (1970). Changing Japan: Field Research. In G. D. Spindler (Ed.), *Being an Anthropologist,* (pp. 238-266). New York: Holt, Rinehart and Winston.

Perlman, M. L. (1970). Intensive Fieldwork and Scope Sampling: Methods for Studying the Same Problem at Different Levels. In M. Freilich (Ed.), *Marginal Natives,* (pp. 293-338). New York: Harper and Row Publishers.

Powdermaker, H. (1966). *Stranger and Friend.* New York: W. W. Norton and Co., Inc.

Rabinow, P. (1977). *Reflections on Fieldwork in Morocco.* Berkeley, CA: University of California Press.

Ruby, J. (1982). *A Crack in the Mirror: Reflexive Perspectives in Anthropology.* Philadelphia, PA: University of Pennsylvania Press.

Sass, L. A. (1986). Anthropology's Native Problem. In *Harper's Magazine.* May: 49-57.

Scheffler, I. (1967). *Science and Subjectivity.* Indianapolis, IN: The Bobbs-Merrill Co., Inc.

Schultz, H. (1961). Blue-Eyed Indian. In *National Geographic Magazine.* 120:1:64-89.

Schwab, W. B. (1970). Comparative Field Techniques in Urban Research in Africa. In M. Freilich (Ed.), *Marginal Natives,* (pp. 73-122). New York: Harper and Row.

Simic, A. (1974). The Best of Two Worlds: Serbian Peasants in the City. In G. M. Foster and R. V. Kemper (Eds.), *Anthropologists in Cities,* (pp. 179-200). Boston, MA: Little, Brown and Co.

Spindler, G. D. (1970). *Being an Anthropologist: Fieldwork in Eleven Cultures.* New York: Holt, Rinehart and Winston.

Spindler, G. D. and Spindler, L. (1970). Fieldwork Among the Menomini. In G. D. Spindler (Ed.), *Being an Anthropologist,* (pp. 267-285). New York: Holt, Rinehart and Winston.

Spradley, J. P. and McCurdy, D. W. (1980). *Anthropology: The Cultural Perspective.* New York: John Wiley and Sons.

Stack, C. (1980). *All Our Kin.* New York: Harper and Row Publishers.

Tedlock, B. (1982). *Time and the Highland Maya.* Albuquerque, NM: University of New Mexico Press.

Tilly, L. A. and Scott, J. W. (1978). *Women, Work and Family.* New York: Holt, Rinehart and Winston.

Valentine, B. (1978). *Hustling and Other Hard Work: Life Styles in the Ghetto.* New York: The Free Press.

Vollmer, H. M. and Mills, D. L. (Eds.) (1966). *Professionalization.* Englewood Cliffs, NJ: Prentice-Hall, Inc.

Whiteford, M. (1974). Barrio Tulcan: Fieldwork in a Colombian City. In G. M. Foster and R. V. Kemper (Eds.), *Anthropologists in Cities,* (pp. 41-62). Boston, MA: Little, Brown and Co.

Yengoyan, A. (1970). Open Networks and Native Formalism: The Mandaya and Pitjandara Cases. In M. Freilich (Ed.), *Marginal Natives,* (pp. 403-440). New York: Harper and Row Publishers.

MANGO PICKLES AND GOAT GRASS:

FAMILY FIELDWORK IN AN INDIAN VILLAGE

Doranne Jacobson *(1)*

Department of Anthropology, Barnard College and
Southern Asian Institute, Columbia University
New York, NY 10027

INTRODUCTION

In the heart of India there is a small settlement of agriculturalists, artisans, and entrepreneurs living in mud-plastered houses nestled at the foot of a forest-covered hill. None of the villagers have travelled outside of India and most have but a dim idea of the location of America, which they call "Amirka," or "Land of the Rich." In fact, some of the least sophisticated of the villagers believe America lies somewhere near the snowcapped Himalayas, as they have heard America is a country of ice and snow, very unlike the tropical region they inhabit. But however uninformed these villagers may be about New World geography, they know a surprising amount about American family life, as they have been able to observe at first hand an American family which has been associated with their village for several years.

The family which--for better or for worse--has provided virtually all of the information upon which these villagers base their opinions of American domestic structure is my own. The villagers have been able to watch the progress of my family-cycle over a span of nearly two decades, and they have met not only me--an inquisitive ethnographer, my archaeologist husband, and my two children, but also a few of my other relatives who have visited us in India. One of the most prosperous village families has recently received detailed reports on us from their kinsmen who emigrated to the United States and have visited our American home several times. While I have studied the villagers and their rich panoply of traditions, they, in turn, have studied us. In the long course of our interaction, we have changed each others' lives in many subtle ways.(2)

31

The special nature of anthropological field research often requires long-term *in situ* study of a group of people, and it has become commonplace for anthropologists to live for years in cultures other than their own, frequently under conditions that would be considered primitive or difficult by middle-class Western standards. Anthropologists' spouses and children often live with the researcher in the field, thus becoming an integral part of the research situation, affecting and being affected by their surroundings.

Anthropology may be unique among the sciences in the extent to which the investigator's domestic unit influences the research and is itself altered by it. Yet, until now, very little has been said about this special aspect of anthropology. Anthropologists have, of course, written about doing fieldwork; particularly in relatively recent years (see, for example, Powdermaker 1966, Spindler 1970, Golde 1970, Freilich 1970, Mead 1972, Beteille and Madan 1975, and Georges and Jones 1980), yet not enough has been written on the place in the research of the researcher's spouse, and even less on the researcher's children. Among the few anthropologists to have openly acknowledged the importance of their children in their research are Gertrude Enders Huntington (1970:206-13, 1981), who worked among Hutterites, and Jeremy Boissevain (1970:69-74), who conducted research in Malta.

That anthropologists' children in the field have been but barely acknowledged in the academic literature can easily be seen as part of Western culture's pervasive segregation of children and other mundane aspects of domestic life from the high-minded realms of business, academe, and other professions. As we all know, crying babies are barred from corporate boardrooms, lawyers' offices, and anthropological conferences.(3)

The separation of the domestic and professional spheres is a major theme in modern Western urban culture, so basic that it is not often subject to serious challenge. It is almost never acceptable for a professional person to openly bring domestic responsibilities into the workplace. Except for an emergency involving imminent or actual death, a person's need to perform family-related activities is seldom accepted without prejudice by supervisors or professional colleagues. Usually, professional and domestic demands upon an individual are seen as being in potential or actual conflict, and the forces of the workplace act to punish those who are deemed to allow their professional work to suffer because of involvement in home responsibilities.(4)

It is with regard to young children that these prohibitions are strongest. Indeed, the child-nurturing urges which parents typically experience do frequently conflict with often overwhelming professional demands that our attention be almost exclusively devoted to work-related matters. Sanctions for transgression must be substantial to be efficacious; these usually involve threats to one's ability to support oneself and one's family.

In the 1979 Academy-award-winning film *Kramer vs. Kramer,* a man's wife suddenly departs, leaving him responsible for the care of his young son.   When the father's involvement with birthday parties and PTA meetings intrudes into the sacrosanct precincts of his Madison Avenue office, his boss and supposed friend fires him from his job.   In real life, professional women have known for years that any mention of their young children to male--and sometimes female--work associates can cause them to fall a notch or two in the professional pecking order.

Mr. Kramer's problem was special because he had had no training in how to actually be actively involved in family duties and yet conceal this fact from his work colleagues.   Women tend to develop such skills over many years.   When a woman being considered for a position of high responsibility is asked for information on her offspring and/or plans for parenthood, she is aware that she cannot admit to devotion to the needs of her own young children and still hope to achieve substantial professional success.   Certainly, an academic woman who discusses her young children at length with colleagues runs the risk of not being accepted as a serious scholar.

Women are, of course, particularly vulnerable to the charge that they may not be able to adequately separate and carry out home and work duties.   Until recent years, with men holding virtually all of the major professonal positions, the separation of realms depended upon women-- wives, maiden aunts, grannies, or servants--working at home to care for children and maintain domestic establishments supportive of men working separately from the home sphere.   Even today, women working outside the home usually rely heavily upon other women, such as domestic employees and day care workers, to carry out essential family-related tasks.   In fact, most women working outside the home still personally bear the major responsibility for domestic work.   Thus, women are usually seen as more responsive to domestic demands than men are, a negative factor to an employer.

Obviously, without appropriate supportive institutions and males who truly share in shouldering domestic responsibilities, along with general acknowledgement of the relevance of home and family life to all aspects of human endeavor, these conflicts will continue.

In fact, the separation of the domestic and the professional is a false distinction, very difficult to maintain.   Anyone with normal human emotions will ponder family problems both at work and at home.   Similarly, involvement in work-related challenges can dramatically affect one's family life.   These two realms are separated by a membrane as thin as that separating the yolk of an egg from the white.   Each moves in response to movement in the other, and the slightest disturbance brings a rupture, inextricably mixing the two.   Still, we are compelled to publicly pretend that the two spheres are, and should be completely separate.

For anthropologists, this can be a rather elaborate pretense, involving deceiving oneself as well as others. It is interesting to note that many anthropologists, like the people whose customs they so carefully analyze, often fail to see the implications of their own taboos. In the case of an anthropologist, particularly a cultural anthropologist conducting field research, these areas are inextricably blended. In a non-North American or non-Northern European society, especially in any non-urban setting, there can be virtually no separation of the domestic and the professional for the ethnographer.

The reciprocal reflections between all facets of their lives should be acknowledged and openly examined by anthropologists. This volume, the conference from which it springs, and succeeding discussions have provided much-needed forums for such examination.

Another aspect of existing domestic-professional tension is the fact that in urban North America today, children are widely considered an irritant to adults, limiting to pleasurable and useful activity. Clearly, most parents love their own children to at least some extent, and the clientele at adoption agencies and fertility clinics is more than ample. Still, many adult Americans avoid contact with children. For example, interviewing retirees in a "child-free" retirement community on Long Island, a reporter elicited the following remarks from grandparents and others:

> "They are precious, as long as they're asleep."
> "Don't get me wrong, I like kids, I just don't like them around."
> "Many of us have children and grand-children, and we don't miss all the crying and screaming and running and jumping. I do love children, though."
> "Personally, I hate kids." (Geist, 1982)

In some urban areas, numerous museums, movie theatres, restaurants, and apartment buildings also ban children or restrict their access. Children are regularly excluded from adults-only concerts, parties, weddings, and funerals as well. Their presence on airplanes is resented by adults who are unbearably irritated by their whimpers and write complaining letters to newspaper editors in order to elicit sympathy for their suffering the little children to sit near them.

Such negative views and restrictions have developed within the context of the American system of age grading, segregation of children from the adult world in general, and the separation of family and work-related concerns.

FIRST FIELDWORK IN INDIA

Carrying a full assortment of cultural baggage with us, my husband Jerry and I departed for India to do our dissertation research. We first went to India in 1964 and remained there until 1967, living much of the time in a village we call Nimkhera, in Madhya Pradesh state, central India. During our first field trip we had no children, but in 1973, with our three-year-old daughter Laurie, we returned to India for fifteen months. In 1979 we spent three months in India, accompanied by Laurie, then eight, and our son Joshua, three.

When we left for India the first time, we little knew how much our professional and private lives would be affected by the fieldwork experience, and vice versa. In fact, the focus of my study was to be Indian dichotomies of private and public: my particular interest was in purdah, the seclusion and veiling of women.

In India, we learned that expectations about public and private realms are very different from our own. Certain aspects of domestic life are certainly to be kept separate from one's public life, if one has a public life (many women in seclusion hardly do). For example, in some parts of India, a man of a traditional family ought not to publicly discuss, or even refer to, the existence of his wife, and the wife herself may be veiled or otherwise shielded from the view of visitors to the home and others outside the close family circle. Yet, in other respects, family life is considered extremely relevant to one's means of making a living. For many Indians, the caste into which they, like their families, are born, is a major determinant of occupational choice. For example, members of the Washerman, Carpenter, Potter, and Tailor castes typically work in their traditional caste endeavors. In other instances, several generations of a family will specialize in a particular business or profession. For example, the Jhaveri family is India's most prominent diamond merchant family. Their name means "jeweler" and is obviously taken from their line of work. In their business, international trading networks follow kin ties.

When Indian college graduates in many fields apply for white-collar jobs, they consider it significant to mention the stations of their closest relatives of importance, and to indicate that they belong to a "respectable family." Government and other office employees of high and low rank regard it as normal to take "casual leave" to spend a week attending a cousin's wedding in a distant city. Indeed, such attendance can be crucial, since the success of some future effort may well depend upon family ties established or reaffirmed at the wedding.

In many situations in India, people who are not related to each other set up fictive kinship ties so that they can treat each other as quasi-relatives. Colleagues and business associates frequently address each other as "uncle," or "elder brother," and children call neighbors "aunt" and "uncle."

In the rural setting in which I conducted research in central India, family and work are completely interdependent. Landowning farmers, contractors, laborers, priests, and craftspeople reside and work closely together. The whole village is seen as a family-like group, with kinship terms used for all, whether or not actually related by blood or marriage. To a larger extent, occupations still follow caste and family traditions, and long-established patron-client relationships between families remain important to many villagers. Villagers typically work surrounded by their kin, including their children, and nepotism extending to family, fellow caste members, and fellow villagers is expected and considered desirable.

The virtues and foibles of several generations of one's family are known to all fellow villagers and are the topics of common gossip. Such knowledge strongly affects responses to an individual in virtually every situation. Unsurprisingly, in this hierarchical society, political leadership and economic power follow family lines.

With family ties so important to one's position, it is accepted that a person will take time off from ordinary toil in order to participate in lengthy weddings, funerals, caste council meetings, pilgrimages to deposit deceased relatives' ashes in the sacred Ganges River, or any of a number of other kin-related activities. Additionally, for women, childbirth and child care are assumed to take precedence over other obligations.

While women work and play apart from men in many situations, children do not. Young children are a part of every event and activity. For example, at a village council meeting, a council member might well have a small granddaughter on his lap. In fact, in certain ritual contexts, young high-caste Hindu girls are acknowledged as embodiments of goddess-like qualities and are worshipped by male village elders. Only as children mature do they withdraw from particular activities in order to adhere to adult sex segregation rules.

My husband and I discovered that for our research work in the village to succeed at all, we had to be adjudged acceptable as human beings and as a family. Our personal characters and the nature of our domestic life would be examined and evaluated throughout the time we lived and worked in the village, and our access to the information we sought would be facilitated or inhibited accordingly.

Nimkhera, the settlement in which we lived, is a village of about six-hundred and fifty people, eighty percent Hindu and twenty percent Muslim, situated some forty miles east of the state capital of Bhopal, and eleven miles east of the district center of Raisen. Fertile fields of wheat, lentils, and rice provide most villagers with a livelihood, while some villagers derive significant income from trucking and construction contract work. In this relatively traditional village, we were fortunate in residing in a private guesthouse, owned by a wealthy village family and made available for our use.

The house, built expressly to provide accommodation for guests, faced the center of the Muslim quarter and backed onto the Hindu section of the village. Like other local houses, the guesthouse had walls of stone plastered with earth and whitewashed, with a roof of hand-made clay tiles. Floored with cement, the structure included two large rooms--one for us, and the other for my research assistant, a well-educated young woman from a city. There were front and back verandahs, a tiny kitchen, bathing room, enclosed rear courtyard with a guava tree, and best of all, a private septic-tank latrine, operated with buckets of water. This latter feature was thoughtfully constructed by our host just before we moved in and saved us from having to trek to the forest or fields for elimination, as most of the villagers did, or use the traditional "sweeper system" favored by some prosperous village families.

Cool well water was brought to us regularly in a special bullock cart fitted with a steel tank and manned by one of our host's many servants. We ourselves had servants; we brought a cook from Bhopal city who did the time-consuming shopping in the market centers and spent about eight hours a day in the kitchen, while his wife dusted, swept, and washed clothes. Our having our own house and servants made it possible for us to set our own routine, more or less, and to eat food that we found palatable. By local village standards, we were living in luxury.

However, even our Boy and Girl Scout training had not adequately prepared us for the need to deal with several serious practical problems. There were constant incursions of rats and mice into our home; Jerry eventually trapped more than five-hundred in our house and courtyard. Scorpions appeared in the latrine, and one frightful night a black cobra hissed its way into my assistant's bedroom. (We killed it and later blocked all possible snakeholes.) Rabies, too, posed a threat--mad dogs kill many hundreds of people in India each year, and several village canines died in foaming fits during our stay. The climate was also challenging. The winter season was pleasant, if sometimes chilly, but the hot season brought temperatures of well over one-hundred and ten degrees amid swirling dust storms, and in the monsoon downpours our roof leaked impressively. All of these conditions threatened our sense of well-being, and the weather particularly affected our ability to work.

Our host, Latif Khan, and hostess, Birjis Jahan, were Muslim Pathans, whose families had originally come from Afghanistan to settle in this region, formerly part of the Pathan-ruled princely state of Bhopal, which merged with India after independence. Pathans consider the giving of hospitality to be an essential virtue, and we were among the fortunate recipients of their largesse.

We were offered hospitality initially because we were introduced to Latif Khan by a government official who requested that we be accommodated. However, as time went on, Latif Khan and his family wanted to know a lot more about us before they extended more than mere Pathan courtesies. Queries about our marital status were of first importance. Were we really married, or were we illicit lovers, as some district official was said to have suggested? This question was significant in a culture where extramarital relations, especially for women, are strongly condemned. Had we not been married, my research work probably never would have progressed very far, nor would we have received the generous treatment we did.

Other queries followed, pertaining to our family backgrounds and to our real purpose in the village--some nefarious aim, or academic research? Were we honorable people? Most particularly, was my husband a man of merit who could be trusted not to take advantage of local women? If he could not be considered a man of "good character," I would have had no women visitors.

Apparently we passed muster, and Latif Khan's family and others who accepted his leadership treated us with great warmth. Latif Khan called me "sister," and Birjis Jahan, normally veiled from unrelated men, received Jerry as a brother.

We were often invited to dine with our hosts, and we rode in their jeep on exciting nocturnal hunts for deer, antelope, leopard, and wild boar in the jungle near the village. Venison and other game were often sent over for our cook to prepare.

In an effort to gain rapport with intially suspicious villagers outside of our host's circle, we provided amateur medical care to several people each day, and we became sadly aware of the high infant mortality rate and the dangers of disease for all villagers. On this first research trip, we ourselves fortunately fell victim only to flu and intestinal parasites. But our jeep was frequently used to rush victims of viper bites, diphtheria, meningitis, tuberculosis, and typhoid to the nearest hospital, eleven miles away. When some of the patients died, we cried with the other mourners, all pretense of objectivity stripped away. Similarly, when a patient lived because of our intervention, we rejoiced. As we became more and more personally involved in the villagers' lives, we became increasingly accepted by the entire village community, and our ability to conduct research was enhanced.

Within our home we had a certain amount of privacy, although visitors were constantly dropping in. Patients arrived every morning at dawn to demand medicines and bandages. One vegetarian, Brahman, found it particularly amusing to visit us every evening at dinner time to watch our carnivorous eating habits. He, like the other villagers, was interested in knowing about our dietary habits, as these are closely linked to caste and religious affiliation in India, as well as to other aspects of status. While we objected to eating on stage, as it were, we realized that these and other visits allowed the villagers to obtain the information about us they needed to categorize and accept us. Of course, the visits provided many opportunities for us to learn about the local culture and to make friends, essential for our work. When we desperately needed full privacy to protect our sanity, it was possible for us to latch the doors and window shutters, although some determined callers could still get in through a chink in the courtyard wall. Later, when our children were with us, we all slept in one big room with our beds in a row, so there was no full privacy as American families know it in their native land.

In conducting his archaeological investigations, my husband and his field crew of local youths usually went off to the jungle for the day, or worked with microliths and paleoliths on the back verandah. During their hours with Jerry, the youths plied him with a multitude of questions about our habits, and he, in turn, elicited plenty of ethnographic information from them. The families of the young men would not have allowed them to work with Jerry if they had not decided that his character as well as his project were acceptable.

In my study of the lives of women who observed purdah--seclusion and veiling--I found that many of these women, sequestered as they were, were at first suspicious of me and my American peculiarities. My being married was a great asset--in that regard they considered me normal, while my unmarried urban research assistant was the subject of much amazed gossip. In this part of India, all rural females who are not severely handicapped are married quite young.

Rapport was hard to develop, but my assistant and I worked at it constantly, and we finally achieved wide acceptance. Still, we found we were unwelcome at family infant blessing ceremonies, rites designed to protect the newborn from death, all too common in this rural area. Since we were initially unknown outsiders, it was feared that we might transmit malevolent influences or bear envious feelings that could bring disaster to vulnerable babies and their mothers. In this most vital matter, the villagers could not afford to make a mistake about us. Their fears were mitigated only very gradually.

In fact, having babies was the women's main concern, and the fact that I had no children bothered them. One old woman, of whom I became extremely fond, one day put her hands on my head and blessed me, saying, "May you have many sons," Clearly this was the best fate she could wish for me. Women constantly patted my stomach and demanded to know when I was going to produce offspring. Even my husband got advice--most memorably from a ten-year-old boy who admonished him that if he wanted to become a father, he ought to increase his sexual activity. Virtually every village Hindu rite I attended was celebration of or a request for prosperity and fertility, eternally intertwined.

Certainly, in this agricultural community, a family's prosperity could not be maintained without children. A new baby was born in the village weekly, and all around us were scores of children. We became especially friendly with a neighboring family of nine charming children who were in and out of our house frequently. During our stay, our hostess, Birjis Jahan, gave birth to her eleventh child, quietly and without fuss, as I watched. After two years of playing with many children and receiving intense pro-reproductive brainwashing, whatever reservations Jerry and I might have felt about having a family had been overcome.

Our fieldwork was challenging but successful. We returned to the United States with full sets of field notes—and a determination to produce not only dissertations but children.

Back at Columbia University, a little counter-reproductive influence from our academic advisors and demanding teaching schedules postponed our becoming parents for a couple of years. But when our daughter Laurie was finally born, we happily sent out proud news to the village. My research assistant went to Nimkhera to distribute sweets on our behalf, as we would have done if we had been there. Our American relatives and friends were pleased, certainly, but from what we learned, I think the villagers were equally pleased.

SECOND AND THIRD FIELD TRIPS TO INDIA

When Laurie was two years old, we went to India for just a month, taking her with us, not only as a matter of practicality, but also to show her off. The villagers were delighted to see her, and they were happy that we had proven ourselves normal enough to have children as they so regularly did.

At that time, Laurie was just learning English, and Hindi was a complete mystery to her. While she was doted upon by all, it was not an easy matter to care for her and conduct intensive field research at the same time. Diapers were a problem, and food, too, was difficult.

A few months later, in 1973, when Laurie was turning three, we returned to India for a stay of fifteen months, this time hoping that Laurie would fully adjust to life in village India. Essentially, she did.

We were, of course, familiar with the Nimkhera village setting and its questionable medical facilities and health hazards. We engaged a new cook from Bhopal, whose wife Selma became our *ayah*, or nursemaid. Selma knew no English, but she came with six children of her own and set up housekeeping in a small house adjacent to ours. Laurie learned to move freely between our house, Selma's house, and our host's home. Latif Khan's teen-aged daughter took a great interest in playing with Laurie and teaching her Hindi, which proved to be a great benefit. With her simple Hindi, Laurie was soon communicating and playing well with the neighbor children.

Laurie occasionally went to the village school with some of her friends, although she was really too young to comprehend the lessons. She happily went around the village and attended rituals with me, and in general became a part of the village scene. She wore the jingling anklets, tinkling bangles, and long petticoats popular in the village and learned the body language of the local children.

Some of the children of poor families treated Laurie with a little too much respect, however, fueling the possessiveness she felt about her vast supply of American and Indian toys. Our host's children considered her equal to them in social standing, but they overindulged her at times, in the same way Indians often indulge their own small family members. They also mischievously taught her some Hindi obscenities, and I was very much embarrassed when I heard her utter these offensive phrases in the presence of visiting government dignitaries!

The nursemaid's little daughter was blissfully unaware of her low status as a servant's child and sometimes called Laurie insulting names, thus providing a healthy antidote to the indulgence Laurie received from others. Without realizing it, the nursemaid's daughter was reacting negatively to Laurie's anomalous, but favored, status as an "American Princess" within a highly hierarchical society. On one hand, I was pleased that my child was enjoying pleasant treatment, but on the other hand, my personal sense of democracy, derived from my own culture, was offended by a system that consigned people at birth to such ranks as "important people," "high-caste," "untouchable," "low-caste," or "low quality," and treated them accordingly throughout their lives. Furthermore, the local people were extremely color-conscious, with fair skin being considered much more beautiful than dark skin. The nursemaid often praised Laurie's light color and derided others for being "black."

I did not want my child to respond to such color preferences or to learn the behaviors required of the favored to keep the disfavored in their place. Animosity between religious communities was another subject of which I wanted my child to develop no personal knowledge. However, I did not want my child to suffer the disrespect often accorded those at the bottom of the social scale. In fact, even though she was an "American Princess" among the Muslims and most of the Hindus, conservative high-caste Hindus considered her (and her whole family) to be ritually impure, and they took care to keep her away from easily "polluted" water pots and cooked foods. Still, as long as I lived in the village and raised my child there, she would learn at first hand, as all village children do, how to be part of this complex hierarchical system, a system which I could accept only as an object of anthropological investigation.

In the midst of India, we tried to give Laurie a sense of her identity as an American. Our family celebrated local holidays with the villagers, and, in turn, invited neighbors to participate in our attenuated American festivities. One Christmas, my mother and sister were with us, and we sang carols to the villagers. Another sister and her husband visited for Thanksgiving. These celebrations, as well as the welcome visits from our relatives, reminded us of who we were. They also pleased our village friends and helped them realize that we, too, had kinship ties and came from a different, but real, culture that had meaning to its members.

Throughout our stay, we feared for our child's health. Obviously, we feared that she might die, an innocent sacrifice to her parents' anthropological ambitions. We had heard of the Hitchcocks' tragic loss of a young son in Nepal (Hitchcock 1970:170), although we knew no details. Microbes, parasites, snakes, and scorpions still abounded in the village, and many children still died. We tried to control Laurie's potential contacts with such dangers, but since both Jerry and I were often away from the house for hours at a time, we had to rely on our nursemaid and host's family. Although Laurie had been vaccinated against measles, she developed a terrible case of the disease (possibly a special Indian strain), and for ten days we dreaded possible fatal complications. During this time our nursemaid was a great comfort, as she read blessings from the Koran over our feverish little daughter. This crisis caused us to question our devotion to anthropology and our acceptance of the sacrifices it calls for. Finally, the fever broke and she recovered.

On another occasion, as we watched from our window, Laurie followed behind a herd of goats and mimicked them by plucking and eating grass--grass sprinkled with goat droppings! We feared the worst possible parasite infestations, but she was plagued by fewer than we were. She did contract some nasty eye infections, leading strangers to ask us if our child was blind. The threat of such a possibility was most unpleasant. All of us were bothered by lice at one time or another, as were most villagers. It was when we asked for help in ridding ourselves of lice and bedbugs that the villagers realized that we were incontrovertibly human!

For various ailments, the villagers often gave us health advice and prescribed folk cures. Whenever Laurie looked the least bit ill, our nursemaid or Birjis Jahan ritually removed the influence of the evil eye from her by waving a handful of chilis and salt over her head and throwing them into the fire. Late in our stay, both Jerry and I became severely ill with infectious hepatitis, which incapacitated us for weeks. Fortunately, a stiff and timely injection of hard-to-find gamma globulin kept Laurie from becoming ill, and sympathetic neighbors and servants took care of her and nursed us back to health. Jerry's disease was particularly tenacious, and an elderly Brahman priest showed his affection for us by making an unsolicited house call to attempt a cure with Hindu prayer and sacred amulets. We learned at first hand the anxieties of the ill and the comfort of having caring neighbors who bring possible cures.

After we were both better, the villagers stepped up their urgings that we have more babies. In fact, I did become pregnant for our second child shortly before we left India.

In rural India, it is only the very young or those cursed by an unlucky fate who do not have children. Thus, our having a child was considered only natural by the villagers and allowed them to view us as adults possibly worthy of respect. Being a mother made me much more acceptable to the village women, since, for them, motherhood is their most valued role. Whereas previously I had been regarded by many as rather lazy, doing no obviously useful work, I could now be seen bathing my daughter and cleaning up her messes. In short, I was now "the slave of a child," as they considered themselves to be. I was called to help at some difficult births by previously secretive families, and I was welcomed at those touchy infant blessing ceremonies. I was even asked to photograph the blessing rituals, conducted at night by veiled women in the dark recesses of their homes. I was also asked for advice on birth control by a few highly fertile women.

As for me, I gained a deeper sympathy for the hopes and sorrows of the village women: their desire for babies, their great fears for their loss, their problems of health and child care, and the difficulties of their labors and of meeting their children's needs. I became extremely sensitive to differences between American and Indian birth and childrearing practices.

If we had first made our appearance in Nimkhera with a child or children, it would have been much easier for us to establish rapport than it was. However, after having spent two years in the village already, our coming there with a child did not enhance too significantly our good relationships. However, if we had remained childless, we would have been pitied and possibly feared by the villagers as likely to bring misfortune or to practice witchcraft to obtain children. Being classed as a barren woman would certainly not have added to my prestige among the maternity-minded village women.

My having a child did not do anything to place me more firmly in the category of women, thus limiting my access to male informants and activities, than if I had not had a child. In rural central India, all post-pubescent males and females are firmly sex-categorized in every context, and it was only by virtue of my foreign origin--and gall--that I could transgress certain rules normally followed by local women. In fact, my having a child, in concert with my wearing a sari and following many local modesty customs, made my transgressions more tolerable to the villagers and thus enhanced my effectiveness as an ethnographer.

One can have children, of course, and still not bring them to the field. Margaret Mead, for example, left her daughter with caring friends while she made her Pacific Island junkets, and at least one American couple I know of left their two-year-old with grandparents in the United States for more than a year while they conducted research in India. We, however, felt that for the sake of our family integrity, we could not be apart from our child for any significant length of time. The fact that we knew the setting into which we were moving gave us the confidence to take her along.

It cannot be denied that the logistical difficulties of arriving new to the field on our first research trip with a small child would have been very great, and it might have been extremely trying for us to be strangers both to parenting and a completely new cultural setting at the same time. We travelled widely around India on our first field trip; such travels would certainly have been difficult with a small child. Even within the Nimkhera region, we limited our travels because of Laurie. On one long dusty trip to Rajasthan--twenty-four hours in a bus each way--when my husband could not accompany us, I took along a manservant as a necessary companion and child-tender. I was tempted to join the villagers on a long pilgrimage to the Ganges but did not because of my child care concerns. I was glad I had already visited the sacred river while unencumbered with offspring. In retrospect, I think our combination of field trips both with and without children worked well both personally and professionally.

FOURTH FIELD TRIP TO INDIA

After a few years, in 1978-79, we returned to India for a short stay of three months. We attended an anthropological congress in New Delhi and then proceeded to Madhya Pradesh for research. While we were in New Delhi, it was easy to retain an American-like lifestyle, as we stayed at the American Embassy Hostel, and Laurie, then 8, and Joshua, 3, ate hamburgers in the American cafeteria. But down in the hinterlands of central India, things were very different. Unfortunately, our stay was too short to allow the necessary major adjustments to be made.

Laurie was older and less pliable than she had been before. After returning from her earlier residence in India at the age of four, she had had to move sharply away from Indian village culture in order to reintegrate herself into American society. "Burger King" and "designer jeans," once nonsense syllables to her, were now what she craved. In the process of re-Americanizing herself, she had so successfully distanced herself from India that on this trip she refused to recall or learn afresh the simplest Hindi words, and she appeared to be developing anorexia rather than eat the Indian food she had once delighted in. In India, refusal to eat is a sign of anger and rejection, and this refusal distressed our generous Pathan hosts, who prepared elaborate meals to tempt her. Finally, Laurie settled on a diet of hot mango pickles with flat breads.

Not wishing to interrupt her schooling--schooling is an obvious problem for an older child--I arranged for her to live in our host's Bhopal townhouse and attend an English-medium school with his daughters, once her playmates. Going from an American open classroom to a British-style convent school did not make Laurie happy. In the school she watched girls being punished by nuns wielding rulers, and she was teased by girls who told her America was inferior to India. Apparently, the city girls treated her with no "American Princess" favoritism. Eventually Laurie did enjoy dressing up Indian style, and she took part in the fun of two weddings. Still, her constant wish during our stay was to go home. Her displeasure was heightened by the fact that I left her in town for several days at a time with Latif Khan's family while I took her brother to the village forty miles away. When I did take her to the village with me for weekends, however, she was not entranced by the somewhat primitive living conditions of most villagers. No longer a malleable toddler, she now had clear opinions of her own, based on standards she had learned in the United States.

As a young child, she had not really been aware of the idea of the caste system and ritual pollution restrictions. She was suddenly confronted with this issue at a Brahman wedding in the village. The thirteen-year-old high-caste bride was being dressed inside her house, and high-caste girls were clustering around her. Laurie joined the group and was rudely scolded by a visiting relative who made it clear she wanted Laurie to get out of the house at once. As village girls of Laurie's age would have known, the Brahman woman feared ritual contamination of the wedding house and prepared foods by the touch of the casteless interloper. Villagers who knew Laurie would have been more polite, but they would have had the same fears. My assistant and I had endured such tactless treatment at many Hindu social functions and had borne it for the sake of anthropological knowledge. Even when I explained the traditions behind the woman's rudeness, Laurie's reactions were not tempered by devotion to science; she simply rejected the whole scene and all its participants. She was getting a taste of the animosities Muslims and low-caste Hindus quietly develop toward upper caste "superiority." What she could not learn was that she should accept such treatment from people living in what she considered sub-standard housing and wearing what were, in her opinion, rumpled and dirty clothes. The idea that she, a well-bathed child of American suburbia, should be regarded as unclean was offensively preposterous. Her conviction that her real place was in another cultural system was reinforced.

Even now, several years after her last India stay, Laurie affects a disinterest in India and dislikes hearing Jerry and me speak Hindi. She states that she has no intention of becoming an anthropologist and wishes to confine her future travels to places like England, Switzerland, or the Bahamas. Nonetheless, she has written school reports on India and has several friends whose parents are immigrants from India. One of her favorite snacks is mango pickles, bought in Indian grocery stores in the United States. As she matures, her attitudes are mellowing.

Josh was never a docile child, even by American standards, and he became very difficult in the village. Completely frustrated by his inability to speak Hindi, irritated by the poking and pestering of the village children, he became wild and unruly. I wanted to show off my fine three-year-old son, but he arranged to embarrass me whenever possible. The nursemaid, rehired for our visit, did her best with him, but of course she spoke only Hindi, and he frequently defied her admonitions not to roll in the mud or walk near the edge of a dangerous well. Because of his misbehavior, I had to spend much of the day with him and conduct many of my more complicated interviews only at night after he was asleep.

I freely admitted to the villagers that I considered my child's behavior unacceptable, so that they would not think I condoned it. His wild antics became a joke among our host's family, and one young man did a hilarious imitation of Josh "when the evil spirits possessed him." In fact, there was some suspicion that there might be a supernatural cause, or at least there was hope for a supernatural cure. Josh and I went with our hostess, Birjis Jahan, to a Muslim holy man to enlist his aid in asking the saints to help calm some hostilities in her family. While we were there, she suggested that perhaps the saints could help Josh too. Ready to try anything, I asked the holy man to blow sacred verses into the child's ears. Thus, my child's behavior led me to relate to a faith healer as more than an object of study; I truly hoped his prayers would help. I regret to say that these cures did not work either for Birjis Jahan's problems or for mine.

Josh did like the special vehicles and animals of the village (no language problems with them). He became quite attached to a puppy-- although he mistreated it--and loved to ride in Latif Khan's jeeps, on his tractors, and in bullock carts. He certainly received plenty of loving attention from older children and adults.

Just as we were preparing to leave the village, Josh was on the verge of making a breakthrough in the language. If we had stayed another month, I feel certain that we would have become a social creature and calmed down enormously.

He now wants to return to India. He remembers the special attention and adventures he had there and proudly repeats the few Hindi words he recalls. The only word he does not like is one he heard often: *shaitan*-- naughty.

Studies of Indian childrearing have indicated that sibling rivalry among young children, particularly between sisters and brothers, appears almost nonexistent, or at least is not manifested in the same way as it is in the West (Minturn and Hitchcock, 1966). This was true in Nimkhera, where groups of young siblings and cousins frequently seemed to perceive themselves as a unit vis-a-vis other family groups. Typically, village children carry about younger siblings on their hip, treating them lovingly and indulgently. Laurie and Josh did not follow this pattern; in fact, they presented a beautiful case study of American inter-sibling hostility to the fascinated villagers. Their squabbles embarrassed me, and also increased my interest in the causes of such sibling rivalry. Whatever it is that we Americans do to our children to produce this syndrome, we do it early and effectively, even if we try very hard not to.

CONCLUSION

My family fieldwork in India has affected my personal as well as my anthropological views in many ways. Most especially, my experiences in India with my own children have made me acutely aware of alternatives to the ways in which American deal with birth, the care of children, and ties of kinship.

In some instances, I have become more appreciative of American customs. For example, the existence of better education and medical care for the majority of the American population, as compared with the Indian population, is a definite advantage. It is indeed sad to see children infected with microbes from unsanitary living conditions sicken and die needlessly, their uncomprehending mothers stricken with grief. When I was a new mother, I was glad not to have to follow the dietary taboos and pollution rules adhered to by parturient women in Nimkhera. (There, for example, new Hindu mothers are forbidden to drink milk, as it is thought to be too "cooling," and they are considered so unclean for forty days after birth that their husbands and most others may not touch them.) I wish that my village women friends had been given the advantage of Lamaze childbirth techniques--instead they often suffer acute pain while giving birth on their well-swept but non-sterile earthen floors. Too many women still die in childbirth, unattended by any trained medical practitioner. I was, as I have said, reluctant to have my children learn about caste and religious biases, which are so much a part of Indian village life and was glad we departed before these issues truly affected them. I was happy too not to have to try to teach my children about the American system of self-selection of spouses in a land where most people consider such activity to be indecent and rely instead upon marriages arranged by elders.

My experiences left me with the feeling, however, that American family and kinship systems lack many important merits common in Indian family structures. In India, large families residing jointly, or groups of kinsmen living separately but still bound together by strong ties of senti-ment and cooperative behavior, typically form caring support groups. Squabbles there may be, but children grow up knowing their relatives intimately and feeling part of a meaningful kinship unit. In contrast, my children see their father's brothers and their cousins rarely, as they live thousands of miles from us. In India, we might well be living together or near each other, providing moral and material support to each other as needed.

In the United States, I broke my leg and was hospitalized and otherwise completely incapacitated for a year when Laurie was one year old. Only my college-age sister was available to help out. All other relatives, both natal and affinal, were too busy or too distant to provide significant assistance. When my sister could no longer stay with us, we had to hire strangers to assist. Had we been Indian, the terrible strains our family underwent that year would have been soothed by a circle of helpful kinsmen. The contrast with the care we received in India during our later bout with hepatitis from people who were not even our relatives was noteworthy.

Experiencing Indian life, in which children are welcome everywhere, and people of all ages work and play together, has led me to be very critical of the American system of segregation of children from the adult world and the American style of age grading. American children are separated from their parents by plastic infant seats and private bedrooms, and as I have noted, are excluded from a variety of significant activities and places, as well as from the hearts of their elders. I keep trying to take my children many places with me, so that they can experience American life in its full variety, even as they experienced life during their stays in India. But in many situations I feel that they are not welcome. While some Americans complain about hearing children's cries on airplanes and in restaurants, most Indians go out of their way to admire and hold strangers' children as well as their own. Indians simply love children and feel that whimpering children are to be comforted, not despised. Having seen Indians' expressions of affection for my children as well as their own, I am acutely aware of this contrast with American behavior.

Anthropological field research is an important and challenging enterprise. Ideally, it should be conducted not only by people who suffer alone the pangs of distress of separation from fellow members of their own culture, but also by researchers who enjoy the comfort of meaningful and intimate family ties, even in the field. Despite the many problems involved, such research can be a most significant experience for all concerned. It can lead to better data collection and analysis as well as a family life based upon a widened consciousness of the variety of life styles the world offers.

All of our experiences in India--professional and familial--today impinge upon our lives on a daily basis. Clearly, for us, as for most anthropologists, our domestic life was and remains an integral aspect of our professional lives, even as the professional is an inherent part of our private lives. Our time together in India has made our family, and even the Indian villagers among whom we worked, much more aware and appreciative of other ways of life, and perhaps, more sensitive to the problems of other people all over the world.

Our family has gained a deep sense that we are part of a world much larger than the particular areas in which American culture reigns supreme. We and the children know that our native culture offers only a small proportion of the many possibilities that exist on earth, and we reinforce this knowledge through frequent reference to and discussion of India and other parts of the globe. We continue contact with our village friends in India and maintain a good friendship with a family of Latif Khan's cousins who have immigrated to the United States.

Our children are aware that the experiences of our family are not those of the average middle-class American family, and this gives them a feeling of being a little different from their friends. With our special perspective gained from anthropological insights into human behavior, my husband and I, like many anthropologists, feel in some ways marginal to our own culture. We are undoubtedly striving to recreate in our own children this marginality, this ability to stand apart, comprehend, and evaluate. This may be part of what my daughter is resisting so strongly--as an adolescent, she wants to be nothing but a full-fledged member of this culture. Perhaps once she has achieved that aim, she will be more receptive to other points of view. Ultimately, she and her brother will recognize that they have been imbued with a global outlook which should increase their understanding of reality and help them to meet the challenges of the future.

REFERENCES

Beals, A. R. (1970). Gopalpur, 1958-60. In G. D. Spindler (Ed.), *Being an Anthropologist*, (pp. 32-57). New York: Holt, Rinehart and Winston.

Beteille, A., and Madan, T. N. (Eds.) (1975). *Encounter and Experience: Personal Accounts of Fieldwork.* Honolulu: The University Press of Hawaii.

Boissevain, J. F. (1970). Fieldwork in Malta. In G. D. Spindler (Ed.), *Being an Anthropologist*, (pp. 58-84). New York: Holt, Rinehart and Winston.

Freilich, M. (Ed.) (1970). *Marginal Natives: Anthropologists at Work.* New York: Harper and Row.

Geist, W. E. (1982). Child-Free Living: Cries and Screams Set Aside, Deliberately. *New York Times*, April 13.

Georges, R. A., and Jones, M. O. (1980). *People Studying People: The Human Element in Fieldwork.* Berkeley: University of California Press.

Golde, P. (Ed.) (1970). *Women in the Field: Anthropological Experiences.* Chicago: Aldine.

Hitchcock, J. T. (1970). Fieldwork in Ghurka Country. In G. D. Spindler (Ed.), *Being an Anthropologist*, (pp. 164-193). New York: Holt, Rinehart and Winston.

Huntington, G. E. (1970). Living with the Colony People. In: The Hutterites: Fieldwork in a North American Communal Society, by John A. Hostetler and Gertrude Enders Huntington. In G. D. Spindler (Ed.), *Being an Anthropologist*, (pp. 206-213). New York: Holt, Rinehart and Winston.

Huntington, G. E. (1981). Children of the Hutterites. *Natural History* 90(2):34-47.

Jacobson, D. (1974). The Women of North and Central India: Goddesses and Wives. In C. J. Matthiasson (Ed.), *Many Sisters: Women in Cross-Cultural Perspective*, (pp. 99-175). New York: The Free Press.

Jacobson, D. (1976). Women and Jewelry in Rural India. In: Family and Social Change in Modern India. In G. R. Gupta (Ed.), *Main Currents in*

Indian Sociology, (Volume 2, pp. 135-183). Durham, NC: Carolina Academic Press.

Jacobson, D. (1976-77). Indian Women in Processes of Development. *Journal of International Affairs* (Special Issue on Women and Change in the Developing World) 30(2):211-242.

Jacobson, D. (1977). Purdah in India: Life Behind the Veil. *National Geographic Magazine* 152(2):270-286.

Jacobson, D. (1980). Golden Handprints and Red-Painted Feet: Childbirth Rituals in Central India. In N. E. Falk and R. M. Gross (Eds.), *Unspoken Worlds: Women's Religious Lives in Non-Western Cultures,* (pp. 73-93). New York: Harper and Row.

Jacobson, D. (1982a). Purdah and the Hindu Family in Central India. In H. Papanek and G. Minault (Eds.), *Separate Worlds: Studies of Purdah in South Asia,* (pp. 81-109). Columbia, MO: South Asia Books.

Jacobson, D. (1982b). Studying the Changing Roles of Women in Rural India. *Journal of Women in Culture and Society* 8(1):132-137.

Jacobson, D., and Wadley, S. S. (1977). *Women in India: Two Perspectives.* New Delhi: Manohar Book Service and Columbia, MO: South Asia Books.

Klass, S. S. (1964). *Everyone in this House Makes Babies.* Garden City, NY: Doubleday.

Klass, M., and Klass, S. S. (1983). Birthing in the Bush: Participant Observation in Trinidad. Paper presented at the annual meeting of the American Anthropological Association, November, Chicago.

Mead, M. (1972). *Blackberry Winter: My Earlier Years.* New York: William Morrow and Co.

Minturn, L., and Hitchcock, J. T. (1966). *The Rajputs of Khalapur, India.* New York: John Wiley.

Powdermaker, H. (1966). *Stranger and Friend: The Way of an Anthropologist.* New York: W. W. Norton Co.

Schwab, W. (1970). Comparative Field Techniques in Urban Research in Africa. In M. Freilich (Ed.), *Marginal Natives: Anthropologists at Work,* (pp. 73-121). New York: Harper and Row.

Spindler, G. D. (Ed.) (1970). *Being an Anthropologist: Fieldwork in Eleven Cultures.* New York: Holt, Rinehart and Winston.

Spindler, G., and Spindler, L. (1970). Fieldwork Among the Menomini. In G. D. Spindler (Ed.), *Being an Anthropologist,* (pp. 267-301). New York: Holt, Rinehart and Winston.

NOTES

(1) Doranne Jacobson, Research Associate in the Department of Anthropology, Barnard College, is also affiliated with the Southern Asian Institute, Columbia University. She is an anthropologist who has focused her research on changes in women's roles in central India. She is senior author of *Women in India: Two Perspectives* (Columbia, MO: South Asia Books, 1977); and has published numerous articles on women, the family, development, and religion in India. She is also a widely-published photographer.

(2) The field research was supported by the National Institute of Mental Health, the American Museum of Natural History, and the American Institute of Indian Studies, for which I am most appreciative. I am grateful to the residents of Nimkhera for their hospitality and cooperation, and to Miss Sunalini Nayudu for her assistance in the field. I also owe a debt to Dr. Leela Dube and Dr. Neera Desai, my academic sponsors while I was in India. My husband, Jerome Jacobson, provided essential help.

Some examples of publications resulting from the research are: Jacobson, 1974, 1976, 1976-77, 1977, 1980, 1982a, 1982b, and Jacobson and Wadley, 1977.

(3) Sheila Klass, a writer and the wife of anthropologist Morton Klass, has written a most engaging account of giving birth to a child during fieldwork in Trinidad (Klass, 1964, see also Klass and Klass, 1983). Researchers' children are discussed briefly in such writings as G. and L. Spindler, 1970; Beals, 1970; Hitchcock, 1970; and Schwab, 1970. A volume edited by Joan Cassell on families and fieldwork, based on a 1983 symposium, is currently in preparation.

(4) The organizers and participants involved in the conference were actually taking a professional risk in initiating open discussion of their domestic and familial concerns within an academic context.

ORDER RULES THE WORLD:

OUR CHILDREN IN THE COMMUNAL SOCIETY OF THE HUTTERITES

G. E. Huntington

Department of Anthropology
University of Michigan
Ann Arbor, MI 481094

"There are four playhouses, but I've only seen
three of them and I think this one is the best. They
have three girls in it but only two girls own it. They
have a dresser, a high chair, a couch, a bed which is
somewhat like a couch, a table, a washing basin and
a lot of other things. But what I found most interesting was that on their dresser they had some
colorless nail polish, and also hidden underneath a
little drape of material there were two pairs of high
heels.... The playhouse belongs to Barbara (age
twelve) who has the keys and to Theresa (age nine)
who just went along with her, who does not own a
pair of keys but is allowed to go in whenever she
wants. They have doll beds and a chest for dolls and
a chest for their own clothes, that they use for
dress-up."

This was our nine-year-old daughter reporting into the tape recorder.
In the course of the summer, she reported on the changing cliques when the
little girls locked one another out of the playhouses and on how the
excluded child suffered the loneliness of not being accepted by the peer
group. Our daughter described how the school girls put on high heels and
talked in loud voices as do "ugly, worldy women." She reported when they
played doctor--everyone was the doctor, everyone was the patient.

The playhouses represent an area of the culture that I , as an adult
woman, would never have seen. I knew the goose houses were used by the
children after the goslings were turned out to pasture, but even though the
little girls unlocked the house and showed it to me, they did not play in the

presence of an adult, nor did I rummage in the locked chests and behind curtains, noting what items the girls had salvaged, what forbidden items they hid there. Were it not for my daughter, I could not have known the extent the playhouses were used, nor how they functioned in the children's development as they played out various worldly and community roles. Though I could observe the world of childhood, I could not participate in it. Our children participated and, depending on their ages, reported or at least gave me an excuse to follow them into that world. As a parent, I noted details of the host culture when I saw my own children taking on new behavior patterns, when I watched them struggle to "fit in" or fight to maintain their own identity.

The topic "Children and Anthropological Research" has two dimensions: "how do our children affect our research?" and "how does our research affect our children?" These are very different questions; both are valid and both deserving of serious study. In this chapter, I will deal primarily with the first question and only with those aspects of my fieldwork that were related to the presence of my own children--primarily parenting and the children's culture.

Considering how many anthropologists have agonized over whether or not to "take the children," it is surprising that so little has been published on the subject. Certainly the demands of parenting will modify fieldwork both on a practical level and on a conceptual level. The need to care for one's own children may influence the selection of a culture, of a geographical location, of the method of study used and even the specific problems examined. It may influence the degree of participation that is possible, or practical, or required of an anthropologist who is also a "practicing" parent. Once in the field the parents may find themselves and/or their child participating more fully than they had foreseen and more fully than is comfortable. Where is the line between abandoning your children to the host culture and remembering that eventually your children must succeed in middle-class America? These conflicts influence one's emotions, one's actions, one's observations and one's awareness, and thus influence one's research. One must be constantly alert to one's own emotional involvement both with one's work and one's child and try to evaluate how this influences what one sees and how one sees it.

Our children lead us into areas of the host culture that we could never explore alone, and even our problems as parents forge bonds with host parents, giving them opportunities to teach us "proper" parenting techniques. Just as members of the host culture may use their own children for the continual socialization of adults (who act correctly because they must be an example for their children), so too, the host culture, while enculturating the anthropologist's children, may use the anthropologist's children to acculturate their parents, by providing specific information on how to conform to community values.

In many societies, if one is to study the woman's culture, it is helpful to have children of one's own for often a woman remains "an older girl" until she has proved her adulthood by bearing children. Among the Old Order Amish, I was treated differently as a bride, a childless married woman, and a mother. Some information was available to me only after motherhood and the pressure for motherhood was strongly felt. When I returned to the field not visibly pregnant after two years of marriage, one of the older women sympathetically told me her daughter had four miscarriages before she had her first baby. Most women were more subtle, but all made me feel that as a childless married woman I was somehow incomplete. I hardly dared return without a baby in my arms.

My experience has been that children are an asset in the field. I have had children of all ages with me from in-utero until their mid-twenties. It was because children have accompanied me so often that, on learning that I was returning to the field alone, my son commented, "How can you go without children?" However, the problems of working and simultaneously parenting are not to be minimized. One must balance the advantage of having children with one, against the question of introducing too many strange individuals into a homogeneous social group. One must assess the time and attention one's own children take from one's fieldwork with the additions they make to the fieldwork. One must take into account the length of time in the field, the unique personality, the age and sex of one's own child and the characteristics of the culture being studied.

When one's own relationships approximate, at least superficially, those considered natural by the host culture, entry is easier. Thus, in my fieldwork among the Hutterites, when I was to stay for an extended time, I had either my mother or my husband with me in addition to my children. Because a Hutterite woman always lives in her home colony, she is to some degree under the supervision of either her mother or her husband until she has grown sons or her mother is infirm. This supervision minimizes defused worry over possible sexual temptation. Having my mother with me facilitated studying parenting by a grandparent, that is the parenting of an adult by his or her parent, a significant role for the older Hutterite.

The Hutterites or Hutterian Brethren are a German-speaking, communal, Christian sect who have lived in North America for over one-hundred years. Today they are located in about three-hundred colonies, primarily in the plains states and provinces. Theologically they are Anabaptists, descendents of the left-wing of the Protestant Reformation, who practice adult baptism as a symbol of acceptance into the church community (Bainton, 1941). They date their origins to 1528 when, while fleeing persecution, they placed all their belongings onto cloaks spread on the ground and introduced the practice of community goods.

Hutterite society is highly structured, they often quote the saying, "Order rules the world." They equate disorder with sinfulness. The closer one approaches the center of the culture, whether spatially or behaviorally, the more ordered it appears. The center of the colony consists of the kitchen with the dining rooms, the baking room, the laundry and the bath; the long houses, in which the families sleep and keep their personal belongings; the kindergarten building and the room or building in which church services are held. The buildings are built true to the compass, due north and due south; they are connected by straight cemented walks, and painted according to use. In the colony I will use as a reference, the living buildings were white with blue trim, the economic buildings (barns, shops, feed mill, etc.) were red with white trim and the provincial school, which is emotionally outside the colony, had been left its original yellow. The uniformity of the color and architecture, the physical proximity of the buildings, the grassy commons, the flowers around the living houses, and the neat walks proclaim visually the orderly existence of the inhabitants.

Our family of five were assigned to the "teacherage," a small building supplied by the colony to house the public school teacher during the school term. We were about forty feet from the nearest family, with whom we shared an outhouse, and about sixty feet from the nearest "long house" consisting of apartments for four families and having a floor plan that has changed little since the sixteenth century.

Time is measured out as discretely as space. There is a proper activity for each moment of the day, each day of the week, each season of the year and for each stage in one's life. Time spent on this earth is used to order individuals within the social structure. The age grades are clear cut with behavior socially prescribed for each stage. Hutterite age grades constitute a sequence of culturally defined distinct phases. Age grades include both males and females and do not involve a group initiation experience. The only group initiation practiced is the ritual of baptism which signifies admission into a spiritual corpus (Hinnant, 1980). The age grades are as follows: House children, birth to two-and-a-half or three years; Kindergartners, three to six years; German school children, six to fifteen years; Young people, fifteen years to marriage; Married couples, about twenty-two years for women and twenty-three-and-a-half years for men, to widowhood or aged; Aged, those retired from active, physical participation in the colony work patterns.

Although school children can easily list every woman and every man in order of age, the children can only vaguely relate the age of a specific man to the age of a specific woman. This reflects the distance between the men and the women in the social structure and the distance between the men's and the women's cultures.

The distribution of work and authority are also regulated by the age grade system. Unmarried men rarely hold leadership or executive positions. Women may retire from the heavier work such as hoeing or cooking when they are forty-five or fifty-years-old, although the headcook generally works as long as she is physically able, and older women are the choice for kindergarten mother. Men may retire after fifty, but depending on the demographic structure of the colony, many of them maintain executive positions beyond this age for most of the hard manual labor is performed by young adult males.   Aged men occupy advisory positions until death. Because of the high birthrate and the practice of forming new colonies when the population numbers between one-hundred and one-hundred-fifty, there are very few aged individuals in any single colony.   The elderly are treated with care and respect.   Often a grandchild will be assigned to run errands and to sleep with an aged member.

During the particular fieldtrip that is used as the basis for this chapter, we had family members in every age grade except the aged and young adult.   There were no aged in the colony in which we spent most of our time, and our school child was admitted to the fringes of the adolescent peer group.   Her worldly experience made her somewhat acceptable, and because of her age, she was not a sexual threat.   My mother spent much of her time in the company of the three grandmothers in the colony; I worked with the married women.   My husband, who was there only a short time and, by Hutterite standards, still had much to learn about carpentry and farming, worked both with the young married men and the older boys. We had a house child, Caleb, age two; a kindergartner, Daniel, who celebrated his fifth birthday in the colony; and a nine-year-old school child, Abigail.

The individual Hutterite's dress establishes sex, age, activity and degree of obedience to the rules of the colony, indicating where each individual fits into the social order.   Our school-age daughter was the first family member to discard her "worldly" clothes.   Our second day in the colony she came back from German school dressed as a Hutterite and from then on refused to put on her own dresses.   Clothing is such an obvious and important symbol, that we could not be participants if we did not put away our "ugly clothes."   Dressing as Hutterites do signified our willingness to accept our age- and sex-determined positions in the colony and to abide by its rules. Looking Hutterite was part of acting Hutterite. It was primarily through our daughter that we were reminded about details of our dress, particularly what was appropriate for which occasion.   Still, any major transgression, such as taking off the heavy black polka-dotted cotton scarf that covered the close-fitting cotton cap just because the temperature in the laundry room was over $100^{\circ}F$, was corrected by any woman present. When my mother suggested that perhaps we could wear only one head covering during periods of extreme heat, she was told, "You can't expect to be comfortable here and there both." (If you are comfortable in this life, you do not deserve to be comfortable in the next.)

Our nine-year-old daughter, Abigail, was an excellent fieldworker and a major channel for the socialization of the rest of the family. As a school-age child under the supervision of the German teacher, she was specifically taught appropriate behavior, from table manners and details of dress to acceptable work and play patterns. Because she had no sisters and the older of her brothers was almost too old for her to sleep with, she was often invited to sleep with other girls in the colony. Children generally sleep with the same-sex sibling closest to them in age. Thus when nine-year-old Sara was at another colony with her mother who was caring for a married daughter following childbirth, Sara's older sister invited Abigail to sleep with her because she was lonely when she slept by herself. With the possible exception of young adulthood, once out of a crib, it is generally considered unpleasant to sleep alone in a bed and even worse to sleep alone in a room. When my son and I returned for a short visit, I slept with one of the baptized, but not yet married, girls; and my son who, as a ten-year-old, was too old to spend time with his mother, shared the bed of boys his own age. Though I knew where each person slept, it was primarily through my children that I learned how people felt about sleeping patterns. Various investigators have suggested that siblings sleeping together strengthens family bonds and contributes to nurturant family life (Caudill and Plath, 1966; Gallimore, Boggs and Jordan, 1974; Werner, 1982). The Hutterites emphasize nurturant behavior for both sexes and all ages, within the family, within the colony and among colonies. Visitors from other colonies share work and beds with their hosts.

Hutterite culture maximizes colony loyalty and de-emphasizes personal and nuclear family loyalty. When a baby is born, the mother of the post-partum woman comes to care for her daughter and her daughter's older children. The grandmother does not specifically care for the baby, but mothers the mother (caring for her grown daughter as one would care for a child) thus freeing her daughter to care for and enjoy her new baby. This grandmother role rewards the daughter when she gives birth with a visit from her mother (who usually lives in another colony) and her mother's almost exclusive attention. It is one of the rare occasions when a woman is treated with solicitous, individual attention. Both women's roles as mothers are reinforced, the women's culture is supported and the nuclear family is de-emphasized by the incorporation of another generation. The father participates little in the care of his wife and baby during the first four weeks.

Special foods are cooked for the new mother, including a sweet zwieback that she is given to pass out to the constant stream of friends who come to visit her and to see the new baby (Huntington and Hostetler, 1966). The newborn is tightly swaddled, often wrapped with a specially woven red cord (the baby bundle resembling a Byzantine Christ child). The red cord is said to protect the child from the evil eye and the swaddling to make him easier to play with. Men and boys are as interested in the baby as are the women.

The situation minimizes jealousy among siblings. They are privileged to have a new baby and the visiting grandmother gives them more attention than they usually receive. She does not participate in colony work and has time for the house children and kindergarten children. The next older baby does not move out of his parent's bedroom. The visitors pay attention to the other house children and reward colony-approved behavior, such as when a two-year-old brings a chair for the visitor, or when a four-year-old child attempts to care for the baby. Jealousy is never used to elicit obedience nor as a method of teasing (Mead and Macgreager, 1951). House children and kindergarten children, including our sons, were often rewarded for good behavior by being allowed to hold a baby. The aversion to making comparisons between or among individuals within the colony was extended to our children. Although there was colony consensus on the differing degrees of "goodness" of our children, they were never compared. Daniel was never told that either of his siblings were better than he was. Rather, Daniel's behavior was related to an abstract model of how a child his age should act. Children and adults are taught to nurture one another, to punish one another when deserved, but not to compete.

Tiny babies are not only considered to be valuable and vulnerable, they, like all young children, are sinless. An individual is determined to have left babyhood and to have entered childhood when he either strikes back (according to a seventeenth-century Hutterite sermon on the "Slaughter of the Innocents"), or picks up a comb and tries to comb his hair. These behaviors indicate purposefulness. The child is old enough to be trained because he understands what he is doing and thus should be punished for misbehavior (Kagan, 1981).

Although the mother takes primary care of the house child, the whole colony participates in his socialization. The father cares for the children during the night. Some women, it is claimed, wean their children early so that the father can give the night feedings and the mother does not have to awaken. The mother carries food from the kitchen for the house child who is fed by the father or mother. Until the child enters kindergarten at the age of two-and-a-half or three, every visitor, every colony adult interacts with the child, greets him and plays with him physically. Hutterites are skilled in eliciting a positive response from the child (Ross and Goldman, 1977). A child is encouraged to overcome any fear of colony members; an older house child may be punished by his parent or caretaker for refusing to go to someone else. In contrast, should a Hutterite house child be approached by an outsider his anxiety response is respected or even encouraged (Kagan, 1981; Werner, 1982).

Toddlers are weaned from their parents by older children who encourage them to join in such excursions as a ride on the wife-wagon to watch the butchering of a sheep. The toddler caretakers usually gather in multi-age playgroups while their mothers sew together; the house children thus have a great deal of social interaction. Sharing and display of affection is encouraged, while all types of aggression are strongly discouraged. Our house child learned quickly to avoid punishment by immediately kissing the playmate whom he had just hit. The first Hutterite word he used spontaneously was "kiss." When two house children both grab for an object they are quickly separated and cuddled by a caretaker. People are more important than things; affection is substituted for possessions.

A Hutterite child's life changes dramatically at the age of about three. Not only is the pattern of his day different, but the response of the people around him changes. The differential treatment of the house child and the kindergartener was impressed on me a few days after our arrival while I was doing our family laundry in the community laundry room next to the communal kitchen. Virtually everyone who came through tried to kiss Caleb (age two-and-a-half), tried to pick him up, to hold him, to toss him around, or to play with him. At first he was a bit resentful. He was not used to so much physical handling, but soon objected less and entered into the play. In contrast, the men and older children paid almost no attention to the five-year-old who was also there. Visitors from other colonies notice, touch, stroke, or handle any young child, but do not even greet a kindergarten or school-age child.

To the Hutterites it is obvious that children have stubborn wills that must be broken. Kindergarten helps teach the children not to be willful or stubborn. As the kindergarten mother applied the Brown Doctor (a leather strap) to a three-year-old who was licking his boot, she commented, "He'll need many *britschen* before his will is broken." Kindergartners have the lowest status in the community, "They can't do anything but memorize." Of all the age groups within the colony, the kindergartners experience the most restricted, most regimented, and least varied existence. In contrast to contemporary educational practice, many colony kindergartens allow no toys, no books, and no paper. Due to perceived physical danger, the children under six years of age are forbidden to touch such objects as pencils, scissors, knives or forks. Children between the ages of three and six spend the whole day in kindergarten, arriving before breakfast and leaving after the midafternoon snack. They learn to feed themselves, to eat quickly, and to use the school outhouse. Children younger than kindergarten age more often use a potty and during the summer may urinate freely outside. The kindergartners memorize about fifteen prayers and perhaps twenty-six hymns, some with more than twenty verses. They recite their prayers and hymns kneeling by the long benches, hands folded under their chins, the girls at one bench, and the boys at another. Rocking rhythmically, they recite very rapidly; the older ones doing so quite loudly. This is the only occasion on which a kindergarten child may raise his voice--he must even cry quietly. He may not answer back to anyone older than he; he has probably already learned not to initiate interaction with adults. Kindergarten children are most frequently punished simply for being in someone's way. They are rewarded for cooperative, docile, passive responses to correction or frustration. Anyone older than six may punish a kindergartner and the school children appear to pass on their punishments. Kindergarten is seen as necessary to wean the mother from her child, to teach the child to obey, to pray, to sit properly, to share, to get along with others and to keep the child out of the way of colony work.

From this contracted description of the kindergarten age grade it is probably obvious that my parenting practices and Hutterite parenting practices diverge dramatically. We had tried to provide our children with intellectually stimulating environments; we lavishly supplied them with toys, tools and books; we tried to answer all of their questions and to explain everything. We did not believe in a stubborn will. Instead, we relished spunkiness and determination. We did not approve of spanking, much less strapping. Had I known more about the culture, I would not have brought a kindergarten child with me, especially a child of Daniel's temperament and personality. If Daniel was to survive in his own culture, he had to be independent and questioning. He needed to retain a sense of control and his zest for life. On the other hand, I also had a responsibility to my hosts not to be disruptive. I believe passionately that anthropologists must always remember that individuals are more than cultural respresentatives or sources of information. We are working with the real lives of real people and we must not "use" either our own families or members of the host culture primarily as "tools."

Five-year-old Daniel could not be a full participant because it would hurt him; he would disrupt the kindergarten. We tried quite ineffectively to protect him and to protect our hosts. Daniel never spent much time in kindergarten without my mother being there also. Because two of the three women in my mother's generation were the kindergarten teachers, it was natural for her to visit kindergarten to be with women her age. In fact, my mother was a school teacher in the outside world. She could manage Daniel, and if he showed signs of being too disruptive, they would leave. I made it obvious that I did not want the adults to strap Daniel, but there was little I could do to shield him from abuse at the hands of the older children who were determined to teach him submission. The colony tried to integrate Daniel into the group, but his stubborn will had not been broken. He did not passively accept punishment at the hands of the older boys. He responded to teasing with anger. If an older boy called him a bad name, he responded in kind. The crueler the children were to him, the harder he fought back and the louder he yelled his objections--a response that is totally unexpected (and altogether unacceptable) in a Hutterite child of his age. In a set of colony rules, written in 1812, members are reminded that "it is very sinful and rude" to call each other such "insulting and contemptuous names" as "pig" or "dirty dog." The very first Hutterite words Daniel used spontaneously were those for "you pig" and "you dirty dog."

Many of the adult men questioned me about our boys being away from their father, because Hutterite boys between the ages of three and baptism are rarely separated from their fathers and do not make long visits to other colonies. This atypical situation meant that Daniel spent more time with his grandmother and mother than was acceptable for a child who was being weaned from his nuclear family. My mother reports one of the milder incidents.

> When we arrived at the garden, I asked Daniel
> and Caleb if they wanted to stay on the tractor
> trailer with the other children (there were about ten

of them) or if they wanted to come to the garden
with us. They started to come with us, but then
Daniel saw that Jonathan (age 10) was going to take
the children for a ride and tried to hurry back and
climb on the trailer, but they would not stop for
him. After the children had driven up the hill and
turned around and come back, Daniel said, "At least
I can go and sit on the trailer." He went to sit on
the trailer, but the children wouldn't let him get on.
He came back to me and said, "They won't let me
get on." I said, "They're just trying to see if they
can make you cry--go back." So he went back and
again the children wouldn't let him get on--they
taunted, "Why do you just go with your grand-
mother--your grandmother--why do you go with
your grandmother." So I called and said, "Daniel--
get on the trailer." Theresa was blocking the way
with her leg, but he started to climb on and when
they saw that I was looking they let him on, but as
he got on the trailer and went to the front, each
child hit him. Then Margaret (age seven) started to
attack him and fight him and one of the kindergarten mothers called from the garden, "Stop the
fighting." I started over toward the tractor and one
of the older children said, "You better go over there
and see that they don't fight."

A Hutterite grandmother would not have been that involved with a five-
year-old nor that assertive. Once Daniel's father arrived his lot improved;
he could follow his father and play with the little boys on the edge of the
men's world. He was now in the appropriate space, his father was nearby
and the teasing diminished. While he was in the colony, however, he never
learned to accept frustration passively nor to interpret teasing as positive
attention. He thought the children his age boring, the older children and
adults cruel and the rules arbitrary and senseless.

A change in social place at about the age of five to seven seems to be
characteristic of many cultures around the world (Rogoff et al., 1975;
Minturn, 1969; Werner, 1982). Among the Hutterites this change takes
place on the sixth birthday when children leave the kindergarten and
become school children under the supervision of the German school
teacher. The gradual shift from nuclear family to colony is indicated by
the eating patterns: house children eat all of their meals in the living
quarters; kindergarteners eat slightly more than a third of their meals in
the living quarters; and school children eat all of their meals with their
peers in the children's dining room. School children are assigned specific
colony work by the German teacher, who is responsible for all of their
colony-related activity.   The girls clean the dining room after the
children's meals and pick peas for Tuesday dinner. The school children

gather potatoes, a job too boring for men and too heavy for women. Individual children may be assigned to help the chicken boss, or the cattle man, or an adult woman who needs extra help. All formal babysitting is by children between the ages of six and fourteen who are assigned to care for the house children during adult meals, church services and most periods when mothers are doing colony work. Our school child learned immediately that the colony expected her to babysit her brothers whenever I was working with the women. The Hutterite practice of older children caring for younger ones is consistent with the patterns observed in cultures where the women make a substantial contribution to the subsistence economy; where women's work takes them outside the home and/or is difficult to interrupt; and where circumstance of residence, birth order and family size make child caretakers available (Werner, 1982; Minturn and Lambert, 1964). The house children have a regular sitter, usually an older sister but sometimes a cousin or an older brother. Although boys are expected to be as nurturant as girls, they are less likely to be assigned as babysitters because they would then miss church regularly. Church attendance is not as important for girls who will never have a religious leadership role. Occasionally a school girl from another colony may be brought in temporarily to help her older sister, aunt or cousin (Weisner and Gallimore, 1977). Babysitters are always consanguineally related to their charges.

School children learn their gender roles through work assignments, formal teaching and in their single-sex play groups. Spontaneous same-sex work groups and play groups are reinforced by the colony (Maccoby, in press). Although kindergarten and house children play in cross-sex clusters, school children are taught to play with members of their own gender. Konner (1981) reports that cross-cultural segregation of child groups by gender tends to occur at five to seven years. When Daniel asked a six-year-old girl living in the adjacent longhouse if she would like to play with him, she responded, "Girls don't play with boys." Had she been a year younger it would have been all right. When the school girls were playing leap frog (seemingly unencumbered by their long dresses), the minister scattered them with, "Girls don't play that way." There was, in fact, quite a bit of interaction across sex-lines, but it often took the form of mild antagonism of girls against boys. Although girls are given considerable latitude to play all over the colony, they tend to stay closer to the living quarters than do the boys. The girls form cliques, excluding one another for any momentarily unapproved behavior.

Among the boys there was more physical fighting; but individual boys were also picked on or excluded by their peers. Within the boys' groups and the girls' groups the children monitored one another's behavior and imposed pressures for conformity that contributed to the differential socialization of the girls and of the boys (Maccoby, in press). In spite of internal bickering, boys and girls present a united front to members of the opposite sex and to adults.

In a Hutterite colony there is no need for males to learn female roles or vice-versa, as there may be in a nuclear family. In the colony there are always individuals of the appropriate sex who can step in during moments of family stress (Minturn, 1969). Socialization for sex roles is clear and consistent. The Whitings (Whiting, 1965; Whiting & Whiting, 1975) relate sex-identity conflict and absent fathers to hyperaggression in males. Hutterite men are always available. They are nurturant and non-aggressive. As far as can be determined, there has never been a murder committed by a Hutterite (Hostetler, 1983).

During church services, during the adult meals and at times when the men are working and the women are hoeing in the garden, the children are together in the colony unsupervised, participating in their own culture. It is at these times that the children discipline one another most intensely. As participating adults, we attended church and adult meals. Had we not had children, we could never have known what went on in the children's culture. We would not have realized how important these specific periods were in the development of the peer group and how different the children's behavior was when they knew they were free of adult surveillance.

> Just as iron tends to rust and as the soil will nourish
> weeds, unless . . . kept clean by continuous care, so
> have the children of man a strong inclination toward
> injustices, desires, and lusts.

It is assumed that children will misbehave (though not shirk responsibility) and that adults must watch over them and correct them. Therefore, Hutterite children out of sight and earshot of adults are relatively free from restraints. Abigail pointed out that it was unfair to expect her to be "good" even when she was not with us--none of the other children were troubled by their unobserved misbehavior nor felt the least bit guilty when participating vigorously in their own subculture.

Caleb, when he became a school child, was as untroubled by breaking rules as were his Hutterite peers. The children knew what the rules were, knew what the punishment would be and took their chances. When several of the boys were late to German school because they had been catching pollywogs, the consensus was that the three straps they received were well worth the fun. The children were not lectured about their behavior, which the adults consider typical for boys who naturally prefer catching polly-wogs to copying German hymns. The punishment was payment for misbehavior, wiping the slate clean. Everyone knew that when the boys were older, they would be less interested in pollywogs than in their colony responsibility. No one moralized, no one worried, no one was offended.

Within the colony, our own children picked up the pattern of both recommending and passing on physical punishment. Thus, Abigail's reports of children's behavior began to include comments that so-and-so should be whipped for some transgression. She became upset that we discouraged her from physically disciplining her brothers. And we did put unrealistic demands on her, for even we adults, in frustration, succumbed to community pressure and briefly tried physical punishment with our child who did not blend in. Immediately, we noted that whenever his younger brother bothered him, he spanked him very readily and told him to be quiet. He did this for small provocations that he had previously ignored. Hutterite parents are aware that children pass their punishment along. They say that that is the nature of children. When commenting on one lively, rather aggressive two-year-old boy, the response was, "After all, he has six brothers that have been picking on him and that's why he's that way." No one was concerned about the eventual development of either the older brothers or the two-year-old, everyone was confident that the children would all grow into cooperative Hutterites. The passing on of physical punishments makes the power structure clear; it protects the adults from annoyance; it teaches the younger ones that anyone older than they can punish them. It also teaches them that discomfort is unavoidable, unpredictable, often arbitrary and not of great significance.

Colony people live in close physical proximity. Depending on the colony, a couple is given a second room when either their fourth or sixth child is born, a third room when their eighth or twelfth child arrives. Sounds pass between apartments and through walls. The close living quarters place a value on quietness. Children are encouraged to play quietly, not to initiate responses from adults (Harkness and Super, 1977; Nerlove and Snipper, 1981), and to talk and cry quietly. Babies who cry when left alone in the crib during work periods have no one to respond to them. A mother of a young baby will ask someone coming into the kitchen if they heard the baby when they passed the house. But no one specifically listens for the child during these periods, so his fussing is often unheeded. The child caretakers are more annoyed than disturbed by the crying of their charges. Crying is a solitary activity and school children do not like to be singled out or stared at, so this too reinforces quiet crying. By the time we left the colony our youngest child never yelled, spoke only in a whisper when strange adults were present (including his surprised nursery school teachers who had taught his assertive older siblings), and even when hurt, cried very softly, if at all. Although Hutterite children engaged in considerable scrapping, they did not fight in the presence of adults. They fought individually, quietly and the younger child usually gave in quickly. Aggressive behavior is contrary to the Hutterite value system and the close living quarters make children's fighting disruptive (Minturn and Lambert, 1964). Personal emotions are minimized and display of strong emotion is not condoned. Until children enter kindergarten, they are discouraged from being noisy, but are usually not severely punished for screaming. Kindergartners may raise their voices only when reciting the prayers or hymns; school children are loud when they are away from the adults; women sing loudly and enthusiastically in church; and the ideal man is described as having a quiet voice.

By participating with our children in the Hutterite colony, we were constantly made aware of the role nonparents have in the parenting of children on both a formal level--prescribing the colony participation of each age grade--and on an informal level. Hutterite children demonstrate clear patterns of differential obedience. Kindergartners obey virtually anyone who is over six years of age. As school children learn the colony hierarchy and the various roles of colony members, they learn whom to obey and when. Thus, a school child would obey others in the following sequence: 1) the German teacher or German mother, 2) the child's own parent, 3) a specific person in the boss category, that is, a child in the pig barn would obey the pig boss but not just any adult, 4) an adult male, 5) an adult female, in relation to her age and consanguineal relationship to the child, 6) the child's own nonadult babysitters, and finally 7) another older child in relation to its age and relationship to the child. Orders are passed in the proper sequence. Thus, a mother would tell me to tell her daughter to come to her, then the mother would tell her daughter that she must babysit her younger sister. Because the child did not want to watch the little one, and I had no authority to make her babysit, she would not have listened to me had I told her she must babysit. However, it is proper for her to return to her parents or the German teacher, if anyone tells her to, and she must obey her mother. Similarly, when the children were playing by throwing one another into the silage pit where they were in danger of being run over by the tractor, no one stopped them because a) the German teacher was not there, b) no parent was present, and c) the field boss was not responsible; he was concerned with the silage, not with the children. The response of one of the young adults on hearing about the incident, was to tell our daughter, "You'd have made a very nice angel."

Conflict between a child and his babysitter or even between a child and his parent elicits response from a third person. The first field note I have about colony pressure on Daniel is on the third day when a seventeen-year-old girl told him, "At the end of the summer I'll paddle you and teach you that you don't get angry at your mother." Aggression against the mother does not fit in neatly with observations made by the Whitings (Whiting and Whiting, 1975). A Hutterite child's mother will cajole the aggressive child, reminding him how she takes care of him. But another colony member will, depending on the circumstances, physically remove the aggressive child from his mother, or threaten him, as Barbara did Daniel, or scold him quite harshly. Should the punishment of a young child by an older child get out of hand, an adult will intervene to protect the young child without undermining the caretaker's status. The most usual form of such intervention is for the adult to pick up the young child and pretend to strike the caretaker. The younger child realizes that the punishment of his caretaker is not in earnest, but he is also being cuddled and rescued and perceives the adult authority as intervening on his behalf. Whether the third party takes the part of the child or the caretaker, the dynamics of the situation are changed and tensions abated (Rabin, 1982).

When trying to explain to a Hutterite mother of a kindergarten child how many hours an outside mother spends caring for her five-year-old, she commented, "I'd certainly like Mickey less, if I had to see any more of him." There are no battered children among the Hutterites. Parents have been socialized to avoid anger; they do not see their children as extensions of their own egos; they are never isolated with their children. Other people are always available, always watching and always interested. Hutterite parents do not experience the type of pressure occasioned by the loss of a job because they do not bear sole responsibility for their children. If they become frustrated with a child, there is always someone to take over. Should a parent appear too severe in punishing a child, another adult will intervene. On a more significant level, overly severe punishment is prevented by constant community restraint. Both the parent and the child are protected by the colony (Korbin, 1981).

Hutterite fathers enjoy children. Fathers get up with the babies at night and some help feed the house children. It is usual for the fathers to assist in putting the children to bed, as it is appropriate for the father to lead the night-time prayers. Both our school child and our kindergartner probably were the butt of greater displaced aggression from other children because their father was not there to give them status and to protect them by his presence. Children are almost never allowed in the kitchen or with the women when they are doing colony work. By contrast, children often tag along with the men and play nearby the working men. If a new building is being erected, the children will be near the site. Abigail reported that the children always turned to their fathers for comfort, especially if they were physically hurt. She felt that a father was the first choice, then an older brother or a sister the second, but not a mother. She thought that mothers were less gentle in their feelings towards their children than were the fathers, that the men enjoyed having the children around when they were working and that the women did not. She also perceived the mothers as busier, doing more exacting work and working harder than the men, who had time for interruptions. Though she dared only discuss it in a whisper, she had become sufficiently socialized into the women's culture to firmly believe that the women's work was not only more difficult but was more important than the men's. In the evenings when colony people are sitting around talking, the men are as likely to be holding children as are the women. I have counted six preschoolers in physical contact with their grandfather as he sat talking to colony members.

Many of the parenting practices of the Hutterites are at variance with those of the American middle-class. The two cultures have different goals: one, communal living in a highly structured, traditional social setting and the other, individualism in a complicated, shifting, unpredictable society. Some of the aspects of Hutterite child rearing that are conducive to communal living will now be reviewed.

Sharing child care is supportive of Hutterite culture. Homogeneity within the colony insures consistency among a child's various caretakers who manifest a common set of socialization goals and a common set of practices in relation to childrearing. The caretakers are explicit about the desired behavioral outcome: that the children grow into adults who will voluntarily submit to the will of the community. Some authors have argued that sibling caretaking restricts the development of individual differences in both children and adults (Levy, 1968; Ritchie, 1956). The socialization goal of the Hutterites is to minimize individual differences and individual achievement in order to integrate the child into the communal social pattern (Weisner and Gallimore, 1977). Werner (1982) reports that diffuse mothering (in contemporary societies by strangers) tends to lead children to orient more toward their peers than toward adults. Among the Hutterites the diffuse mothering is effected by relatives and neighbors, but Hutterite children also are oriented more toward their peers than toward their parents. They are more neutral toward their parents than are non-Hutterite children (Schludermann and Schludermann, 1971). In many cultures children who have important household and childcare tasks to fulfill, who interact mostly with kin and neighbors, tend to be more altruistic, nurturant and responsible (Werner, 1982). Adult Hutterites are non-aggressive, are not self-centered or assertive; within the colony they are altruistic, nurturant and responsible. Strong sex role identification smooths role acceptance in a society in which the social structure makes it unnecessary either to act aggressively or, as may be the case in today's isolated, nuclear families, for an individual man or woman to fill, even temporarily, the role of the opposite sex (Minturn, 1969; Whiting, 1965).

How did having children in the field affect my field work among the Hutterites? Our children were relatively adaptable; they had traveled, camped and lived on Amish farms. The Hutterite social structure is such that my children took less of my time than they would have in many cultures. Hutterite child care patterns free the mother to work outside the living quarters. Our oldest child could care for the younger ones and still be abiding by community norms. All food was prepared by the colony, and, although I helped in the preparation, I did not have to raise my own food, shop or cook for my family.

Observing the difference the presence of their father made in our children's experiences within the colony alerted me to many aspects of fathering that I would otherwise have missed. It also illustrated comparative roles of father and husband, in that my husband's presence had a greater affect on the colony response to the children than the colony response to me. (Although, had I not been married I could not have participated as I did.)

My daughter's acculturation helped me understand how the women's culture is perpetuated, as well as how it is effected. She was more sensitive than I to the distance between adult men's culture and the adult women's culture and how women should behave in front of men. "Mother, you should not have laughed when talking to Leonard. Women don't laugh in front of men." And when she was explaining that women's work was more essential to the colony than men's work, she whispered. Men must never know that their superior position could, even momentarily, be questioned by anyone--even a schoolgirl. "I'm sorry, women just are inferior to men. They just are not up to men. It says so right in the Holy Scripture--it's too bad, I feel sorry for them, but that's just the way it is."

A most obvious area in which our children were essential was in the study of Hutterite children's informal culture. The rigidity of Hutterite social structure kept me away from the children's culture: As an adult participating in the system, I was never free to observe them when the children were most actively engaged in their own culture, i.e. when adults were at church or at meals. One is expected to go to meals and sit in one's place even if one eats nothing and healthy women are not allowed to miss colony work just for children. But even if I had been free to observe them, the children would have scattered physically to avoid my watchful eye or would have behaved differently just because an adult was at hand. Not recognizing this can produce an outsider's description that is limited to just one dimension of their culture. For example, as part of my preparation for fieldwork, I talked to a psychologist fieldworker who had never taken his own children with him and had never spent more than a couple of days in one colony. He described the Hutterite children as gentle, friendly, obedient, and docile. He had observed the 'in front of adults', the 'in front of strangers' behavior, but had never experienced the Hutterite children participating in their own culture. In some ways the children's group responds in the presence of an adult as the colony does in the presence of the outside culture.

From my perspective as a field anthropologist, taking into account the cultures that I have studied and the problems that I have found most interesting, my children have been an invaluable asset. They proved to be able assistants and constructive critics.

REFERENCES

Bainton, R. (1941). The Left Wing of the Reformation. *Journal of Religion*, (21):124-134.

Caudill, W., and Plath, D. W. (1966). Who Sleeps With Whom? Parent-Child Involvement in Urban Japanese Families. *Psychiatry*, (29):344-366.

Fonder, A., and Kertzer, D. I. (1979). Intrinsic and Extrinsic Sources of Change in Life-Course Transitions. In M. W. Riley (Ed.), *Aging from Birth to Death: Interdisciplinary Perspectives*, (pp. 121-136). Boulder, CO: Prager.

Gallimore, R., Boggs, J. W., and Jordan, C. E. (1974). *Culture, Behavior and Education: A Study of Hawaiian-Americans*. Beverly Hills, CA: Sage.

Harkness, S., and Super, C. (1977). Why are African Children So Hard to Test? In L. L. Adler (Ed.), Issues in Cross-Cultural Research. *Annals of the New York Academy of Sciences*, (285):326-331.

Hinnant, J. T. (1980). Age Grade Organization: An Explicit Model for the Aging Process. In C. L. Fry and J. Keith (Eds.), *New Methods for Old Age Research*, (pp. 146-154). Chicago: Loyola Press.

Hostetler, J. A. (1974). *Hutterite Society.* Baltimore: Johns Hopkins University Press.

Hostetler, J. A. (1983). *Hutterite Life.* Scottdale, PA: Herald Press.

Hostetler, J. A., and Huntington, G. E. (1968). Communal Socialization Patterns in Hutterite Society. *Ethnology,* (8):331-355.

Hostetler, J. A., and Huntington, G. E. (1980). *The Hutterites of North America, Fieldwork Edition.* New York: Holt, Rinehart and Winston.

Huntington, G. E. (1965). Freedom and the Hutterite Communal Family Pattern. In *Proceedings of the Fifteenth Conference on Mennonite Educational and Cultural Problems,* (pp. 88-111). Bluffton College, Bluffton, Ohio, June 10-11.

Huntington, G. E., and Hostetler, J. A. (1966). A Note on Nursing Practices in an American Isolate with a High Birthrate. *Population Studies,* (19):321-324.

Kagan, J. (1981). Universals in Human Development. In R. L. Munroe, R. H. Munroe, and B. B. Whiting (Eds.), *Handbook of Cross-Cultural Human Development,* (pp. 53-61). New York: Garland STPM Press.

Kanter, R. M. (1972). *Commitment and Community: Communes and Utopias in Sociological Perspective.* Cambridge, MA: Harvard University Press.

Konner, M. J. (1981). Evolution of Human Behavior Development. In R. L. Munroe, R. H. Munroe, and B. B. Whiting, (Eds.), *Handbook of Cross-Cultural Human Development,* (pp. 3-52). New York: Garland STPM Press.

Korbin, J. E. (1981). *Child Abuse and Neglect: Cross-Cultural Perspectives.* Berkeley: University of California Press.

Levy, R. I. (1968). Child Management Structure and Its Implications in a Tahitian Family. In E. Vogel and N. Bell (Eds.), *A Modern Introduction to the Family,* (pp. 590-598). New York: Free Press.

Maccoby, E. (in press). Social Groupings in Childhood: Their Relationship to Prosocial and Antisocial Behavior in Boys and Girls. In J. Block, D. Olweus and M. R. Yarrow (Eds.), *Development of Antisocial and Prosocial Behavior.* New York: Academic Press.

Mead, M., and Macgreagor, F. G. (1951). *Growth and Culture: A Photographic Study of Balinese Childhood.* New York: Putnam.

Minturn, L. (1969). A Survey of Cultural Differences in Sex-Role Training and Identification. In N. Kretschmer and D. Walcher (Eds.), *Environmental Influences on Genetic Expression,* (pp. 255-264). Washington, D. C.: U.S. Government Printing Office.

Minturn, L., and Lambert, W. (1964). *Mothers of Six Cultures.* New York: Wiley.

Nerlove, S. B., and Snipper, A. S. (1981). Cognitive Consequences of Cultural Opportunity. In R. H. Munroe, R. L. Munroe and B. B. Whiting (Eds.), *Handbook of Cross-Cultural Human Development,* (pp. 423-474). New York: Garland STPM Press.

Rabin, A. I. (1982). Supplementary Parenting in the Kibbutz Childrearing System. In M. J. Kostelnik, A. I. Rabin, L. A. Phenice, and A. K. Soderman (Eds.), *Child Nurturance, Volume 2: Patterns of Supplementary Parenting*, (pp. 265-267). New York: Plenum Press.

Ritchie, J. E. (1956). *Basic Personality in Ratau.* New Zealand: Victoria University.

Rogoff, B., Sellers, M. J., Piorrata, S., Fox, N., and White, S. (1975). Age of Assignment of Roles and Responsibilities to Children: A Cross-Cultural Survey. *Human Development*, (18):353-369.

Ross, H. S., and Goldman, B. D. (1977). Infants' Sociability Towards Strangers. *Child Development Quarterly*, (48):638-642.

Schluderman, E., and Schluderman, S. (1971). Adolescent Perception of Parent Behavior (CRPBI) in Hutterite Communal Society. *Journal of Psychology*, (79):29-39.

Schwartz, T. (1976). *Socialization as Cultural Communication: Development of a Theme in the Work of Margaret Mead.* Berkeley, CA: University of California Press.

Weisner, T. S., and Gallimore, R. (1977). My Brother's Keeper: Child and Sibling Caretaking. *Current Anthropology*, 18(2):169-190.

Werner, E. E. (1982). Child Nurturance in Other Cultures: A Perspective. In M. J. Kostelnik, A. I. Rabin, L. A. Phenice and A. K. Soderman (Eds.), *Child Nurturance, Volume 2: Patterns of Supplementary Parenting*, (pp. 207-237). New York: Plenum Press.

Whiting, B. B. (1965). Sex Identity Conflict and Physical Violence: A Comparative Study. *American Anthropologist*, 67(6), Part 2:123-140.

Whiting, B. B. (Ed.) (1965). *Six Cultures: Studies of Child Rearing.* New York: John Wiley and Sons.

Whiting, B. B., and Whiting, J. W. M. (1975). *Children of Six Cultures: A Psycho-Cultural Analysis.* Cambridge, MA: Harvard University Press.

Whiting, J. W. M., and Whiting, B. B. (1975). Aloofness and Intimacy of Husbands and Wives: A Cross-Cultural Study. In T. Schwartz (Ed.), *Socialization as Cultural Communication*, (pp. 91-115). Berkeley, CA: University of California Press.

RESEARCH AND EXPERIENCE WITH MY DAUGHTER IN ECUADOR:

AN ODYSSEY OF ETHNIC MOBILITY(1)

Barbara Butler

Department of Sociology and Anthropology
·University of Wisconsin at Stevens Point
Stevens Point, WI 54481

INTRODUCTION

An idea at the heart of anthropological theory is that the social and cultural differentiation of human groups is maintained by the socialization of new members. The symbolic nature of that socialization process can be powerful in the context of ethnic diversity. Competition for control over it by individuals of differing groups, or the disruption of its course, can raise emotional issues for those concerned, particularly if the ethnic groups are arranged hierarchically. Such was my experience between 1977 and 1979 when I took my one-year-old daughter Marisa along to Highland Ecuador for my dissertation research. As the personal and professional situations occasioned by fieldwork demanded, we became temporarily immersed in three different cultures, practiced three codes of etiquette and demeanor, and adopted three competing group loyalties (cf. Gonzalez, 1974). This paper examines the issues raised and the meanings created by my daughter's involvement in these groups for me and for members of each group who had a morally sanctioned interest in her. It is, simultaneously, a subjective account of personal experience and an objective illustration of the symbolic power of the biological, social and cultural links between generations within groups in social hierarchies. Finally, it is a tentative exploration of the relationship between the subjective and the objective; that is, between an anthropologist's personal experience during fieldwork and her subsequent anthropological analysis.

The three hierarchically arranged socio-cultural groups with which we interacted during field research were white, middle-class North Americans, represented particularly by my family of origin; middle-class mestizo Ecuadorians,(2) represented by my husband's(3) family of origin; and impoverished, Quichua-speaking Indian peasants from Otavalo, Ecuador,

73

who were the focus of research. This hierarchical ordering of the groups is a matter of considerable agreement among them. Most members of each group would confirm that the greater wealth and political power, lighter skin color and superior education of the North Americans gives them a higher position on the world hierarchy than all the Ecuadorians. By the same criteria, Otavalo Indians rank lower than the Hispanic-Ecuadorians. Despite the recognition of this ranking, certain beliefs cushion the impact of an inferior placement for both groups of Ecuadorians. Ecuador's international status as an underdeveloped nation is sometimes attributed by the Hispanic majority there to the presence of the underdeveloped Indians within the country's borders. The most negative, and quite common, evaluation of Indians by the rest of the Ecuadorians is that they are uncivilized, animal-like and worthy only of exploitation. On the other hand, Indians in Otavalo sometimes reject the relevance of this hierarchy, since it is a part of the Western cultural system from which they claim to be separate.

It is important to recognize that this characterization of the three groups involves factors of class as well as ethnicity, although ethnicity receives greater attention. For example, socio-economic class distinguishes Otavalo Indians from middle-class Ecuadorian Mestizos as much as does ethnicity. Although the American middle class does not constitute an ethnic group per se, ethnic factors do distinguish it from the Ecuadorian middle class, and cultural factors related to middle class status differentiate it from other classes in the United States.

The fact that anthropological research is affected by the researcher's personal life and that his or her personal life is in turn affected by the research is an obvious truth whose importance is nevertheless frequently overlooked in print. If a discussion of the interplay between personal and professional factors were a standard feature of ethnography, such major controversies as those between Redfield (1930) and Lewis (1951) over Tepotzlan, and Mead (1928) and Freeman (1983) over Samoa, would be considerably demystified. However, these discussions are usually confined to works, such as this volume, with fieldwork itself as the central theme. In this paper such background information helps make clear the nature of my involvement in Ecuadorian society. Because of the particular combination of personal and professional interests, my daughter's and my ethnic mobility during fieldwork was not a figment of our own or our informants' cultural imagination but a socially significant process.

While I was still an undergraduate, my research interests in cultural differences, development and Latin America co-evolved with my relationship to the Ecuadorian graduate engineering student who became my husband. After graduation in 1971, we went to live in Ecuador, first in the largest city and coastal port, Guayaquil, and then in the national capital and largest highland city, Quito. We returned to the United States in 1973 in part so I could attend graduate school in anthropology. Although I had expected my field research to provide an opportunity for us to return, together with our new daughter, to Ecuador for a time, factors related to his career prevented my husband from leaving the United States for such a long period.

The ideas for research on ethnicity, hierarchy and interethnic mobility had grown out of my experiences while living in Ecuador between 1971 and 1973. Like other social scientists from the United States who spend time in Ecuador or related culture areas, I found the hierarchical nature of the society and the racial, cultural, economic and political aspects of its structure and operation to be of particular interest. This may be due both to the objective and ideological differences between the internal social structures of the United States and such areas, and to the great disparity between the positions of Ecuador and the United States in the international political-economy. These facts heighten the sensitivity of both Ecuadorians and North Americans in Ecuador to issues of hierarchy in general.

The choice to focus the study on Indians reflected the traditional emphasis of anthropology on indigenous people; the fact that Indians represent a polar, and therefore conceptually key position on the hierarchical continuum of Ecuador; and my own tendency to "side with the underdog." The fact that the communities selected were in Otavalo, some 120 kilometers north of Quito, was the result of factors to be explained in a later section. Two communities of Indians, each with a different ethnic identification, were chosen. Both communities were in Otavalo *canton* (similar to the United States county). The research examined ethnic mobility over generations by comparing the developmental cycles of domestic groups among migrants from these two communities to the domestic group developmental cycles among non-migrant community members. Most permanent migrants from Otavalo had moved to Quito.

Although there is a regular flow of individuals from the Indian to the Hispanic ethnic group in Ecuador, the ethnic boundary and its accompanying power differential are institutionalized in rules for interethnic interaction. Such prescriptions and proscriptions for social interaction are a universal feature of ethnic boundary systems, although the extent to which they are enforced varies depending on the total social context. For example, the rules are more elaborate and more strictly adhered to in rural Otavalo than in more urban areas. In 1969 Barth suggested that ethnicity is both superordinate to other statuses and imperative in the presentation of one's own social identity, or in the acceptance of an identity proposed for one by another person. By superordinate he meant that one's ethnic identity, as one aspect of one's total social identity, overrides and influences almost all other roles an individual may assume. Ethnicity is imperative because it can not be overlooked in favor of another definition of the social context. Otavalo Indian ethnicity in Ecuador approaches this model of a superordinate and imperative status.(4) Most Otavalans wear items of clothing or a hairstyle which serve as a insignia of their ethnic identity at all times. Therefore, no ambiguity of ethnic classification by others exists, although an Indian and a non-Indian may disagree on the social and cultural consequences of its recognition.

Nonetheless, there are culturally-appropriate contexts in which alternative ways to present one's identity or to categorize another person are acceptable. As a result it is possible to engage in interethnic interaction which deviates from the usual pattern of dominance and submission. For instance, most of the face-to-face interaction between Indians and ourselves was of a negotiated, non-customary type. Such alternative interaction is possible for a number of reasons: hairstyle and costume can be changed; other relevant indices of ethnicity and rank, such as skin color, wealth and authority may not necessarily coalesce in a single individual in a typical way, making categorization difficult, particularly among strangers; criterial indices are usually relative, not absolute, leading to a certain flexibility in the classification of actual individuals; and any one person belongs to other ranking systems, such as those based on age, kinship seniority or specialized knowledge, that might take temporary precedence. When two strangers meet, one person may not have enough information to override the ambiguities occasioned by the changeable, multiple and relative indices of ethnicity and to rank the other person as those with more information might rank him. Other reasons besides ignorance can provide the motivation to engage in more egalitarian interethnic encounters. If one is a young, as yet socially marginal, non-Indian reformer; a person deeply in love; a member of a millenarian movement; or an anthropologist, one might allow other roles, such as those based on age, to take temporary precedence over ethnicity in classifying another person.

THREE CULTURES AND SPHERES OF INTERACTION

There was never a question about whether or not my daughter Marisa would accompany me to the field. Because of the different characteristics of our work and because I was her mother, I had been the primary parent. My husband and I thought that it would be less disruptive for her to come with me. We also believed that children were inevitably an asset to ethnographic research, based on vaguely remembered remarks by other anthropologists. Finally, we were anxious for Marisa to experience her Ecuadorian heritage, despite her young age. In fact, Marisa's Ecuadorian relatives became an important force in her socialization there.

The Indians in Otavalo also became concerned with Marisa's welfare. During the first few months of our stay we established a fictive kinship relationship with a larger extended family in one community through a local institution of godparenthood, thereby creating bonds more like the ones between us and our other kin. Nonetheless, the impact of their involvement with us was somewhat different for me from that occasioned by the other relatives. The Indians had less right to direct my behavior than did my own and my husband's family. In addition, the Indians' every act or belief was direct contribution to the research in which many of them were genuinely interested. For these reasons my relationship with them was less ambivalent, more completely positive than that with my other relatives, towards whom I often felt anger for their unwanted influence.

The substance of people's concerns for Marisa's welfare varied among the different groups. As far as my geographically distant family was concerned, Marisa was to be socialized as a North American. Two sources of worry for them were her removal from the proper agents of North American socialization during fieldwork, with the exception of myself, and her exposure to two cultures there, which they saw as possible sources of improper socialization. They also feared what they believed was an unhealthy physical environment.

My relatives-in-law, who lived in a different region of Ecuador from the research population, saw Marisa as a North American/Ecuadorian child for whom the most advantageous mixture of their culture and my own was anticipated. They believed themselves to be responsible for her appropriate Ecuadorian socialization. Exposure to the unacceptable Ecuadorian Indian culture was considered potentially harmful.

Among the Indians in Otavalo with whom we had become fictive kin, the concern was that we establish a lasting relationship of social, if not economic, equality with each other. Such a relationship would affirm the worth of their own identity as Indians. They attempted to give Marisa a partial Indian socialization and believed that the members of the Hispanic-Ecuadorian culture posed the greatest threat to their goals.

The American Relatives

The socio-economic position of my natal family is important here for two reasons. Class status in general is a good indicator of what techniques parents believe necessary and what outcomes they consider desirable for the socialization of their children. Secondly, since social norms constrain interaction between members of different classes, my family's class status affected their ideas about and relationship with the other characters in this narrative. My family is solidly middle-class, white, Anglo-Saxon, Protestant. My father has been very successful in manufacturing and business, and now has an income vastly surpassing anything I knew as a child when his career was beginning and funds were distinctly limited. Frugality has never been unfamiliar to me, but identification with anything other than the middle class has also been unknown to me.

Between 1971 and 1973, my parents and my sisters had each made at least one visit to Ecuador. However, neither they nor I had then established any relationship with people who identified themselves as Indians. Because of this lack of knowledge and their predominant orientation to Ecuador as tourists, they saw Indian areas as a very strange, undeveloped environment. Both Marisa and I also had special significance to my parents, Marisa as first grandchild and I as first child. To my one

surviving grandparent, we were first great-granddaughter and first grandchild; and for my sisters, first niece and oldest sister.

Among my family and friends, what Marisa and I were doing was
considered novel, dangerous, exciting, exotic and either brave or foolish.
One major aspect of this novelty was that I, a woman, was voluntarily
separating myself from home and husband for career reasons, unlike my
trip to Ecuador in 1971 when I had followed my husband in *his* career move.
Since I could not necessarily expect to ensure my future income from this
enterprise, my academic goals could even be classified as merely a form of
self-fulfillment.

In those days of feminist excitment, my husband and I were proud, if
not completely happy, with our pioneering endeavor. We were also very
aware of the potential and actual disapproval of others. My husband's
colleagues were politely and passively horrified. My friends and colleagues
in the department of anthropology supported the plan with some reservations.   More distant colleagues did not discuss the issue, presumably
because of the unwritten rule to maintain domestic and public or professional spheres totally separate (see Jacobson in this volume). Other friends
and neighbors maintained polite but worried non-involvement.   A
tremendous burden had been placed on me to ensure a successful outcome
for this risky enterprise. The most emotion-laden measure of such an
outcome to most relatives and friends was Marisa's returning the normal,
healthy and happy middle-class North American toddler she had been
expected to become.

Four foci of concern on the part of North Americans about the
effects of field research in Otavalo on Marisa were fear of a dirty and
unhealthy physical environment, fear of an improper cultural environment,
fear of the effects of a separation from the culturally appropriate home
environment, and fear of the social disruption of the nuclear family. All
four fears are common elements of ethnic boundary phenomena. Physical,
social and cultural elements of the life of the ethnic other are feared,
being particularly dangerous for those new and vulnerable members. When
ethnic boundaries are being crossed, group members are concerned that
new members will not only be hurt but be lost to them. In this case we
worried that Marisa would become more Ecuadorian than North American.

People in all societies anticipate that their children will grow up to
have certain valued behaviors and characteristics. Efforts to produce
these effects are both implicit and explicit parts of socialization practices.
Among the individuals of diverse ethnic origins who have come to belong to
the middle class in the United States, the symbolic processes involved in
socializing new generations are very similar. One quality of middle class
American socialization is the exaggerated responsibility parents and other
concerned adults are given for the development of the behavioral, intellectual and social abilities of each child. Success in school is held to be an
important measure of those abilities. For middle class Americans, children

partially represent a product of the household whose high quality must be ensured for family and household prestige. In contrast, among much of the world's poor, particularly agriculturalists, children partially represent a resource for ensuring household viability and old age security, whose quality the individual parents are rarely expected to control. Our worries over the course of a child's development are connected to our beliefs about its nature. Middle class North Americans believe that childhood development has the following characteristics: it is very vulnerable to noxious influences; it is predictable of adult life and success; and it is more or less irreversible. Thus the exaggeration of fears for a child's welfare and attempts to control a child's development are part of the socio-cultural complex that actively distinguishes middle class North Americans from other socio-cultural groups.

When considering the concern about the physical environment, it is important to note that dirt or lack of cleanness is, for North Americans, one overwhelmingly potent example of the negative and dangerous aspects of foreign societies, particularly those they may consider primitive or underdeveloped. This category of dirt can mean soil, in the absence of water to wash it off, water in the absence of purifying techniques, bodily exuviae such as feces and urine in the absence of proper disposal techniques, and even small creatures from germs (viruses and bacteria) to insects. These substances can be harmful in both a physical way, exemplified by legitimate public health concerns, and even in a somewhat "mystical" way. In 1956 Horace Miner made this point about North Americans in a somewhat exaggerated but no less telling way. He wrote that a people he called the Nacirema (Nacirema is American spelled backwards) had raised the preservation of cleanliness to a semi-sacred activity.

In Ecuador the frequent lack of pure water and the profusion of disease-carrying insects like ticks, mosquitos, chiggers, fleas and lice; arachnids like tarantulas and scorpions; helminths like roundworm, hookworm and tapeworm; and intestinal protozoa like those causing amoebic dysentery worried me greatly as they would most, if not all, North Americans. For many of those not trained, as anthropologists are, to put aside those beliefs that maintain inter-ethnic distance, this fear can be culturally magnified beyond rational limits. During fieldwork, I zealously guarded Marisa from these dangers, even more than myself. That effort and the good medical care I sought out ensured a fairly successful outcome. She suffered relatively few infections and each time she recovered completely.

My North American relatives never clearly specified what aspects of the foreign environment and of the separation from the proper native environment were the greatest cause for alarm. Instead, a diffuse anxiety on my relatives' part over Marisa's social and cultural environment only became allayed when she was back where she belonged in the United States. One means we agreed upon for alleviating these concerns was to give Marisa a home environment in Ecuador that was as similar as possible to a North American one. While Marisa and I were in Ecuador, my mother and even I, the sometimes self-conscious North American in situ, made efforts to provide Marisa with plenty of educational toys and to celebrate North American holidays for her. Her Easter basket was lavishly stocked; on her second birthday she had two parties with cake, ice cream and presents; and for Christmas she even had a decorated evergreen tree. Our apartment in Otavalo had water, electricity, and even a tiny refrigerator that my father had thoughtfully carried along when he came to visit. I attempted to provide as temporally and socially ordered an environment as possible. This my mother advocated and I agreed seemed to meet Marisa's and my own needs.

Among North American concerns was the use of Spanish almost to the exclusion of English in our Otavalo household. This concern was mitigated by the recognition that Spanish is her father's native language and that bilingualism is an educational advantage. However, Marisa's exposure to a third language, Quichua, which the Indians spoke, was considered unnecessarily confusing for her and in no way beneficial.

Finally, my servant was a source of some discomfort to my parents and husband, although she was a trustworthy, even indispensable, helper for me. Among middle class North Americans, it is considered undesirable for a servant to care for one's child, even though it is more or less acceptable if one hires another middle-class mother to babysit. A servant is one who commits the unpardonable offense of publicly accepting a role as a social inferior, thus compounding any social inferiority she may have had because of birth and upbringing. As an inferior she would impart an inferior socialization to her charge.

The fourth focus of concern was the disruption of the family. The separation of Marisa from her father, my husband from myself and my parents and relatives from Marisa and me was a situation that could only be remedied by ceasing fieldwork. However, after one year of research, a number of factors led me to accede to her father's request to return her to the United States. The responsibilities of fieldwork and parenting made such impossible demands on my time that the quality of my performance of both was effectively diminished. I was also convinced that fathers have the same right and responsibility to parent as mothers. Finally, my husband and my family were becoming increasingly dissatisfied with the situation as a whole. I saw her twice, for two weeks each time, during the next six months. While Marisa seemed a happy and extremely outgoing baby in Ecuador, and even more relaxed and happy when we visited her father at home, her time at home without me left her depressed. In addition, her father never adjusted to single parenthood. Although I was able to throw myself wholeheartedly, if brokenheartedly, into research during this period, the emotional cost to the entire family was high.

The major factor that has kept these events emotionally alive for me to this day is that Marisa did not return the normal, middle-class toddler everyone had expected. When the field research period was over, she was approximately three years old and the signs of major developmental lags, which had been noticed before, became impossible to ignore. Then began an involvement with diagnostic, educational and treatment professionals that has since become a way of life. Marisa is hyperactive and has an attention disorder. My opinion, shared by some but not all professionals now, is that Marisa is neurologically impaired. She is seriously learning disabled and the learning that is disabled, both delayed and distorted, is motoric, cognitive and social. However, the etiology of such a syndrome is particularly ambiguous, since some of the features can be caused by a large number of factors and since, in this case, as in many, there is no recognized and specific trauma or condition to which to attribute the problem.

The result was that professionals in both medicine and education, and relatives in the United States, attributed Marisa's difficulties to our recent adventure in Ecuador, sometimes tentatively and sometimes with great conviction. Her problems were not perceived as the result of abnormal brain functioning, but the result of abnormal experiences. The supposed dangers of prolonged exposure to the strange physical, cultural and social environment of the underdeveloped Indians, and of the separation from the beneficial social, cultural and physical environment of our own society were culturally potent enough as symbols to fill in the uncomfortable etiological gap. The geographic, cultural and social distance between societies became transformed, as is so common, into the distance between the poles of a continuum uniting the most desired and the least desired social environments. The United States symbolized a civilized, safe and eminently human social order and Indian Otavalo represented a dangerous, polluting and uncivilized disorder. Besides the need of experts to have an answer for every problem, the middle class North American's heightened concern with producing a "perfect" child created the emotional climate for seeking a scapegoat.

The Ecuadorian Relatives-in-Law

Like my own family, my ex-husband's family is middle class. His parents came from the lower-middle class of a small coastal city, but my husband's father's business success allowed them to rise to the petty aristocracy for a number of years. However, a national economic crisis, and the untimely death of my husband's father during my husband's early adolescence, led the family to Guayaquil in much reduced circumstances. Having passed through a number of precarious years, they are now solid members of the urban middle class. Their middle class status is due to the educational and occupational achievements of the now-adult sibling group, which were made possible by the efforts of their mother.

Two of my husband's brothers are married to North Americans, and during the research period, they lived in the United States. Both have incorporated North American attitudes and view the Third World as unhealthy and undesirable, although one is acculturated to the white middle class and the other to the lower or working class of the North American minorities. Just before Marisa and I left for Ecuador, the former reportedly cried all through one night at the thought of what the "savage Indians" might do to Marisa, particularly steal her. He has refused to take his own two young sons to visit his native country.

For the relatives in Ecuador, an extended family I had come to know between 1971 and 1973, the concerns for Marisa's well-being during fieldwork were far less extreme. After all, as Ecuadorians themselves, they were convinced that health and well-being were ensurable, even for children, in their own country. Although it was distinctly unusual for a married woman to travel alone doing social science research, there were a number of reasons why that became a less emotionally-charged issue for the Ecuadorians than for the North Americans, despite the considerably greater freedom for women in the latter country. First of all, Marisa was considered part-Ecuadorian with a North American mother.   When in Ecuador, she was where she belonged, not in a strange, foreign country as she was for her maternal grandparents. In fact, it was my husband's not following us home that was the focus of his relatives' criticism, not my fieldtrip.   Furthermore, my mother-in-law had long felt that North American women had rights that women everywhere deserved. In general, since North Americans are very much admired by middle-class and lower-class Ecuadorians for their wealth and political power as a nation, and by extension, for their presumed greater 'civilization' as persons, my in-laws were slightly more disposed to view favorably my unfamiliar goals and actions as a North American, than my own relatives in the United States were to view those of the Ecuadorians, their underdeveloped South American neighbors.

There were two stages of involvement in the field trip on the part of my husband's relatives. During the first stage of research, which lasted about three months, my mother-in-law lived with us. Marisa and I landed in Guayaquil in late September of 1977 and stayed one week in my mother-in-law's home. Only unrelenting pressure on my part took the three of us-- Marisa, my mother-in-law and myself--to Quito the following week to stay at the house of the parents of my brother-in-law's wife. There I began to make contacts, formulate specific plans and do library research. After two weeks in Quito, I reluctantly rented a two-room furnished house in one of the wealthier new neighborhoods for a longer stay. Although eventually dividing our time between Otavalo and Quito, we maintained that lease for about three months. During the second stage, the remaining sixteen months of research, I periodically either called my mother-in-law in Guayaquil by phone from Otavalo or travelled the several hundred miles for a visit. I rarely made the effort to visit the few relatives in Quito. In the first stage of research the conflicts of value between my mother-in-law and myself were more acute due to closer contact. In general the issues of concern were assuring proper social status, ethnic distance, kinship solidarity, health and safety, adequate household management and appropriate child socialization.

One of the main concerns of the family at all stages of the research was that their good name and reputation be maintained for the sake of everyone, themselves as well as Marisa, my absent husband and myself. In fact, they hoped that the whole family's social position would benefit from the kinship to the more prestigious North Americans. What made this particularly difficult were my plans to study people who were considered by most Ecuadorians to be vastly inferior in both class and ethnic identity. My mother-in-law's cousin's husband, a minor career diplomat and perhaps the highest status person in the family, was enlisted to change my research plans away from the socially less desirable rural areas and Indians. He first tried to encourage me to work in Quito, but failed immediately. He then decided to ensure that I go to do research among the most "civilized" Indian group by general Ecuadorian criteria, those in Otavalo. He succeeded by calling a potential financial sponsor for the research, the director of the Instituto Otavaleño de Antropologia, who in a subsequent interview promised me a large number of benefits. This dissuaded me from a research site already selected in another province, although I never did get any funding from the anthropology institute.

During this early period, all the Ecuadorian relatives made a concerted effort to take care of Marisa and me, as was culturally appropriate towards a woman of the family who is without her husband. One brother-in-law, the eldest sibling then living in Ecuador, provided many services, wanted and unwanted: he helped me buy a crib; he arranged for us to stay with his in-laws in Quito; he looked in on me frequently when we had moved to the tiny house; he offered to drive me in search of field sites, which became Sunday outings for his wife, children and in-laws; he introduced me to his excellent pediatrician and he even lent me his car for two months, much to his wife's dismay.

My mother-in-law gave full time and attention to Marisa's and my lives during this early period. This led to some conflicts between her expectations of me as a daughter-in-law and mother to her granddaughter and my own behavior and expectations. One major cultural incongruity in the household in Quito concerned the issue of disciplining Marisa and providing order in her life. In Ecuador it is commonly held that babies, particularly those who do not yet walk, talk or control their excretion, must be humored and indulged. Otherwise, it is thought, the strong feelings of anger and frustration that result from the obstruction of their desires will make them ill. They are seen as lacking any cultural means of handling these dangerous emotions and as physically vulnerable. In my tradition, in contrast, one begins some discipline as soon as possible lest the child become "spoiled," expecting her own way and unable to defer to others' needs and wishes. Marisa was hyperactive and impossible to distract when a powerful stimulus presented itself to her. In addition, she seemed both incapable of establishing any order in her own life and likely to experience increasing discomfort and disintegration of control when schedules and limits were not imposed for eating, sleeping and play areas, among other things. The more tired she was, the more likely she was to loudly and miserably refuse sleep altogether. My mother-in-law could neither believe in my philosophy nor command the energy to implement it. When Marisa's hyperactivity and resistance to mild direction began to annoy or tire her, she quickly turned responsibility over to me. Rather than hide or forbid fragile possessions from Marisa and risk her frustration, my mother-in-law would allow Marisa to handle and almost inevitably break them, then require me to replace them. It is worth pointing out that sensitivity to such disagreements was probably increased by everyone's incipient but unacknowledged concern with Marisa's extreme behavior and delayed motor development.

Both my mother-in-law and I were ill and exhausted when she returned home to Guayaquil after about six weeks, nearly a month earlier than she had planned. Marisa, however, was healthy. I had had parasites which led to anorexia, exhaustion, acute bronchitis, and then anemia and a lingering infection. My mother-in-law suffered a flare-up of chronic ailments that her children and doctors in Ecuador and the United States alike consider largely psychosomatic. In addition, both of us found the 9,000-foot altitude taxing, and she never physically adjusted to it. As she felt increasingly ill, she restricted her activities to sweeping, babysitting, and giving me advice and direction. Marisa and I did the daily marketing at a store about one mile straight down (and back up!) a steep hill (the neighborhood was too new for any stores or good bus service). I cooked the three-course main meal at noon, which I could rarely force myself to eat; fed and changed Marisa, carried water from a tap at the road when water failed in the house; spent a minimum of one and a half hours helping Marisa go to sleep every time she was tired; and contrived to spend a maximum of two hours a morning and four in the afternoon chasing authorities, bureaucrats and documents all over Quito by bus. Added to that daily schedule were the frequent shopping trips which satisfied both my mother-in-law's recreational needs and her idea of my equipment requirements for setting up house in Otavalo. In addition to the usual trying responsibilities of a working single mother, I had the benefit of a babysitter and the considerable burden of a boss in what I considered my own house.

One of the reasons I was forced to adjust to these cultural patterns, from child socialization practices to class and ethnic hierarchies and social separation, was because of Marisa. Although I had an affinal kinship connection to an extended family of Ecuadorians, the responsibility to foster Marisa's consanguineal ties was far greater than my own interest in the relationships, particularly in the absence of my husband. Even more important was that I needed help in childcare. My mother-in-law's help then was invaluable and she intended to stay until she could be sure the right domestic help had been hired to take her place.

I had decided to take a domestic servant from Quito to Otavalo with me.   I thought a Quitena would be comfortable with foreigners.   In addition, a person native to Otavalo and imbedded in its social life could involve me and my household in such things as factional disputes or tests of ethnic loyalty without my knowing until I had achieved a better under- standing of local social life.   The eighteen-year-old woman I eventually hired was an orphan who had been in domestic service since the age of seven.   She was part-Indian, although not raised as an Indian, and from a distant part of the country.   She was also intelligent, trustworthy and mature.   Most important to my mother-in-law, she combined a sufficient knowledgeability and interest in proper middle-class life and a respectful, if not docile, attitude that would prevent her from ruling or taking advantage of me.   Although she and I developed a more egalitarian and friendly relationship than is usually acceptable in Ecuador (she ate at the same table with us, for example), the fact that I was the ultimate authority over the household I financially supported, over my child, and over my own personal and professional life, was far more congenial to me than the earlier situation with my mother-in-law.   This was particularly so since my research involved a continuous intimate, egalitarian association with Indians that my mother-in-law would have found intolerable.   In addition, my domestic assistant was eager to agree that the common practice of forbidding maids any disciplining of their charges was detrimental to children's character and household order as well.   Later, in Otavalo, the non-Indian townspeople frequently reported that they had seen my servant speak harshly to Marisa or slap her hand, which they found intolerable. After vainly protesting that I approved, I would promise to look into the matter.

As a final note on the early concerns of my Ecuadorian in-laws, their fears about the dangers of the physical environment for Marisa's and my health were by no means as deep as were the North Americans'.   The preoccupation with intestinal parasites is an example; my mother-in-law still views skeptically the medical diagnosis of amoeba histolytica as a cause of illness.   A generalized belief does exist, however, that the highlands harbor more and different illnesses than the coast, the rural area more than the urban, and the environment inhabited by Indians more than the one inhabited primarily by Mestizos.   Nevertheless, since exposure to all those added risks was unavoidable in the research I insisted on doing, effort was directed toward providing a comfortable apartment with a reasonable landlord, abundant water, cleaning utensils, cooking facilities, a well-stocked market nearby, light, privacy, and adequate furnishings.   The pediatrician in Quito and the hospital in Otavalo were considered sufficient to provide for our needs when sick.   All these amenities were symbols of a minimally acceptable Ecuadorian middle-class life style as well.(5)

During the second stage of field work, when my mother-in-law and I were separated by many miles, the same concerns persisted, but with far less immediacy.   When we were in contact, I was criticized for neglecting to call or visit her and all my other in-laws as frequently as a proper fulfillment of family duties would require. From my point of view, however, the fact that we spent one Thanksgiving, one Christmas and Marisa's birthday in Guayaquil was a fairly generous gift of my time, considering my professional responsibilities. The "deterioration" of my Spanish from contact with Quichua-speakers in Otavalo was another frequent topic of conversation. The fact that Marisa knew a few Quichua words was a source of embrassment and they feared that I might be tempted to dress her in Indian clothing. In other words, our neglect or violation of three very important mechanisms for the maintenance of the social hierarchy in Ecuador, particularly the Indian/non-Indian ethnic boundary, were singled out for censure. These three mechanisms were the composition and interaction of kinship networks, costume and language.

Although my relatives in Ecuador subscribed with greater or lesser conviction to the prevailing Ecuadorian belief in Indian inferiority, during my research, they went out of their ways to extend to those Indians I worked with non-discriminatory treatment and to aid my work wherever possible. During her school vacation, my sister-in-law visited for a week, to help care for Marisa and to see another part of her country. She never came with me to the Indian village, but in my home she made a successful effort to interact cordially with those few Spanish-Indian friends who visited. Later that year my mother-in-law unexpectedly came one Saturday with her Chilean lodger and his visiting mother to see us and to attend the colorful weekly Indian market. With my Indian fictive kin (*compadres*), we ate in a restaurant that is relatively fancy by Otavalo standards. Later that day we met my parents, who were visiting Ecuador at that time. We all ate together at a first class tourist hotel in Quito, much to the surprise of the management and serving personnel. Another time, my Indian *compadres* and I stayed overnight at my mother-in-law's house in Guayaquil. That time we bought Kentucky Fried Chicken and brought it home to eat. As persons we represented three status levels in these encounters. But our financial expenditures were most appropriate to the highest level of the Americans, and our language and general etiquette were most often those of the middle level of non-Indian Ecuadorians. Indian cultural elements were not a part of our interaction, another indication of their social unacceptability outside the Indian community.

Without Marisa's presence, I doubt if I would have appreciated the extent to which a deep concern for the eventual social identity of the children of Ecuadorian families constrains relationships with their social inferiors. In the Ecuadorian middle class, younger generations are expected to surpass their elders in social status, if possible. In an attempt to gain the most advantageous social ranking, they must acquire the right accent, companions, manners, and clothing. In my husband's family, as among most Ecuadorians I knew, relative darkness or lightness of the skin color of one's own children, grandchildren, cousins, children's friends, neighbors and others is frequently discussed. Non-Indian neighbors in Otavalo often commented that it was good that Marisa's skin color was lighter than her father's and a shame that it was darker than mine.

Although this prolonged intimate contact with Mestizos was partially due to my need for help in child care and to my desire to acquaint Marisa with her paternal kin (and vice versa), I was simultaneously aware that the contact was a source of data for understanding ethnic boundaries and status mobility in Ecuador.

The Hispanic Ecuadorians in the Otavalo area, who unlike my husband's family, have daily contact with Indians, made their belief in Indian inferiority much more explicit, for example in their attempts to maintain social, and even spatial, distance from them. Physical contact with Indians is considered disgusting by Hispanics. Any such contact, even on a crowded sidewalk, can be considered an offense for which the Indian may be rebuked, struck or even kicked. While non-Indians in Otavalo often sought out contact with Marisa, they shunned the children of my assistant and other fictive kin. On the bus non-Indians would play with Marisa if she attempted to touch or talk to them. They would roughly push Indian babies away and harshly rebuke their mothers if they were even accidentally touched. In another incident, the local mestizo town treasurer had come to my assistant's house to oversee the harvest of corn that would be used to pay back taxes. At meal time his entire family arrived with an elaborate cooked meal. They insisted that Marisa and I share their food. Although they were offered the food that had been prepared in my Indian assistant's house (which I ate), they refused it and offered nothing at all to my assistant and her children. After eating, the treasurer's children, age six and eight, begged to be allowed to stay and play with Marisa, but ignored the Indian children there who were the same ages, except when they wanted to grab a toy from their hands. All of these incidents were extremely painful for me. But, like the idea that ethnically different people steal children, these behaviors brought home to me how early and rigidly the training in the social separation that upholds the status hierarchy is begun.

The Indian Community and Fictive Kin

The Indians among whom I did research are very poor peasants who, only a few generations ago, re-acquired ownership of the land they had worked for others since the Spanish conquest. That land continues to be the focus of their identity and subsistence, although a shrinking land base relative to population and a greater access to cash is currently challenging their traditional isolationist strategy. The Indians live in endogamous communities surrounding a small non-Indian town, Simon Bolivar, which functions as an administrative center. The Indians emphasize their self-sufficiency and independence from Hispanic Ecuadorians, as do the latter from them. In fact, they are highly interdependent in local economic, political and religious activities. In the Otavalo area, interethnic inter-action is paternalistic at best and brutal at worst, with the Indian almost always the humble victim of socially sanctioned insult and oppression. No Indians in the community, although some in the town of Otavalo, can be classified as middle class by economic criteria. There are, however, many Mestizos in the area whose poverty equals or surpasses that of the Indians.

The Indian community is hostile to outsiders. Although an introduction by the Otavalo Institute of Anthropology allowed me to establish
rapport quickly, a certain amount of distrust lingers to this day. Introductions to the woman who would become my assistant were made in
January. I began daily visits to her community in February. She gave birth
to her second child and first son on March first and the following day she
and her husband asked me to be the godmother at his baptism. Furthermore they proposed to name the baby after my husband and Marisa's
father. Thus, two months after starting research, we became fictive kin.
According to their rules of godparenthood, the most important relationship
established in the baptism ritual is that between the parents and the couple
who become godparents. We became *compadres*, co-parents, to each other.
Indeed, by extension, everyone in my husband's and my cognatic kinship
networks then became *compadres* to everyone in the kinship network of my
assistant and her husband. In an endogamous community of approximately
1,000 people, the latter networks are impressively large.

This relationship, taken seriously by me, my *compadres*, and most of
the community, changed my primary position from white stranger, to whom
no social responsibilities were owed and toward whom fear and hostility
were the primary orientation, to the position of respected white kinsperson
to whom courtesy and interaction were religiously sanctioned duties.
Although they had originally felt ambivalent about establishing a close
relationship with someone who would leave in less than two years, they
decided to make my time there meaningful. At the same time, fictive
kinship could ensure a continuing relationship even after the end of my
stay. In addition, material benefit through gifts of goods and labor is
always an important motive for establishing *compadre* relationships, particularly with non-Indians. It was clearly one reason for establishing and
maintaining this one. The visits by various members of my consanguineal
and affinal kinship networks that took place then and continue to take
place are part of this reciprocal responsibility. Even my second husband, a
native of India who speaks no Spanish, was incorporated into the sytem
during a recent visit.

Marisa's presence in the field was useful to me in many ways. She
was both a catalyst in my relationships with the people of the community
and a participant in relationships as a person in her own right. In addition,
Marisa was treated by local non-Indians in a far different manner than
were my *comadre's* children. All these things provided revealing data. In
the first six months of research I carried Marisa, then in her second year,
with me in a backpack on my daily trips to the community. But as she got
older, heavier and more mobile, and as I became more involved in serious
house to house interviews, she was usually left at home. She still saw my
assistant and *comadre* and her family when they frequently visited our
house in Otavalo or we visited them.

The fact that I was a married woman with a child was extremely
important to my research. In Otavalo, the fact that my husband and I

owned a house in the United States was also significant. Marriage, children and house ownership, with its accompanying household headship for the couple are the bases of adult status. Questions concerning whether I had fulfilled those criteria were consistently the first asked. Had I not been such an adult, it would have been assumed that I shared no basis of mutual interest or expertise with Indian adults and that I was socially unqualified to interact with them as equals. Informative communication would have been much more difficult than it was. We had this strong basis for shared social intercourse when they could temporarily ignore the countless signs of my difference from them, such as my foreignness, white skin or far superior status in the local social environment. Both my position as fictive kinswoman and my increasing skill and willingness to abide by their rules for interaction encouraged them to do so.

Perhaps even more importantly, I early demonstrated my willingness to share my child with them on a social basis. Both Indians and non-Indians in Ecuador teach their children to maintain social distance from the opposite ethnic group by telling them that those others steal *our* children. Many Hispanic Ecuadorians had warned me seriously that Marisa would be stolen if I took her to Indian communities. Knowing this, the Indians in the community used Marisa as a sort of "hostage" to test and perhaps ensure my goodwill and trustworthiness. Several times as I walked with my assistant through the community in the early days of the research, people ran out of their house compounds, grabbed Marisa and ran off with her into their houses. The mime part of the action was obvious since it was done with nervous laughter right in front of me and their kinswoman. Although I knew that people did not want me in their house compounds, I chose, with my assistant, to interpret this act as an invitation to follow (see Perlman, 1970: 306). Clearly a mother belongs with her baby. However, I did not try to seize Marisa back. My willingness to let them try to amuse Marisa, a very friendly and cheerful child, convinced them that I considered them human after all and that we could have human interaction of a sort very different from the usual interaction with non-Indians.

In other ways they repeatedly violated taboos concerning the inter-action between Indians and non-Indian children. For example, they frequently dressed Marisa in Indian clothes for fun and often asked me to buy her an entire outfit. For the festival of San Juan in June when everyone gets a new set of clothes, I bought one for Marisa, too. She wore it occasionally, to the great pleasure of the people of the community and to the frank and often vociferous horror and disgust of the non-Indians in Otavalo. Although the Indians know that Mestizos despise their food and that I obviously limited Marisa's opportunities to try it, they often forced the issue. Then I would allow them to feed her, despite the unsanitary conditions of the food's preparation. Because I did not live among them, I felt that I did not need to stand absolutely firm on such issues in order to maintain my responsibilities as a North American mother. Indians also knew that other Ecuadorians rarely admit knowledge of any Quichua words and do not want their children to speak that language. But they made a continuous game of drilling Marisa in the few words she picked up. Her first word for dog, for example, was in Quichua. Although other people's children are not normally the constant object of attention, Marisa was carried on their backs, sung songs, taught to dance and in many ways sought out for the intimacy that is otherwise denied with white children.(6)

Marisa was treated like a princess. She was allowed freedom to act differently from others, no matter how negatively it would normally have been interpreted, because she was of a supremely privileged class of people. She was indulged and humored beyond what native children ever would have been. For those who were brave enough to visit us at our apartment in Otavalo, Marisa's room with crib, walker, stroller, high chair and lots of toys was the favorite attraction. The jack-in-the-box soon made its way to the village where it was used to frighten adults visiting my *compadres'* house. All this privilege, this ownership of space and property even in babyhood added to her status as a very special person of a different sort from themselves.

Although the Indians enjoyed playing out a fantasy of socially incorporating Marisa since she was, unlike me, still basically unformed, in fact they were as acutely conscious of her social superiority as they were of my own. To the Indians, she and I represented the highest level of the status hierarchy. They themselves represented the lowest. The response then to our egalitrianism or, put another way, our exaggerated kindness and consideration, was sometimes exaggerated respect, gratitude and even obeisance. In reference to myself I once overheard two older, and perhaps slightly inebriated, women suggesting that the juxtaposition of my obvious social and material superiority with my humility and willingness to learn and abide by many of their distinctive customs, probably meant that I was the Virgin Mary returned to earth. The only context in which the socially superior and behaviorally humble could co-exist was supernatural, and the only person who could combine the two was divine.

The Indians in Otavalo considered many aspects of my childrearing techniques odd. However, since Marisa was a bigger and healthier child than their own, they considered these techniques to be satisfactory for us. Although they commented gently to me about these differences, and I occasionally overheard more skeptical remarks, they did not criticize me directly. One example was my attempts to feed Marisa and put her to sleep at relatively fixed intervals. In their experience, children demand food when hungry and fall asleep when tired. For those who believed me when I said Marisa had weaned herself from the breast to a cup at age one, this was another sign of our different nature. This was all the more strange when it became clear that she had been weaned to a milk-substitute formula, that was difficult to find and expensive to buy, because she was allergic to cow's milk. Finally, when Marisa was left behind in the United States with her father at 26 months, they reassured each other that she had in fact been weaned. But the most difficult fact to assimilate was that, at such a young age, she had been left with her father (male) rather than my mother (female).

Both Indians and Mestizos in Otavalo noticed Marisa's hyperactivity and her slow development of such milestones as walking, talking, feeding herself and toilet training. Many seemed to believe that we as North Americans were just different, in both socializing practices and natural development. After all, she was the same height and weight as most children one to two years older than she. On the other hand, my godchild was far more active than other Indian children as a baby. To them this was a perfectly reasonable result of his new kinship with us active North Americans. My own tentative explanations then were that he was relatively more healthy and well-fed than most Indian babies, and that he was in daily contact with me, a caretaker with a vastly different view of normal adult-baby interaction. Perhaps, in retrospect, he was copying Marisa as well, although she did not always accompany me to the village. To be fair, however, this child is now, at five, no more active than others who have no North American godmother, and his baby brother is far more active than he ever was.

Although as a North American I saw in the physical environment risks to Marisa's health that our hosts did not recognize, our host saw risks to us, and themselves, that we did not. Because of that ignorance, I sometimes jeopardized the well-being of all of us. An example was my continuing ignorance about the association of dangerous or evil spirits with particular places. A combination of factors encouraged that ignorance. I lacked both a belief in spirits and a research focus on such matters. Perhaps more importantly, Indians are careful not to reveal those supernatural beliefs that outsiders might consider ignorant superstitions. Once I unknowingly set my godchild down on the ground in a cemetery, which could have made him gravely sick. Luckily I felt ill later that day which suggested to them that, as a weak foreigner, I had absorbed and succumbed to the evil forces in that place rather than my godchild. More dramatically, my *compadres* once accompanied me on a trip to a large waterfall that serves as a tourist attraction for young North Americans, but which most Otavalo Indians believe is the abode of very powerful and dangerous spirits. Curious to visit the spot, my *compadres* were publically skeptical about the spirits, but as we got closer it became obvious that they privately gave them more credence than they were willing to admit. Marisa somehow fell off my lap almost into the river; she hung on to the grasses halfway down the steep bank until my *compadre* saved her. The fact that Marisa was safe suggested to Otavalans that the spirits had only wanted to warn us. Nonetheless, the fright our souls had experienced and our proximity there to powerful soul-stealing spirits left us all highly susceptible to potentially fatal fright-sickness. This time no one succumbed, which led to a re-evaluation of my constitution as quite strong. Both my *compadres* were scolded, shamed and switched by their parents when they got home for so willfully endangering their own and our lives.

SUMMARY AND CONCLUSION

What did the experience of fieldwork mean for Marisa? There is very little one can say with any certainty because she was so young at the time. The separations in the family that were part of fieldwork seem to have left a legacy of insecurity about the continued presence of her parents. Marisa is confident with strangers, sure that she can make adult friends wherever she goes. This outgoing behavior may have been encouraged by her early experiences with travel and participant observation, or, as one possible diagnosis suggests, it may simply be another feature of her particular neurological makeup. Certainly she takes even solo plane travel in her stride and seems unsurprised but intrigued by contact with different languages and visibly different people. The multilingual and multicultural environment may have increased the difficulties with learning she already had, but most likely in a minor and transitory way. Since she was still a baby during my research, the messages of ethnic and class separation that so powerfully affected me escaped her completely. What seems to have had the greatest impact on her are the loving relationships she formed with kin fictive and consanguineal, among the different peoples of Ecuador, relationships that last for her and for those others until today.

Just who Marisa became as a person was important for the social identity of both sets of her grandparents, whose children had made an interethnic and international marriage, and for us parents as well. The unusual social context of her socialization while I did fieldwork was of concern to all of us. Particularly for the Ecuadorian relatives, too close an assimilation to the poor, powerless and primitive research population, for example, would damage not only her social fate, but that of many others. For the relatives in the United States, the belief in parents' responsibility and need to assure an arbitrarily defined optimum early childhood and the fear of the effects of the Third World on a young child's early development were strong enough to make the experience in Ecuador a plausible explanation for major learning disabilities.

For the Indians in Otavalo, a close association with Marisa allowed them to enact and practice new, more egalitarian interactions with non-Indians and a more positive self-image in a local environment of changing and tense ethnic interaction.

For me, the necessity to continually shift interactional styles and general demeanor to fit the social situation was exhausting (cf. Gonzalez, 1974, p. 32). The strain was increased because of the competing and often contradictory claims of those who had both the vested interest and moral right to order Marisa's material, social and cultural life. The fact that a coincident process was the unfolding and gradual realization of abnormal development only served to heighten the strain. It reached a peak after fieldwork when experts in the United States claimed a causal relation between the first and second processes.

As for my research, Marisa's presence during fieldwork increased my learning and understanding of the importance of a family's control over the socialization of its children. Creating proper descendants vindicates the life paths of persons and perpetuates groups based on ethnicity, class and nationality. The meaning of this process was heightened because the three groups were both ranked in prestige and representative of three levels of power in a world political economy. Marisa's kinship to me and others, and her dependence and vulnerability as a baby brought these issues home.

While my immersion in the drama of ethnic mobility provided me with good data, it is impossible for me to know how much my view of the local reality was biased by my own particular experiences and emotional reactions, colored as they must have been by my own cultural training. For example, the description and analysis of ethnic mobility in my dissertation made more of the relationships between parents and children than I had anticipated. Nevertheless, it remains difficult to distinguish cause from effect. For example, the expressed ideas of both Indians and Hispanics about Indian children and ethnic mobility seemed particularly revealing. In the majority of conversations I witnessed between Hispanics and bilingual Indians, the Hispanics were pleased when they could encourage the Indians to criticize their parents for their outmoded, uncivilized ways. While Indians often acquiesced, in private they admitted that such situations were a cause for great anxiety. They told me in emotionally loaded stories what they thought of "losing a child" (their words) as a result of the child's attempt to pass as non-Indian. They called such passing "denying one's parents." There is an apocryphal story that describes young adults, who sport brand new Western clothes and hairstyle and an ignorance of Quichua, returning to their home area to wander in the streets, claiming in Spanish "where, oh, where are my parents? I have no parents here," in the hearing of their families and both Indian and Mestizo neighbors. Did my emotional involvement trigger these stories or make them seem important? Or was my own emotional involvement in the competition for Marisa's and my ethnic loyalty the result of its importance for the Ecuadorians themselves?

Clearly, fieldwork with one's family is different from fieldwork alone. The most important difference is the amount to which ethnographers accompanied by their families remain involved in their cultures of origin. They cannot set aside as many of their own cultural assumptions and requirements as can a lone ethnographer. There are two reasons for this. On the one hand, wholesale and unilateral imposition of complete cultural relativity on a family would leave the members without the cultural tools necessary to continue the communication among members that any social system requires. Secondly, like other adults, parents who are anthropologists have been trained in certain socialization goals and practices and chosen others that cannot easily be discarded, even temporarily, to facilitate research. The socialization of children is a continuous process.

This involvement in family social life forces ethnographers to reflect continually upon the discrepancies between the cultural patterns of their own and the host society. Although exhausting, this effort can be extremely productive. Not only may ethnographers accompanied by their families thus learn more about the society under study than may a lone fieldworker, but they may also develop considerably greater insight into their own groups of identification. The presence of ethnographers' families may also increase their sensitivity to the interaction between observation and prior cultural expectation, which is the source of ethnographic data.

Furthermore, families are significant units of society everywhere, and among many of the societies anthropologists study they are by far the most important. Having a family along during fieldwork can increase the anthropologist's empathy with informants and thus add to the knowledge of what concerns family members in the society under study. When the ethnographer's family is itself bicultural and when the ethnographer has a research interest in ethnicity and social mobility, as is the case here and in Kleis's contribution to this volume, this effect may be taken one step further. The motivation to exchange information on those topics, particularly as they affect the children, is increased for both the ethnographer and his or her informants. This can be a rich source of data.

Ethnography can benefit from all types of fieldwork teams and from all points of view. However, as has been proclaimed in nearly every treatment of fieldwork published to date, (e.g. Agar 1980; Dumont, 1978; Frelich, 1970; Powdermaker, 1966; Rabinow, 1977 to name only a few) the only way this benefit can be made available is if as much as possible of the social and psychological context of every fieldwork experience is made public. Participant observation, even more than other research techniques, always involves people's personal lives as much as purely scientific goals. In fact the ethnographer's personal life becomes a research tool. Few things are as personal and important to the individual as parenthood. Although there is a taboo in our culture on public self-disclosure, the demands of anthropological fieldwork should override it. Personal accounts by anthropologists are not self-serving, but necessary for the advancement of knowledge. This includes accounts of fieldwork with our children.

REFERENCES

Agar, M. H. (1980). *The Professional Stranger: An Informal Introduction to Ethnography.* New York: Academic Press.

Barth, F. (1969). *Ethnic Groups and Boundaries.* Boston: Little, Brown and Company.

Dumont, J. P. (1978). *The Headman and I: Ambiguity and Ambivalence in the Fieldworking Experience.* Austin, TX: The University of Texas Press.

Freeman, D. (1983). *Margaret Mead and Samoa: The Making and Unmaking of an Anthropological Myth.* Cambridge, MA: Harvard University Press.

Freilich, M. (1970). *Marginal Natives: Anthropologists at Work*. New York: Harper and Row.

Gonzalez, N. L. (1974). The City of Gentlemen: Santiago de los Caballeros. In G. M. Foster and R. V. Kemper (Eds.), *Anthropologists in Cities*, (pp. 19-40). Boston: Little, Brown and Company.

Lewis, O. (1951). *Life in a Mexican Village: Tepotzlan Restudied*. Urbana, IL: University of Illinois Press.

Mead, M. (1928). *Coming of Age in Samoa*. New York: Morrow Press.

Miner, H. (1956). Body Ritual Among the Nacirema. *American Anthropologist*, LVIII:503-7.

Perlman, M. (1970). Intensive Fieldwork and Scope Sampling: Methods for Studying the Same Problem at Different Levels. In M. Freilich (Ed.), *Marginal Natives: Anthropologists at Work*. New York: Harper and Row.

Powdermaker, H. (1966). *Stranger and Friend*. New York: W. W. Norton and Company.

Rabinow, P. (1977). *Reflections on Fieldwork in Morocco*. Berkeley: University of California Press.

Redfield, R. (1930). *Tepotzlan, a Mexican Village: A Study of Folk Life*. Chicago: University of Chicago Press.

NOTES

(1) For their support of the research which made this chapter possible, I would like to thank the Organization of American States (Fellowship No. BEGES 56441); Wenner-Gren Foundation for Anthropological Research (Grant No. 3277); and Neslab Instruments, Inc.

I would also like to thank my parents, my ex-husband, my mother-in-law, my friends and former servants Zoila and Sra. Isabel, and my *comadres* Isabel and Dolores for their support, help and love before, during and after dissertation research.

(2) Choosing terms for the socio-cultural groups in Ecuador is a continuous problem. Since the characteristics, names included population and even ranking shift according to the relative status of the speaker, any term carries with it the biases of one group or another. Since not all the Indians referred to here have a name of wide recognition, the term Indian is most often used. This is a category by which people of Western culture affiliation and/or ancestry refer to the diverse peoples of Native American cultural affiliation and/or ancestry. That term, of course, has perpetuated Columbus's mistaken identification of the continent on which he landed. The same problem of terms holds for the other Ecuadorians. Many terms exist but they refer primarily to either cultural affiliation (Hispanic) or ancestry (white; *mestizo* [mixed]). For that reason, I prefer the awkward but neutral term non-Indian. Most Ecuadorians, including my husband's family, are mestizo in ancestry and so that term is sometimes used here. However much the culture, too, may be mixed, when Ecuadorians contrast it to the Indian culture, it is considered overwhelmingly Hispanic. This

cultural component of the ethnic categorization is crucial, so the term Hispanic is also used for those who are not Indian.

(3) Marisa's father and I have since been divorced.

(4) Only the Indians of one of the two communities studied, both in *canton* Otavalo, are called Otavalo Indians. One characteristic of them is that they expend more energy to keep the ethnic boundary between themselves and Hispanic Ecuadorians explicit than do the Indians in the other community. Since the bulk of my participant-observation was done among these Otavalo Indians, the text refers to them primarily, unless otherwise specified.

(5) However, they were less than what I had been used to in the United States and my own parents found them pitiful when they came for a visit.

(6) The only Indians employed as nannies in Otavalo, for instance, are girls aged seven to twelve who, more often than not, are required to wear Western clothes and are forbidden the use of any Quichua words with their charges.

WHAT HAPPENED WHEN MY DAUGHTER BECAME A FIJIAN

Diane Michalski Turner *(1)*

Department of Anthropology
Michigan State University
East Lansing, MI 48824

From October, 1979 through April, 1981 my husband and I conducted anthropological research in a Fijian village.*(2)* Our research site was a wet-zone village in Viti Levu, the largest island in this archipelago in the southwest Pacific. In this account I have focused on my feelings of exhaustion, resistance to the host culture, and being unable to control the fieldwork situation. It is an accurate assessment of the way I sometimes felt, especially during the initial months of fieldwork. I worried, unnecessarily as it turned out, that these early phases would represent the entire experience. The unsettling confrontation with a foreign culture has provoked in others a similar response, which has come to be known as culture shock:

> a syndrome...which includes frustration, repressed or expressed aggression against the source of discomfort, an irrational ferver for the familiar and comforting, and disproportionate anger at trivial interferences (Golde, 1970:11).

While I was experiencing culture shock and during the rest of the research period, my hosts were tolerant of my cultural differences, were willing to contribute to my research, and welcomed me into their lives. My first responses to Fijian culture have not prevented me from understanding it or admiring Fijian people. Indeed, my initial adverse reactions prompted me to compare Fijian culture with my own and to question the assumptions underlying American beliefs and values. I am very grateful to my hosts for their great kindness, instruction, and patience.

The memory of our arrival in the village is still vivid in my mind. We had traveled from the capital by car to the end of the road and proceeded upriver by boat. I saw the village five hundred yards before we came to the landing. It was composed of brown thatched houses amidst ornamental plants and closely-cropped lawns. Smoke from cooking fires created a haze over the deep green hues of the plants and trees. On the shore, children were queued and ready to carry our belongings into the village. Adults came to the path to greet us. Shaking hands, moving along the path, we could barely hear their salutations, "*Bula*," good health and life to you, above the clanking and pounding sounds of heavy metal mortars and pestles being used to grind a dried pepper root for the ritually and socially important beverage, *yaqona*. We came to the house where we would stay for the next sixteen months, put down some belongings, and then continued on the path to the paramount chief's house. There the paramount formally welcomed us and promised us his protection as part of the ritual of *yaqona* drinking. As I drank the *yaqona*, the solemnity of the senior men, the stillness and the darkness in the house at this twilight hour contributed to my feeling that I was in a church and receiving communion. I kept thinking about all the times that I had read about drinking *yaqona*. Now I was holding a coconut shell filled with it, swallowing it. A neighbor was holding our daughter Megan outside the house, while only my husband and I sat with the senior men. All those years of preparation were for this moment. I felt peaceful. My sense that nothing could ever go wrong here lasted a week or so.

I planned to do a general study of women's roles in a rural village. I was especially interested in the economic activities of women, their participation in decision-making processes, and their sentiments and obligations toward their natal and affinal kin. My research proposal was submitted before I was pregnant. By the time I received notification that I had received funding, I was four months pregnant. Then I began to realize that modifications in my research plans would be necessary. I could not, however, anticipate either the extent or direction of the changes that lay ahead. When we embarked for Fiji, our daughter Megan was nine months old, walking and trying to talk. She was, and is, an extrovert, blessed with more energy than any two adults.

We spent our first month in Fiji in the capital, Suva, making final arrangements for our field site and acclimatizing. Our stay in the city was a harbinger of things to come. In the United States, Jim and I had divided childcare and housework. In Suva, Jim ran most of the errands and called at administrative offices. Megan stayed at our apartment building because Jim and I had determined that she needed to be able to nap, to stay out of the sun, and to have time and place to move about. Because I was nursing her, I stayed with Megan.

There was another factor that kept me housebound--laundry. There were no laundromats in Fiji. If urban people did not own washing machines, they either hired someone to wash their clothes by hand or did it themselves. Our own observations and assumptions told us that laundry was woman's work. I decided to wash our clothes. I did not want to continue the stereotype of European women employing Fijian women to perform household work so that they could spend their time as "ladies." A month of laundering while keeping my daughter safely occupied, however, led me to consider hiring a "housegirl" to assist in the village so that I could engage in my research.

Two-hundred and fifty people lived in the village. Our presence was easily observable by most villagers, and given this and Fijians' propensity to visit travelers and guests, we naturally became the focus of attention. A constant steam of women and children visitors in our house, the presence of our landlord at every lunch and supper, and the guests who stayed late into the evening vaporized my initial sense of tranquility. I was physically tired from what seemed like perpetual hosting of my new neighbors. We were often too exhausted to record the day's conversations and observations. This was the first of a number of sources of strain that would soon affect me.

While we were swept up in the visiting marathon we were also being taught basic Fijian skills that we were expected to use immediately. Our closest neighbors explained to us that Fijians viewed these skills, indeed their culture in toto as superior to our own. Fijians define their culture as the ways Fijians behave, "in the way of the land." The phrase "in the way of the land" (vakavanua) implies the notion that customs stem from time immemorial. Among other things, I was taught how to eat like a Fijian, how to sit like a Fijian, and how to nurse a baby like a Fijian. It was an idyllic situation for an ethnographer--the members of the host culture instructing the neophyte in thier customs and ways. But after a bit, I was overwhelmed by having to do everything in the Fijian way. It was exhausting to change habitual behavior. I did not like to appear clumsy and unskilled and often failed to join my neighbors' laughter at my behavior. I felt that I was being directed at every turn. This socialization process reminded me of my eculturation in a Polish-American neighborhood. As did Polish-Americans during my youth, Fijians stressed obedience to elders, generosity, and concern for others and de-emphasized personal independence. Fijian and Polish-American adults enculturate children by explaining processes and events and closely directing their development. I could visualize how my daughter would be enculturated. I wanted my daughter to learn to be generous and caring as Fijians and Polish-Americans are. But I also wanted her to experience a less directive socialization and more independence.

In Fiji, another spector from my past emerged. I was bothered by my cultural marginality and reminded that I had from time to time felt the same in the United States, where I had made a cultural transition from my background in a Chicago Polish-American neighborhood to the cultural milieu of the academic community. There I had been reminded by my ethnic fellows how "we" behave and alternately made to feel "ethnic" by my university colleagues.

My inter-cultural sojourn was not easy. It has not been a consistently unidirectional journey. I wanted to be accepted as a mainstream, middle class person, yet I valued aspects of my natal cultural tradition and behavioral repertoire and sought to retain these. It was confusing and unsettling to shuttle between sets of values and kinesic and linguistic styles. As my values and ambitions changed through my young adulthood, I suffered in varying degrees from cognitive dissonance. My parents understood me less and less; and my social network was splintered. The cultural conflicts, the marginality, the disparate loyalties, the sensations of floating culturally, socially, and, especially, psychologically without recourse to a mooring place plagued me after college graduation. These feelings subsequently surfaced when demands of graduate school and my natal family collided and when I married and experienced a clash between my own and my husband's expectations and traditions. These alternate ways of doing things, of being, of feeling had eventually found a rapprochment within my life--that is, until I went to Fiji.

I grew up in an extended-family household. My maternal grandmother spent most of her time and took all of her meals with my family, although she slept in her own apartment in the building that was jointly owned. We lived in a neighborhood where a majority of the residents were Polish immigrants or these immigrants' children. Ours was a neighborhood where the residents' general orientation to social life was to attend to or to seek some form of involvement in others' affairs. Specific values, circumstances, and gossip facilitated this. For example, adults, whom we addressed as Mr. or Mrs. or as Aunt or Uncle (if their relationships with our parents permitted it), reprimanded all errant children. Thus, children came to expect that others would take an interest in their behavior and they in turn came to note and comment on others' actions. All of this was enhanced by widespread gossip. News, as gossip was euphemistically called, flowed during conversations between people leaning out of windows in adjacent buildings, by telephone, at daily gatherings on front porches in clement weather, and between old women after daily mass before they separated for their homes.

All this involvement in others' lives, this reciprocal concern, supported an ambience described by several neighborhood residents as, "we were like in an egg." The expression refers to a sense of being protected from participation in anti-social behavior as the contents of an egg are restrained from moving about by the eggshell. But the interwined sense of protection and restraint was also applied by neighborhood residents to our participation in the larger society. It was our ethnicity and Catholicism that shielded us, in one sense, but prevented us, in another sense from mingling with others. On occasion, some individuals spoke about having to "break out of this shell" and to change values and behaviors in order to succeed in American society.

I never thought that a visit to an exotic place would remind me of my Polish-American neighborhood. But Fijians, like my Chicago neighbors, constantly checked on each others' movements, commented on behavior and recapitulated at evening gatherings everyone's activities during the day. They even believed that I should inform the local administrator when I intended to leave the village. What was new about the situation in Fiji, however, was that I had a daughter and I had consequently shifted my focus from my own social containment to a concern for how such an experience would affect her.

Once again I sensed the queasiness of being between value systems and behavioral expectations. There were, however, differences in my two cross-cultural experiences. In America, the cultures were not as dissimilar and I wanted membership in each. In Fiji, I was supposed to be a participant observer, someone who interacted as much as possible with Fijians and tried to abide by their customary ways but who did not internalize their values so that accurate descriptions of their behavior could be made. Yet I was having a familiar sensation of being sucked into a swirling deep black funnel of culture conflict.

Our housegirl was most responsible for my Fijian acculturation. We needed a housegirl at first because we were unfamiliar with the preparation of local foods and had a rudimentary knowledge of the language from our study of the few texts available in the United States. Our housegirl was a *goneyalewa* (girl, an unmarried female). Single females form a labor pool that can be tapped for domestic and agricultural work by their parents and various other kin. Girls should do what adults, i.e, married persons, tell them to do. In the domestic hierarchy, they are supervised by married women. Although expected to work like adults, girls are treated as children. The girls can be paid and their income may be appropriated by those who have rights to control their activities.

For the first week, two girls, one seventeen and the other twenty-two, arrived at six thirty in the morning to haul water from the pipe in front of our house, launder, cook, and serve meals. The girls shared the role of female household head, the role that I should have played. This meant that they controlled the food supplies and interacted with villagers who brought us portions of cooked food in the custom of *i takitaki* (sharing). After awhile the girls began to give our store-bought food to others who came to ask for them, but without consulting Jim or me.

I had not had experience with domestic help, had no inclination to have any, and had uppermost in my mind a concern that I do nothing to alienate my hosts. I was eager to establish egalitarian relations with the girls, who by local values and attitudes I should have supervised. The girls and I had almost reversed our expected social roles. It seemed that I had become what I had tried hardest to avoid--an insipid, indolent European lady disapproved of by her domestic help because she does not work and has no power of her own. People of the interior do not respect women who do not cultivate, fish, and collect firewood and they do not respect powerless people. I was caught in a classic dilemma. I could not engage in traditional village women's work because I needed to attend to my research. However, since the villagers initially viewed research as exclusively my husband's work, they perceived my interviewing and other activities to be the same as the behavior of the quintessential non-working European wife. It is not surprising that I was eager to develop village women's skills and prove to them that I was an industrious, competent and worthwhile person.

The girls also took over much of what I felt to be my role as Megan's mother. *Goneyalewa* are supposed to tend young children so that their mothers are not overburdened with work. By caring for Megan, however, I felt that they were doing the parenting and that I was reduced to being a child. I wanted to feed Megan, but they would take her from me. I wanted Megan to eat enough protein, that is, fish or meat. They assured me that she required "real food" *(kakana dina)*, taro, which they mashed and spooned unremittingly into her mouth.

When at the end of our first week, one girl stopped helping at our house, Siteri became our official housegirl. It was, ironically, by being with Siteri that I learned about the status of girls in Fijian society, and it was she who underscored how childlike I felt in the village. In some sense Siteri and I were structurally equivalent in our household--neither children nor quite adult women.

How much choice Siteri had in being our housegirl remains unknown. Although she was placed in our household by her relatives, and portions of her salary apportioned by her father and her classificatory father, with whom she lived, Siteri still had some income and some freedom, in comparison to other girls. Initially, Siteri appeared pleased with her position as household intermediary and occupant of the household's adult female role. Siteri's camaraderie then withered, and we began to perceive her as mischievous. Siteri, like most villagers, had mixed feeling about working as a domestic. They all liked the income but did not like being employed as servants. Villagers like some European foods and envied Fijians, such as housegirls, who ate them regularly. But they chided Fijians who did not eat indigenous foods as Fijians should. Some villagers, especially young men without any regular sources of cash, begrudged her her small salary and teased her by calling her "housegirl." Various neighbors must have intimated that perhaps she was becoming too much like a European by being in our company so much and by eating our food (oatmeal, jam, and tinned butter), because as time went on Siteri had to reassert to use all those early lessons on the superiority of Fijian culture. She wanted to do things *vakaviti*, Fijian-style. This was acceptable to us, since we said that we wanted to live like Fijians in order to understand them. But I felt that her insistence on "acting Fijian" was not done in an instructive manner but to separate us into our respective categories. Unintentionally, we may have contributed toward her change in behavior. Her salary was too low; it was set at this rate at the suggestion of a young woman who worked outside of the village and whose knowledge and wisdom we initially respected.   In a society where largesse and generosity are praised, we must have been seen as very stingy.   Additionally, our housework was too routine; it did not provide Siteri with the customary variety of tasks, and it separated her from other young people during the day.

In our third month in the village, the hot season was at its zenith and with it came flies that infected my mosquito bite-covered legs. When my legs ulcerated, I became gravely concerned that I would become sick and not be able to take care of Megan or finish my research. At this point, Siteri became an extremely important person to me. She was an example of all I needed to be--healthy, competent linguistically, and skilled in the local tasks and abilities. My needs and deficiencies made me feel like a child and made me view Siteri as the capable adult. My accumen, my skills, what I felt competent in doing belonged to another world. My perception of myself was particularly irksome in regard to my relationship with Megan. I did not feel that I could behave as Megan's parent when I considered myself something less than a responsible adult, as locally defined. I could not do what Fijian adults (and children over five) did: for example, walk through mud and creeks without getting bogged down, cut the grass around my house with a cane knife, and haul firewood without bruising my back and losing my balance on the hillside. To indicate my willingness to integrate into the community, I wanted to speak Fijian to Megan; I could not do this fluently. My Fijian resembled the speech of a Fijian child and therefore I lacked the ability to convey many concepts that adults and parents easily transmit to the young. Siteri could do all the things that I could not. My daughter could do 'Fijian' things better and faster than I. She easily walked barefoot across log bridges while I had to learn to balance and to overcome my fear simultaneously. Her flawless Fijian accent and lexicon were often compared by villagers to my own. Megan was learning things that I was not teaching her, Fijian ways and language. For these reasons, I did not see myself as being her parent--I was not actively inculcating in her my traditions, my language, and my cultural identity. I was learning what Megan was learning. We were, in my view, both children in the village.

Siteri and I vied over socializing Megan. For instance, I wanted to avoid stimulating Megan before bedtime so that she could sleep and I could write fieldnotes.   Siteri wanted to hide in the curtains that drape the sleeping area and to leap out when Megan tugged at them. Megan loved to play this game and she loved Siteri. Our respective relationships to Megan reflected other concerns. We were employed and employee, representatives of the colonizer and colonized dyad, and members of distinct cultural entities. Megan was the prize whose cultural allegiance would represent the superior enculturating prowess of the victor and mark the successful conclusion to a game ranking peoples and their cultures.

Siteri gave Megan language lessons with a deep dose of Fijian culture. Etiquette, rhymes, counting, songs, dances--everything that Siteri could teach Megan, she would. Siteri had a coterie of siblings and other young relatives who came to visit us and play with Megan. They taught Megan her place in village society; she was the youngest and so they teased her by saying that they would take her clothing, her mother's milk, or her other belongings. In their play, Megan learned how to hit cats, dogs, and chickens. Fijians explained to me that small children will not hurt the animals, but by hitting them children will learn to be unafraid and physically assertive with these creatures. I did not like these behaviors, but I could not prevent Megan from getting these lessons.

Megan was so keen to learn how to speak that she babbled constantly. Jim and I could not discern any meaningful sounds. A neighbor, from whom we were taking census information one day, noted Megan's first discernible communication. As we asked this woman questions and she responded, Megan vocalized in chorus. Abruptly, this woman stopped telling us about her husband's family to say that Megan was talking about pawpaw fruit. Megan had noticed a pawpaw tree and kept repeating *leti*, the last two syllables of the Fijian word for pawpaw, *weleti*. To realize that I had missed my child's first words because they were spoken in a language that I did not understand well as a bit of a shock. Megan had been speaking for a week or so and we did not know it because we were expecting English to gurgle forth. I felt a sense of estrangement and of discontinuity between Megan and me because her mother tongue was not mine (even though I was bilingual as a child). It was Megan's increasing fluency in Fijian, my minimal competency in this language, plus the other cultural differences that would become apparent as time went on that made me empathize with immigrants' experiences and their wish to transmit their cultural history and linguistic identification to their children and grandchildren (cf. Nader 1970:112).

I wanted my child to be part of my cultural universe. I wanted a cultural solidarity with her that I shared neither with my earliest reference group nor with my university colleagues. Fijians noted that cultural dissimilarity between Megan and her parents and thus intensified my feelings about this. Villagers said that Megan would become a Fijian because of her village residence, or at least would be so while living there. Some indicated that they wanted this outcome for Megan. Eventually, I came to approve of Fijian and American cultural values being included in my child's socialization, although such splintering of cultural loyalties and my daughter's adoption of Fijian culture had initially caused me to feel that my youngster and I were becoming estranged. This feeling of cultural distance between us recalled my own youthful intercultural odyssey and the conflicts and disquieting marginality to two traditions that accompanied it.

Megan wanted to be Fijian. She imitated their posture, their manners, and their greetings. She tried desperately to comb her blond, wispy hair so that it would take on the shape of their hairstyles. Against the drama and excitement of our neighbors' way of life, Jim and I presented a rather drab alternative. All the really interesting, socially acceptable things were Fijian for Megan. So much of our energies were channeled into our research that we did not engage in the entertaining activities with her that our fellow villagers did. Her father did not ride her around our house on his back, or lay her in his lap and sing her lullabies while rocking her across his knees. We did not have a houseful of relatives to provide her with playmates, and I did not oil her hair and try to fluff it up into a Fijian coiffure.

Most essentially, her father and I did not have much of a cultural or social context to make our lessons or ways very important to Megan. She was often not with Jim and me together. Our respective activities kept us apart for most of the day. Megan accompanied me among the women and children. And Megan regularly fled our house alone to go to her *nana leva* (mother's older sister), her *nei* (father's sister), her *bubu* (mother's mother). Each morning after her first birthday, for example, she toured three other households, at her own initiative, for three consecutive breakfasts. It was exhausting trying to keep track of Megan and engage in the multitude of tasks that research requires. Jim spent little time at home, following village men's pattern.

Our neighbors were immensely pleased by Megan's efforts to make them her behavioral and linguistic models. She was a living statement of what they believed they knew--the greater desirability of Fijian culture over all others. Villagers took every opportunity to teach Megan "the true way of being," Fijian-style. They also made constant efforts to teach Jim and me how to care for her (cf. Huntington, this volume). For instance, they reprimanded us for picking her up by hooking our hands under her armpits. Fijians maintain that a cough is produced in a child by this kind of treatment. I was also berated when she developed a heat rash our first month in the village. Since the month was October and I was physically and psychologically reflecting a northern hemisphere autumnal feeling, I thought Megan should be too. I dressed her too warmly at night and produced prickly-heat blisters on her back.

Despite commenting favorably on Megan's adoption of Fijian ways and striving to inculcate these in her, villagers did not always treat Megan as they did their own children. There were two reasons for this. Because she was a European they catered to her more than they did to their own children. For instance, I once heard a woman tell her child to give Megan a toy because she was a European. As a European, Megan was a representative of a power elite. Fijians respect authority and power, although they do not readily acquiesce to those who have these attributes. The other reason that Megan was given special treatment was because she exemplified the Fijian concepts of *wacece* (cheeky or spirited) and *yalo kaukauwa* (a strong, solid, demanding spirit). Fijian socialization is designed to produce persons who understand their places in the social hierarchy based on age, gender, and rank. However, when a child resists this process and does not display the general childhood social awkwardness, such behavior is encourage. Once at a gathering our landlord looked around for a small child to carry a bowl of *yaqona* to an adult. He selected Megan because, he said, she was not afraid, walked with conviction, and had strong, steady hands.

I had been ambivalent about taking Megan overseas. She was my only child. I had, therefore, more than the usual parental concern about her health, until I came to understand how healthful the Fijian environment was. I alternately castigated myself for possibly jeopardizing my child's health and relished fieldwork. If I had been firmly planted in one cultural tradition, if I had internalized only one set of norms, or so I have believed for some time, I would not have questioned taking my child into the field. But I have kept recalling my earliest reference group's values, those of my neighbors, friends, and relatives. For these people, I have always been somewhat unique, and taking my child out of the country on such a mission merely capped my career of unusual activities. Their values had an added significance for me when I became a parent and began to be concerned about my child's wellbeing. My concerns about Megan were increased when my mother wrote me that one of my cousins said that he would never take his child out of the country because he valued her too much.

When another cousin wrote that her two-year-old played with puzzles and knew the alphabet, I pondered the effects of having Megan in an environment without many educational toys. I was thinking so much about providing Megan with an American education that I was not immediately cognizant that she had been taught by neighbors to count, recite verses, recognize kinship relationships, and know about the village school and its organization. The fact that Megan could also cut her food, bathe herself, and use her toilet unattended when she was a bit over a year did not strike me as remarkable until I returned to the United States.

Even though I understood them, I did not like some aspects of her Fijian socialization. For instance, the personality traits that earned Megan regard for her self-confidence also brought her criticism; they were more acceptable for a boy than for a girl. Thus she was labelled *viavia levu* and *viavia tagane*, respectively, "someone who wants to be bigger" (i.e., higher in rank or age) and "a female who wants to act like a male and assume the masculine gender's privileges." As Megan began her second year, Jim and I noticed that villagers tried to modify Megan's personality in order to make her more like an acceptable Fijian girl. We were worried that they would squelch her enthusiasm, curiosity, assertiveness, and abilities to think and to choose for herself.

The interactions of young, subordinate members' of households with Megan were the ones that concerned me the most. They appeared to want to instruct Jim, Megan and me in their culture. In some cases, they had the right to correct our behavior according to the kinship system in which we were members. For example, a young man whom Megan addressed as "father's younger brother" reprimanded Megan for being noisy in church as we left the vestibule. He followed us out and stopped to talk to us on our front porch. He began admonishing Megan for her actions and he slapped her face. The slap was hard enough to make her cry. I was angry because he hit her, and particularly because it was in the face, which was an act of humiliation from my viewpoint. When I tried to make her swat him back, something that I should not have done, she was afraid to do so and I became angrier. Then he began to kiss her cheeks. His use of corporal punishment was annoying enough for me, but when he presented her with what I considered confusing signals--"I hit you because I love you"--I was furious. Abruptly, he left the house.

The second example of behaviors that I did not like is illustrated by a young woman who pinched Megan's nose as I nursed her. This woman did it because she believed, as did most villagers, that a child should be weaned soon after its first birthday. Prolonging breastfeeding is said to prevent the child from eating other foods that will make it strong. There is also the connotation that such extended nursing keeps the child in babyhood and develops a weak, simpering person. Fijians are often eager to have another child and believe the first child should be weaned before the mother becomes pregnant. What bothered me about this interaction was that, according to my assumptions, it would teach Megan that she could not count on having her needs met when she indicated that she wanted to nurse. This frustration, I hypothesized, would indicate to her that the world and its human occupants were capricious. Thus, she would not have the emotional security that comes from knowing she would obtain a desired response when she signalled her needs, and her self-confidence would suffer.

It seems that those villagers described above, who occupied the lower rungs of this society, particularly represented Megan because she was a member of a people whom Fijians viewed as more powerful than themselves. Older Fijians did not make as many comments about the disparity of power and wealth between themselves and Europeans.

In retrospect, I know that I should have been pleased that we were accepted into the community enough to be given the same treatment as other villagers. But there were times when I sensed that Megan was being disciplined by villagers, especially the children and young people, as a means of showing their displeasure with her parents (cf. Huntington, this volume). In the early months of our stay, I made every effort to keep Megan with me as I made my daily rounds in order to prevent situations in which she might be treated in ways that we did not condone. After residing in the village for a year, we rarely viewed villagers' interactions with Megan as objectionable. Perhaps a number of things explain this phenomenon: Megan, my husband, and I had learned village standards of behavior. Megan was older and better socialized. Our neighbors may have accomodated us by treating Megan according to our values and wishes. Maybe all of these occurred. I noted the decline in the number of distressing incidents while reviewing fieldnotes and diary entries after I returned to the United States.

One further incident will serve to illustrate the extent of the conflict that I felt when trying to conduct research and simultaneously shield Megan from situations that I perceived as unpleasant. One morning Megan and I sat talking with other women and children in a neighbor's house. While we were sitting there, my neighbor's brother-in-law handed her a bat through an open doorway. It was a flying fox that had been killed in the forest. An adolescent girl began to play with the bat as if it were a doll. I knew by her sly looks in my direction, and others' previous comments about the squeamishness of Europeans, that they were waiting for my response. I lived up to their expectations. As she made a slight move in my direction with the bat in her hand, I involuntarily--or so I say now--leapt to my feet. The others chuckled.

I was not the only one who found this creature unsettling. The young children, including Megan, were initially frightened by the fox-like face in its black leather cape. All the children were made to touch the bat as women and girls held it and commented that it was "nice." Soon all the children were capable of at least coming near the little creature.

I was concerned about what the cadaver might transfer to Megan. I was also worried that they might ask me to handle it. They smirked at my reticence to play with the bat. But I did not want to lose rapport with these individuals by leaving. I trusted my neighbor in whose house this occurred and convinced myself that, if it was a harmful activity, she would not allow the children to engage in it. Handling the bat was meant to teach the children not to fear animals, to learn to be animals' masters, and to help the children develop fortitude, strength, and courage, traits Fijians value highly. The children also learned to share and to be kind that morning--the bat was given to a woman whose household had not eaten this delicacy in a long time.

During fieldwork and immediately after it, I thought about this event. I had shrunk from the bat, had feared it would contaminate my daughter, and had been disgusted with myself for allowing her to remain in a potentially harmful situation for the benefit of my research. I believed that because I had been negatively affected by the women's play with the bat that the objectivity of my research would be compromised. I now recognize that the negative emotions elicited by this event prompted me to examine it more closely than I might otherwise have done, yielding new insights into Fijian culture. I will return to the issue of objectivity in the conclusions that follow.

CONCLUSIONS

In those first months of fieldwork I felt like a child, needing others' assistance and unable to function in what I considered an adult and competent manner. It is not unusual for an ethnographer to be in a childlike position during the early phases of fieldwork. Indeed, a childlike status is sometimes perceived to be appropriate to learn the hosts' culture and to open one's mind to its assumptions and meanings. It is often expected that ethnographers will be as ignorant of their hosts' customs and language, and as much in need of tutoring in these, as are the hosts' children. This perception of the researcher's position is sometimes established by creating fictive kinship ties. Being assigned as someone's offspring is a logical solution to two fieldwork problems - the integration and the guidance of a stranger (Briggs, 1974, writes poignantly about such an experience). Who better to take such responsibility than a 'parent'? Slipping into the ingenuous child's role may be especially easy for a female, particularly if the hosts protect a foreign woman as they would a child (Fischer, 1970:278).

Assuming a childlike role during research is not the only connection between childhood and fieldwork. The psychological states provoked by immersion in a foreign culture may recall other situations experienced by the ethnographer. Some ethnographers can find specific childhood events or interests that led them in selecting their professions (e.g., Weidman 1970:241). For example, many anthropologists' biographies indicate youthful concerns about social relations and rebelliousness in the family (Kluckhohn, 1957; Roe, 1953; and Wintrob, 1969). An analogy exists between fieldwork and childhood that facilitates recalling one's youth--in each case the person is insufficiently socialized (Freilich, 1970:19) and recognizes a lack of full-fledged members' knowledge and skills. Given this connection between childhood and the research situation, it is understandable why some ethnographers dream about their youth (e.g., Nader, 1970:111-112) and why in certain cases their dreams recapitulate their biographies before reflecting the present fieldwork situations (Andersen, 1971). Finally, researchers may experience *deja vu* in the host community. Cesara, for example, reports that "on those occasions that were heavy with emotion, she relived her past in most vivid terms" (1982:8).

My sense of powerlessness during fieldwork is attributable to the structural and cultural implications of my gender. Other women anthropologists have also indicated their gender's influence on their research. For example, Landes (1970) wrote that Brazilians tried to direct her movements because she was a woman, and Friedl (1970) reported that Greek villagers viewed her as her husband's secretary even though she was the principal investigator.   Some anthropoligists have suggested that women fieldworkers may experience culture shock differently than men (Mead, 1970; Fischer, 1970). Perhaps women have written about fieldwork more because they have been

> left with the task of conjuring the impurities of experience. The have had to cope with the blook, sweat, and tears aspect of fieldwork--feelings and sentiments included--while the men were exclusively doing "the real thing" (Dumont, 1978:8).

My experience of crossing cultural boundaries was made more difficult by my feeling the need to enculturate an infant into a cultural *system*. American parents perceive an obligation to socialize a child to "fit in" American society. When the anthropologist-parent during fieldwork is floating between mores and institutions of two (or more) traditions, there seems to be nothing concrete to transmit to a child. The parent may want to provide a tradition for the child, a version of the parent's natal culture, but will be faced with the predicament of having modified that culture during the fieldwork (or before, as Kleis, this volume, indicates). In a foreign situation, the parent's concern about ethnicity and cultural continuity can become significant for self-identification. The hosts' alternate patterns for the child can be resented. And during this time the supposedly distinct roles of professional anthropologist and parent are blended.

The culture shock I experienced during field research probably increased my understanding of American and Polish-American cultures (and how I responded to them) said that an aim of cross-cultural research is to critically examine one's own cultural assumptions and to reflect on one's behavior. This is a positive result of cross-cultural fieldwork and a test of objectivity. The things that initially concerned me about Fijian culture were some of the same things that had bothered me about Polish-American culture. On the other hand, the Fijian and Polish-American values that I appreciated made me more aware of those aspects of mainstream American culture that I have never fully understood - the positive value placed on privacy and solitude and the expectation that individuals will want to be alone during periods of fright, pain, and mourning. What I liked about my life in the village was the involvement of others in my life and the acts of caring and advice-giving. I loved the gregariousness, the collective activities, the intrigues, the gossip, and the excitement of communal events. In some way, my time in Fiji was like returning to the neighborhood of my youth.

In the village I enjoyed others' concern as I did in my natal community. Some of my securest moments as a parent came when women knocked on the door at night to ask why Megan was crying and if they could help me. I will always remember my elderly neighbor, squatting beside the lantern that cast ghastly shadows on her face and projected her distorted silhouette on the wall, singing a nursery rhyme as I walked around the house in a tiny circuit carrying my measles-covered baby. She stayed until Megan fell asleep.

As soon as I boarded the flight back to the United States, I recognized the difference between Fijians and Americans in regard to children; no Americans interacted with Megan on the plane and their chilly response to the presence of a child was palpable. Other anthropologists have described similar experiences (Beals, 1970; Jacobson, this volume).

Fijian adults appear more ready to interact with children than to Americans. One reason for this cultural difference is that Fijians, unlike Americans, do not believe that such responses will "spoil" children. When I reflect on this, I wonder how secure American children feel about their world and what their commitment to others is like. I also recall how concerned I had once been that Fijians would affect Megan's confidence in herself and others and my impression that Fijians were not as self-confident as Americans. I then juxtapose these thoughts against the vision of American, not Fijian, children sometimes carrying 'security blankets' to provide themselves with some form of comfort. What kind of self-confidence does this reflect, and self-confidence for what? Do children learn to comfort and care about others as people have cared for them? In the village I did not initially see that Fijian children attain self-confidence too. Fijians learn to believe in their physical capacities and in their ability to get others to assist them. And through the cultural emphasis on kinship and the value of collective action, they learn to depend on others. Fijians do not turn to themselves or an object for comfort because they know that others can be depended upon for succor.

The fact that these insights into Fijian and American cultures were the results of my emotional involvement call into question the basic assumptions beneath the concept of objectivity in anthropology. Objectivity is variously measured in anthropology and the different assumptions underlying it are infrequently examined. There is a tendency to equate objectivity with the concept of cultural relativity. Cultural relativity is the anthropological tenet that all cultures are equally valid if viewed from the perspective of their internal logic. Objectivity, then, means reporting the logic structuring a culture. Any critique of a culture's patterns and their supporting values indicates subjectivity. Similar is the notion that any negative affective response to another culture makes the anthropologist subjective. A positive emotional response is not usually acknowledged as lessening objectivity.

There are anthropologists who maintain that the ethnographer's affect should be part of the analysis of events. These events, after all, include the researcher and are dialectic in nature. Cesara has written of her African field experience that "Had the Lenda left me unaffected, I could not have claimed that I understood them" (1982:9). Genuine participation in the hosts' lives may rely on an "emotional acceptance" of their assumptions and values (Weidman, 1970).

> This is not a facile process where the fieldworker is to all intents and purposes unchanged by the experiences. To some extent it involves alterations in the very structure of the ego (Weidman, 1970:262).

This prescription differs from the one where objectivity is defined as reporting on others' behavior without allowing any aspect of the observer's behavior or personality to intrude. This latter orientation is based on two premises: one is that the reality that is being reported has no dialectic relationship to the ethnographer, and the other is that the ethnographer can record others' behavior without any personal interpretation. The corrective to this perspective on objectivity has been to focus on the second premise and to assert that such fieldworker has biases that filter data collection and analysis because "The anthropologist is a human instrument (fraught with frailties) studying other human beings and their societies" (Powdermaker, 1966:19; cf. Devereux, 1969, Bennett, 1960). There has also been the recognition that personal, subjective factors color all research, regardless of its purported objective, empirical design (Nadel, 1951).

The proposed corrective that fieldworkers acknowledge their biases and personal characteristics in their reports, however, has practical limits. In reality, researchers will not always be able to specify their biases and misconceptions or to indicate data that they ignored or failed to perceive. The missing information and the personal quality of the viewpoints expressed may be apparent when several ethnographers' works are contrasted. As Weidman stated:

> I feel that whatever I have described from my field experience accurately reflects patterns that I observed. Another investigator, with a different cognitive and perceptual organization, would undoubtedly be able to describe other facets of Burmese life more fully (1970:253).

Honigman suggested that variations in anthropologists' interpretations of a culture have "value as well as debatable points" (1976:249). Objectivity, then, should be viewed as a goal of ethnographic study measurable on a scale with no achievable point of complete objectivity.

My concern with my child's development and villagers' input into this process did pervade my perceptions and analysis of Fijian village life. As I mentioned earlier, villagers in Fiji did not view my position as that of a professional anthropologist, but as the anthropologist's wife and his child's mother. How well I fulfilled these roles determined my worth in their eyes. This assessment is not different from an American view that professional women are worthy of respect if they are first good wives and mothers. Men, on the other hand, satisfy the requirements of their professional duties (Shreve, 1984). Since I was constantly reminded by villagers of my status as woman, wife, and mother, it is no wonder that my daughter's welfare became the focus of so much of my emotional and intellectual energies.

By accepting Fijians' definitions of me and to some extent acculturating, I understood villagers better. If I had maintained more cultural distance between us, I would have lost some knowledge but avoided some of the difficulties of culture conflict.

REFERENCES

Anderson, B. G. (1971). Adaptive Aspects of Culture Shock. *American Anthropologist*, (73):1121-1125.

Beals, A. R. (1970). Golpalpur, 1958-60. In G. D. Spindler (Ed.), *Being an Anthropologist*, (pp. 32-57). New York: Holt, Rinehart and Winston.

Bennett, J. J. (1960). Individual Perspective in Field Work. In R. N. Adams and J. J. Preiss (Eds.), *Human Organization Research*, (pp. 431-440). Homewood, IL: The Dorsey Press.

Briggs, J. L. (1970). *Never in Anger: Portrait of an Eskimo Family*. Cambridge, MA: Harvard University Press.

Cesara, M. (1982). *Reflections of a Woman Anthropologist: No Hiding Place*. New York: Academic Press.

Crapanzano, V. (1980). *Tuhami: Portrait of a Moroccan*. Chicago: University of Chicago Press.

Devereux, G. (1967). *From Anxiety to Method in the Behavioral Sciences*. The Hague: Mouton and Co.

Diamond, S. (1974). *In Search of the Primitive: A Critique of Civilization*. New Brunswick, NJ: Transaction Books.

Dumont, J. P. (1978). *The Headman and I*. Austin, TX: University of Texas Press.

Fischer, A. (1970). Fieldwork in Five Cultures. In P. Golde (Ed.), *Women in the Field*, (pp. 267-292). Chicago: Aldine Publishing Co.

Friedl, E. (1970). Fieldwork in a Greek Village. In P. Golde (Ed.), *Women in the Field*, (pp. 195-220). Chicago: Aldine Publishing Co.

Golde, P. (1970). Introduction. In P. Golde (Ed.), *Women in the Field*, (pp. 1-18). Chicago: Aldine Publishing Co.

Honigmann, J. J. (1976). The Personal Approach in Cultural Anthropological Research. *Current Anthropology*, (17):243-261.

Landes, R. (1970). A Woman Anthropologist in Brazil. In P. Golde (Ed.), *Women in the Field*, (pp. 119-143). Chicago: Aldine Publishing Co.

Mead, M. (1970). Fieldwork in the Pacific Islands, 1925-1967. In P. Golde (Ed.), *Women in the Field*, (pp. 293-332). Chicago: Aldine Publishing Co.

Nadel, S. F. (1951). *The Foundations of Social Anthropology*. London: Cohen and West.

Nader, L. (1970). From Anguish to Exultation. In P. Golde (Ed.), *Women in the Field*, (pp. 97-118). Chicago: Aldine Publishing Co.

Powdermaker, H. (1966). *Stranger and Friend*. New York: Norton.

Shreve, A. (1984). The Working Mother as Role Model. *The New York Times Magazine*, (September 9, pp. 39-43, 50, 52, 54.

Weidman, H. H. (1970). On Ambivalence and the Field. In P. Golde (Ed.), *Women in the Field*, (pp. 239-266). Chicago: Aldine Publishing Co.

Wintrob, R. M. (1969). An Inward Focus: A Consideration of Psychological Stress in Fieldwork. In F. Henry and S. Saberwal (Eds.), *Stress and Response in Fieldwork*, (pp. 63-76).

NOTES

(1) For their editorial help, I want to give special thanks to Ann Millard, Loudell Snow, Susan Zach, and James Turner. And for his useful insights, I thank Ade Otieno.

(2) This research was made possible by National Science Foundation Grant BNS 78 16262.

RECIPROCAL RELATIONS: FAMILY CONTRIBUTIONS TO

ANTHROPOLOGICAL FIELD RESEARCH--AND VICE VERSA

Andrew Hunter Whiteford and Marion Salmon Whiteford

Administrative Director/Research Curator
School of American Research
Santa Fe, New Mexico

INTRODUCTION

The arrival of a child inevitably changes a couple's life. The first child has the greatest impact, and the extent of the repercussions seem generally to dwindle with the arrival of each subsequent child, perhaps up to some unidentified optimum number. The diminution of effect results, of course, from the parents' experience and their development of more enlightened attitudes and tactics to cope with the diversity and quantity of situations, problems, and young people they have created. The entire procedure is, as every parent learns, challenging (a marvelous word), stimulating (to say the least), enlightening, deeply rewarding, often discouraging, and frequently exhausting.

People have to learn how to get along with each other according to the patterns of their particular cultures. In our society the development of an effective *modus vivendi* for both parents and children is greatly facilitated as the diverse members of the family learn to fit and to function with each other, with their living facilities, their neighbors, and their various associations. Familiarity with all these elements is more likely to breed comfort than contempt. Simple routines eliminate many of the ad hoc decisions and choices which are required in daily living and they help to release time for new explorations and ideas. Routine also enriches most lives by making it possible to look forward to the pleasant and desirable events in the family cycle: birthday parties, winter sports, summer vacations, Christmas with grandparents, and other things to anticipate.   Even when children, and parents also, may feel more or less coerced into the patterns which family life tends to develop, they usually become aware that the benefits exceed the frustrations which may be generated. The possession of a real home location, a sense of place in the structure of the family, the expression of self in peer groups, and the appreciation of some consistent pattern of expectations help to provide both children and parents with personal security and some measure of optimism about the future.

This desirable state of being is not always attainable because it is the product of a complex and delicate balance of many factors, which come into effective relationship with each other usually, if at all, through a continuing process of learning and adaptation by all members of the family. The delicate balance is easily upset. One of the most disturbing things which can happen to the balance of relations within any family is the loss of the home base, with its consequent disarrangement of personal relationships in the neighborhood and with peer groups. Families which are forced to relocate their homes because of job demands, education, or other compelling reasons recognize the human problems of moving, and most of them would avoid the consequent period of readjustment if they had a choice. Many families which are at the mercy of a fluctuating job market, or which are forced into a state of intermittent migration in search of a livelihood, suffer constant or recurrent disruption of their relationships with friends and kin. Many children in such families grow up with no sense of either a "home base" or a predictable future. In such circumstances it is only the exceptional parents who are able to create a pattern of relationships within the family which will be sufficiently stable and satisfying to provide their children with any sense of security and continuity. It is very difficult!

There are also other families which do appear to have a choice in the matter, but because of innocence, ignorance, curiosity, ambition, or some other forces, elect to remove themselves and their children from their homes and transport them to foreign places. These are, for the most part, the families of anthropologists and other scientists who are engaged in foreign research, but many businessmen do the same thing and share the same family problems. People who are working abroad for their governments share many of the same concerns, but there are often elements of volition and special circumstances which make their experiences somewhat different.

In any case, adaptive strategies of various kinds must be devised to ameliorate the negative effects of the sudden changes in family circumstances. Some strategies succeed in reducing the feelings of loss and insecurity likely to be felt by both parents and children, and some strategies provide the ingredients necessary to facilitate adaptation and renewed growth. But no strategies are always effective and members of the family, especially the children, suffer and are unhappy. In any move away from the home base, every family must contend with hazards and difficulties which cannot be predicted. This is inevitable, but many problems, such as those mentioned here, will almost always occur; they are predictable and every family preparing to live abroad should anticipate them. Each family is forced to deal with them. In some cases they are dealt with consciously and with basic understanding of their nature and causes, in other cases families deal with them only on a "crisis encounter" basis, attempting to solve or combat each particular problem as it occurs.

Regardless of the extent to which the efforts to deal with the strains of family adjustment are successful, every member of the family will be required to arrive at his or her own accommodation to the new conditions. The pressures of learning new behavior patterns, meeting new people, and perhaps coping with different living conditions and a strange language, will have immediate, and probably enduring, effects on the children; effects which may be either beneficial or deleterious. The parents are subjected to most of the same stresses, with the additional worries about the welfare of the children. In the midst of dealing with the problems of family life in a strange culture, the undertaking which was the prime reason for the relocation of the family may be neglected and the research itself may be compromised.

These things we know. We know also that the situation has occurred many times and has been dealt with in diverse ways in the past. No one approach is applicable to every case, but the attempt to describe some of the specific instances, and to evaluate some of the strategies employed, as well as their effects upon the families and upon the research, may provide some helpful hints and guidelines for other anthropologists and kindred souls who are confronted with the problems of taking their families into the field with them.

What are the reasons, if any, for deciding to take children into the field while doing anthropological field work? There are surely many different reasons, or rationalizations, for such a decision, but it is unlikely that many of them envision a substantial increase in efficiency or productivity for the research, although this may be an end result. It is an undeniable fact that being accompanied by children, of any age, necessitates increased travel expenses, enlarged living space, intensified health care, sustained parental attention, and the invention or discovery of amusements and facilities for education. These requirements are almost minimum. The researchers' freedom of movement tends to be restricted, participation in certain kinds of activities may have to be curtailed, and the prospect of unpredictable crises is greatly increased. And, of course, some field situations are much more difficult, or even more dangerous, than others. Considering these factors, and adding the problems of adjustment which children and other members of the family must make while adapting to unfamiliar conditions, it hardly seems possible that concerned and intelligent parents would voluntarily move their children into any strange environment, far less that of a foreign country.

In our particular case we took our children (who are, in birth order, Scott, Mike, Linda and Laurie) with us for six different periods of field research, which lasted from three months to more than a year. In some sessions we were accompanied by four children, in others the numbers were reduced to two, and finally to one. Because the period involved covered some thirteen years (1951-1974), the children were obviously of different ages during the various field seasons. The most compelling reason for taking them with us was that the only alternative was to be separated from each other, an option which was so distasteful to us that almost anything else seemed acceptable. We had both been away from our young family for one period of six weeks (1947); Father had been away from the family for two sessions of field work each lasting nearly four months (1949, 1950); and we realized that foreign field research would either have to be done together or it would have to be abandoned. We decided that together was better than nothing.

It must be recognized that we were the usual young anthropological romanticists for whom the call of far places, strange cultures, and exciting adventures held predictable enchantments. But we were also sustained in our decision to go as a family by the conviction that we were undertaking a research task which was of some significance, and we truly believed that the experience would benefit our children. It might seem ridiculous to believe that foreign experience would be a good thing for children between the ages of four and nine, as they were when we first took them to Colombia, but we were convinced that there were advantages. The first advantage was that they would be with their parents and with each other instead of being separated. We felt that this provided them with an essential condition of security. The other advantage we envisioned reflected our strong convictions that it was enlightening, broadening, and challenging for children to live in a culture different from their own, to cope with a new language, and to learn how to relate to new customs and new people. For the most part it was a new experience for us too, and sharing it with each other and with our children was an attractive prospect which became a fascinating reality. We took them with us because we hoped that it would be so, and it was. We anticipated various problems and were deeply concerned about health, social adjustment, and education, but these misgivings were outweighed by our positive expectations.

The foreign situation into which we took our family the first time (1951) was not inherently dangerous. We were not intending to settle them in the depths of the tropical jungle or in a desert encampment; we went to the lovely little city of Popayan in the upper Cauca Valley of southwestern Colombia. And it was not a totally strange place to the children, because their father had been there three times before, and had lived there for almost half a year. They had heard a great deal about it, seen many slides of its streets and mountains, and knew the names of various of their father's friends whom they were about to meet.

After leaving Miami on their first flight, they were greeted enthusiastically in Bogota by their father's Colombian colleagues and taken out to a friend's *finca* (a ranch) where they could run loose for a while and take turns riding a small burro. With this introduction to Colombia the family then packed again and flew down to Popayan, with a short stop-over in Cali.

In Popayan the children found themselves in strange, large, bare rooms, but they were located in a warm friendly little pension where their father had lived before, and where they were welcomed and entertained by the German couple who owned it. The first sights were intriguing: the snow capped mountains all around, the many trotting horses in the streets, the school girls in their crisp uniforms, and a man walking casually under their balcony with a body of a mountain lion slung over his shoulder.

After a month in the Pension Victoria, which gave everyone a chance to become acquainted with the city and to meet some friends, the family managed to move into a house and settle down. Here the children soon became part of the neighborhood group, the boys playing *futbol* in the street, and Linda, age four, playing dolls with a number of girls her own age. From this base, the boys, who were six and eight, undertook their own explorations and established some friendships which have been retained through the years.

This review is, of course, an idealized synopsis. There were a number of complications along the way, none of which, so far as we are aware, seriously affected the children. We would have been better prepared, particularly in the language, if the opportunity to return to Colombia had not dropped, more or less, out of the blue: a grant, which we had hoped to get a year later, suddenly became available, and it did not seem advisable to turn down the opportunity it offered. Getting everything in order had to be done in a very short time and only the necessary items could be taken care of; a year of preparation would have been appreciated. It would have made it possible also to investigate matters sufficiently to discover that, not only was the Civil War going on in Colombia, but the very region in which we planned to work was at the heart of it. None of this was in the local papers in Wisconsin.

The original research grant was for a survey in the Llanos Orientales near Villavicencio. When we arrived in Bogota, we were barred from entering the region. It became apparent that the situation was not going to improve in the foreseeable future. After many inquiries we decided to go to Popayan instead, if the foundation which was supporting us would approve of such a change in plans. We left for Popayan with no assurance that we would have any funds to work with, and we stayed over in the pleasant warmth of Cali because one of us was "indisposed." But none of this seemed to cause apprehension among the children, nor did they become unhappy when we were delayed in finding a house and furnishings for it. We finally succeeded in moving them into a strange, bleak place which had none of the color, comforts, conveniences, or space they had at home. They seemed to be amused by the peculiarities of their new accomodations, settled themselves quickly into their own sections, and proceeded to examine the neighborhood.

Settling in was much more demanding on Mother than on anyone else in the family. While Father was occupied almost immediately with research preliminaries (relations with government, police, university, etc.), she took on the task of getting us set up as a household for a year of residence. Rental houses were very scarce in Popayan, and the one she was able to secure was completely unfurnished. There were no furniture stores as such, so it was necessary for her to seek out local craftsmen who could make us some tables, chairs, and basic bed frames. This required a great deal of time and endless walking, as well as the maximum exercise of a limited facility with the language. Some new friends were extremely helpful, particularly in arranging to have mattresses made, in purchasing the necessary bedding, pots, pans, dishes and other household necessities-- no two of which were sold in the same store. Finally, still with the help of friends, she managed to get all her new purchases assembled in our little house and set about learning to shop for food in the market and to ask the correct questions of the Indian girls who wanted to work for her. In the end she worked it out and the family was housed and fed for the remainder of the year.

Several factors played parts in the relatively easy adjustment our children made to their new and strange circumstances. Prior familiarity, having heard a great deal about Colombia and having seen pictures of places and people, reduced the sense of leaving home and going off into a completely unknown void. They were assured that Colombia was a beautiful and interesting place where they would meet warm and charming people. (They were too young to have read the news about La Violencia, even if it had appeared in the local press.) Even more important, in our estimation, was the sense of security they felt in being together as a family. We had lived in the relative isolation of a farm with the boys, we had taken them off to live in graduate student quarters at the University and to a cottage on an island in Lake Superior. We had also camped together several times. On all of these occasions they shared the work with us to the best of their capabilities, and we sang silly songs, played games, and read or told stories.

In Popayan the stories were important parts of our family life. We took boxes of books with us, some for the boys' continuing school-work, but others for fun. Three story or reading resources were especially effective. The first was *Anthology of Children's Literature*, a large, thick book (1100 pages), illustrated with paintings by N. C. Wyeth, that contained folk tales, adventure stories, poetry, myths, legends, and fables. Each child had favorite parts, and we read some of them almost every day. The second resource was an unexpected and endless stream of comic books sent to the children every week by a perceptive maiden aunt. They provided hours of Little Lulu and Old Witch Hazel, as well as many Disney characters and others. They also formed an important link between the boys and their potential friends because comic books had not yet arrived in Popayan. Their universal fascination quickly drew boys from one end of the block to the other, who first asked to share them and later settled themselves down in Scott's and Mike's bedroom at all hours to peruse the growing accumulation. The final resource was our own stories, some real and other imagined. The most successful was a continuing series of adventures of a squirrel named "Chitter-chatter Carusoe" who was invented by Mother. Those stories were especially fascinating when she took all children out of the cold clammy house to sit together in the warmth of the little *plazuela* in front of the great church of San Francisco.

Each of these occasions of reading or telling stories captured the children's complete attention and linked them intimately with one of their parents, temporarily shutting out the strange new world and such uncertainties and demands which it invoked. Each story session belonged exclusively to the family. Another exclusively family time, which was important in reinforcing the link between the boys and their mother, was the morning school hours. Scott was being prepared to enter fifth grade upon our return and Mike was getting ready for his second year of school. To this end, we had consulted with many teachers and had gathered together a large supply of readers, work books, flash cards, and enough educational paraphernalia to equip a small school. School time became another "family hour." The family bond was further reinforced during the long walks we took together. Some of these were part of Father's exploration of the city and surrounding territory. Others were for our own pleasure, particularly on days like Sundays, when there was often nothing else to do. A final important family activity, which provided both pleasure and a valuable period of refuge from the demands of coping with a strange world, was the periodic expedition to the movies. At home the children had gone to the movies only rarely, so it was a new and exciting thing for them. An additional attraction was that the movies were in English. Some times they went with friends or took friends with them, but generally it was another family activity, especially on Sunday afternoons.

In retrospect it appears to us that the strong sense of family ties, family support, and family fun were the most important factors in the pleasant and untraumatic introduction our children had to a foreign culture, and the activities we have described above were some of the significant elements which contributed to this basic sense of security. It may be important to mention that we had always enjoyed doing things together. Before going to Colombia we camped, fished, and played as a family. The two of us always enjoyed our children, and we tried conscientiously to maintain pleasant relations and to cultivate bonds of regard and affection. It was our conviction that a close family relationship helped to provide individuals with the security needed for personal growth. We regarded family intimacy and activities as important elements of "the good life" and well worth some care and attention. Our family life in Colombia was as much a continuation of our "normal" relations as we could make it. It is not too much to say that our changed physical conditions were relatively unimportant so long as the family continued to be together.

Of course the family was not the only influence. First among the other forces which combined to create a happy and satisfying experience for all of us were the people of Popayan. Father was able to introduce the family to a few people from his experience in former years, but we met many more, particularly after we moved into our new house on the Street of Heroes. Here the children immediately made friends. In the house to our right lived four little girls and one small brother. The girls ranged in age from two to nine and their curiosity and interest in Linda, the little blonde foreigner who had moved in next to them, was demonstrated at first by a few furtive glances as they passed either our doorway or the grilled windows which were adjacent to the sidewalk. Within a few days the oldest sister had led the others in shy attempts to communicate through the grillwork and to a showing of dolls. Soon they were all sitting on the neighbor's stone steps playing together, and Linda was in their house almost as much as she was at home. They were lovely and charming little girls, closely supervised by the family and a maid, and we never had any qualms about allowing our little girl to be with them. The girls always seemed to get along well, but we never developed a close relationship with the rest of the family.

Another immediate contact, which developed into a continuing relationship of importance to the research program and also to the Whiteford family, came from the other end of the block. The family in the large house on the corner had five boys and three girls. One of the boys was Scott's age, another was Mike's age, and the second girl was exactly the same age as Linda. Our first introduction to this family was through a chance encounter with the mother, a charming self-possessed aristocratic lady. She regarded us with curious and friendly eyes and greeted Mother with the meager English she had learned in school. This simple meeting on the street was enough to lead to a visit from the four-year-old daughter as soon as she could escape from her nursemaid; her two-year-old sister also headed for our open doorway at every opportunity. We soon had a seemingly endless procession of nursemaids and/or older brothers and sisters coming in to find the young ones. They too wanted an opportunity to meet the new people on the street, and to have a look inside their house. It did not take long for the younger Whitefords to be returning home with the messengers, and before long they were nearly as much at home in the Velasco house as in their own. The girls played house and pretended they were ballerinas and other things. The boys played noisy games of *futbol* in the street, had a "Detective Club" that met in the house of a slightly older boy, who was the leader, and got involved in catching fish for an aquarium and trying to raise young chicks brought in from one of the family farms.

Scott and Mike were also very much involved with their horse. Before coming to Popayan, they dreamed of having a horse. The possibility of having a horse had been one of the most discussed attractions of being in Colombia. Once in Popayan we made it come true by buying a white gelding of uncertain age, with good paces, a slightly swayed back, and a most patient and gentle disposition. The boys participated in his purchase, the buying of the tack, arrangements for pasture, and took over the task of feeding and grooming. They promptly named their horse "Amigo," which, for some reason, greatly amused everyone who heard it. They were devoted to Amigo's care and the two of them, sometimes with Father or a friend, would take a rope and the bridle down to the enormous pasture nearly half a mile away and bring Amigo back to the house to be fed. In a very short time they were galloping across the pasture and through all parts of the city, Mike usually hanging on behind his brother and sometimes standing on Amigo's broad haunches. All their friends were experienced riders and Amigo would often be seen trotting down the street with three or four youngsters attached to his back.

It appeared to us then, and in retrospect it still seems, that our three children had a pleasant introduction to Colombia. It was tinged with excitement, but not blemished by any specific or enduring fear that we are aware of. For the remainder of the year in Popayan, life for them became easier, more routine, disturbed very little by boredom, frustrations, or homesickness, in spite of the fact that our activities were somewhat restricted by lack of transportation and by Mother's pregnancy. There were many diversions, such as frequent religious and military processions, the observations of Christmas and the Holy Week of Easter, occasional visits to friends' *haciendas* (ranches), parties such as the elaborate costume affair which occupied all the attention of local mothers and daughters for at least a month; a small visiting circus; bicycle races around the central plaza; and the constant stream of Guambiano and Sibudoy Indians in their bright *ruanas* (ponchos).

So far as lasting effects can be detected it must be noted first that all of our children, including Laurie, who was almost born there, have returned to Popayan more than once. Three of them have become professional anthropologists with Latin America as their region of specialization, and Mike returned to Popayan for two seasons of research which were published in his book *The Forgotten Ones*. In May, 1983, Mike returned to Popayan and stayed for two weeks with a friend who had been his closest playmate in 1951. His visit was in response to the devastating earthquake which destroyed the center of the city early on the morning of *Jueves Santo* (Holy Thursday of the Easter week). He carried with him funds that all the members of our family had gathered as a contribution to assist the city in reducing suffering and recovering from the calamity. Our family of anthropologists has spent literally years doing research in Colombia, Mexico, Argentina, Honduras, Costa Rica, and other Latin American countries. It is surely clear that their early experiences in Colombia infected them with a lasting affection for Latin Americans and their countries.

And what of the research during this first season with the family? It may sound as though the two of us spent our time doing nothing except taking care of the children, but other things did get done, and the children were often participants in them. The first, and most obvious, effect of arriving in Popayan with the entire family was a clear expansion of people's acceptance of Father. Colombians are very strong "family people" and they were not only interested in seeing his family, but regarded it as an expression of confidence in them that he had returned once again to Popayan, and had brought his wife and children with him for an extended stay. There was a good deal of friendly curiosity about our reasons for being there. People whom Father had hardly known in previous years went out of their way to ask about us, and also to offer their help in looking for a house and learning about the city. As a "family man" Father was suddenly a more respected citizen than he had been before. Old friends and acquaintances came out of their homes as we passed and introduced themselves to Mother and made friends with the children.

The open and friendly acceptance of the family was due largely to the presence of the children, and they continued to open doors for us throughout the year. In some instances, as described earlier, we met families because our children played together; in other cases our friendship with families was strengthened because they could bring their children when they called on us, or vice versa. With these families we had something fundamental in common, and through them we met their brothers' and sisters' families, and also their fathers and mothers. In a short time we found ourselves in touch with an important segment of the living network of kinship in the community and on friendly relations with at least three generations of Payaneses (people of Popayan). The two previous field seasons had disclosed certain aspects of the network, but now we were actually living with it and participating in it. We had the great advantage of a close-up, inside view of family life: parent-child relations, sibling relationships, the status of the elderly, patterns of family recreation and coping with crisis, the problems of running a household, treatment of servants, etc. There seemed to be almost no aspect of life in Popayan from which we were excluded. Even during the religious processions of the Easter Holy Week friends asked us if it would be against our Protestant religion for our boys to carry candles; all their friends were participating and there seemed to be no reason that the Whiteford boys should be left out. They were not, but it was only because friends thought it was fitting for them to participate.

Most of our intimate relationships at this time were with families which belonged, socially and economically, to the upper or the middle class. In previous field sessions, when Father was working with the Colombian anthropologists, Virginia and Roberto Pineda and Gregorio Hernandez de Alba, a great deal of data had been gathered in the poorest parts of the city and contacts had been established with a number of families in those *barrios* (neighborhoods). New insights into the lives of these people came when Father and the boys arranged to record the music of a traditional *Chirimia*. These groups played in the streets, their members usually wearing Indian costumes and producing a great deal of noise with several drums, rattles, and other rhythm instruments which accompanied the melody emanating from a lone flute or ocarina. All the men in the *Chirimias* lived in the poor barrios of the city. And we learned about some of the other artisans when the boys had to have their horse reshod by the blacksmith who had his shop under the arch of a bridge. The very presence of the boys facilitated contacts and led to conversations which might not have taken place without them.

This was very true as we walked from block to block through the city making notes and taking pictures to record a number of block-by-block cross sections of the city. Sometimes one or both of our boys would carry a camera or the tripod. Almost always they would stand at the end of the block holding a clipboard with large numbers written on it in order to identify the street and block in the photograph. Our progress along the street was always observed with interest, and women in the windows or men passing along the sidewalk would often stop and ask us what we were doing. Wherever there were boys playing in the street we accumulated a fascinated and curious flock, part of which would sometimes join us for an hour or so. They would often talk to our boys, and persistent followers were often rewarded for their company by being allowed to carry the tripod or, the greatest thrill of all, to stand beside Scott or Mike while they held up the numbers and had their pictures taken. Many of them have been preserved for posterity in our photo files. In the process we learned where they lived, where they went to school, what their fathers and mothers did, etc.: bits and pieces of information which helped to define the details of the neighborhoods through which we were passing, and in which they lived.

Such participation in the research was interesting to our boys, especially when their playmates were all in school, and they learned a great deal about Popayan as we walked together from one end to the other. They also learned something of the nature of the research and learned to recognize events and situations which might be important. During their trots around town on Amigo they saw a great deal. The sound of a horse galloping down our cobblestone street and stopping in front of our door meant that one of the boys would come running into the house with the announcement that "something important was happening in the Barrio Alfonso Lopez" and Father should go and see. Father would then spring into action, slinging his camera and other equipment over his shoulders and rushing out into the street. The two Whiteford couriers and their dear Amigo would quickly disappear around the corner leaving Father to trot after them to the other end of town to observe whatever it might be that had excited the interest of the boys: a local wedding, a small procession, a funeral, or simply some sort of family gathering with music and *aguardiente* (sugarcane brandy). They were keen scouts and they produced many items of interest for the research which would have otherwise have been missed. There were, of course, other times when Father arrived on the scene panting and exhausted only to find that the gathering had dissolved shortly before he arrived.

Even in such cases Scott and Mike might have made their own inquiries and had been able to report during our evening review of the day's events. They were acute and perceptive reporters and we learned a great deal about our neighborhood, and also about the city as a whole, from their comments, their questions, and their patterns of interaction with their friends. Even at this early stage in their development the research was greatly enriched by their observations and also by their interpretations. Anyone who has experienced the intense and perceptive curiosity of young people between the ages of four and twelve will realize that our children saw things that we never noticed and that they asked questions about people and events which would never have occurred to us. Without their comments and questions we might never have known where the local morgue was located, that gentlemen of the aristocracy cultivated fighting cocks, that all small boys had to have a bag of flour for the fiesta of the Wise Kings at Christmas so they could throw it on young ladies they passed on the streets, where sky-rockets were made, and many other bits of essential information. Our boys had gone with a group of their friends to peer through the windows of the morgue at the body of a recent murder victim; they had walked to the cock pit with one of our elegant upper class friends, who happened to be carrying his fighting cock under his arm; they had participated in the activities of every event during the Christmas season; and they had talked with the local *cohetero* (rocket-maker) because they thought it might be a good idea for us to buy some for the next fiesta. Explanations were required for questions which covered an enormous range: why did families have so many servants; why did the lovely girl down the block kick her nursemaid; why did our maid's rural family leave an egg or a few potatoes on the table when they came in at five o'clock in the morning to have coffee and wash their feet on market day; why was our maid so upset when we had a Guambiano Indian friend in for dinner; why were sky-rockets set off at birthday parties, etc., etc.? The questions were endless, and the explanations were not always immediately available. Often we had to do a bit of inquiry, observation, or reading to settle the matter. This was good for all of us.

On a somewhat superficial, but still important, level we all became very interested in how *Payanes* friends dressed and behaved. We did not mind being recognizable as *gringos,* but we knew that we would have to blend to a certain extent simply to be accepted. Mother worked very hard, with the assistance of some friends, to get her own little girl prepared for the Easter styleshow. All the houses on the block were buzzing with talk of materials and ribbons, and floral hats, and new shoes, and our little girl was not going to be left out. However, we made the common mistake of assuming that the whole thing was going to be basically as it was at home, with the result that our ladies were prepared for Easter Sunday only to discover a little too late that everyone wore their finery for the services in the churches on Holy Thursday. We were not quite ready, and we had forgotten to inquire.

Linda very quickly became a little *Payanesa,* practically indistinguishable from the other little girls. The boys' blue jeans made them stand out, and were objects of great envy--blue jeans had not yet arrived in Popayan and had only been seen in cowboy movies. We all became aware that even the very little boys in the city were fully equiped with something called "manners," and Scott and Mike had to learn something about this matter simply to avoid being gauche. The two sons of one of our closest friends were the same age as our boys, and they were so well trained, so completely equipped with the proper manners for every occasion, that they became our role models. They were somewhat resented by Scott and Mike, but even they could not deny that Juan and Victor possessed a kind of grace and aplomb which helped them to cope with practically every occasion. They learned, after they had known Juan and Victor for a while, that they were also noisy, raucous, tough little boys in the street, but they controlled this special coating of "manners" which could be quickly applied when the occasion required it. Scott and Mike never became quite as adept as Juan and Victor, but they acquired a sufficient amount of Latin American manners to get by in Popayan and to make them objects of curiosity to their peers in Beloit, Wisconsin, and a delight to their friends' mothers. They became the Juan and Victor of the local Wisconsin scene and it took quite a time before their Latin demeanor began to wear off.

Following our experience in Popayan, Father was in Mexico in 1955 and 1957, but the family did not return to Latin America until 1958. The earlier surveys in Mexico had been conducted in an effort to locate another small city which possessed at least the basic characteristics of Popayan. This meant an urban center of approximately 50,000 inhabitants, very little or no industry, a rich historical background, a university center, and at least the vestiges of a stratified society. We hoped to make a comparative study of two communities, and also to define some of the basic elements of Latin American urbanism to provide a base which might serve for future studies of the effects of industralization in these cities or in others. Considering the differences, historical and otherwise, between Colombia and Mexico, we knew that finding any place closely similar to Popayan would be impossible; but, after two summers of survey, we settled upon the city of Queretaro. It was located in almost the exact geographical center of Mexico, was about the right size, was only in the nascent stages of industralism, had been settled in 1531, had been a major center for government and trade during the Colonial period, and had played an important role in the history of the nation. It also had a university and had been a major church center before the Revolution.

The city was different from Popayan in various ways, and our research group was also different. In Queretaro we were part of a field school from Beloit College, with one unit doing archaeological research and the other involved in a study of the community. Interaction with the college students was frequent and, after we left the main group and moved into a large house on the highway, our "family" consisted of the two of us, four children, a nephew about to graduate from high school, and an Ecuadorean college student. By this time, Scott was a fifteen-year-old high school student, Michael was thirteen, Linda was ten, and Laurie was five; we were older, too.

Social integration was more difficult for us in Queretaro because here North Americans were nothing unusual; we were unable to find a house in an urban neighborhood and were forced to be relatively isolated; we did not stay as long as in Popayan; our group was much larger; and, except for Laurie, our children no longer possessed the simple innocence of childhood which led them into so many casual encounters in Popayan. In an attempt to enrich the experience for the children, and also to bring us closer to the life of the city, we enrolled them in local schools. Linda and Laurie, along with a slightly older daughter of another faculty member, attended a medium-sized Catholic school for girls. They went only in the mornings and appeared to enjoy it sufficiently to refrain from strident complaints. The effects were not very clear. They made very few friends and, although they learned some Spanish, the experience was badly broken up because a new school building was just completed and everything was in chaos while the old school was shut down and all operations were transferred. They were in attendance for only a month or so before the summer vacation closed the school.

Through the influence of an important family in the city our boys were enrolled in a large private institution for a short time. Here they played *futbol*, made a few friends, and learned almost nothing that they could report at home. As a result of the friendships they were invited out to some family *haciendas* (ranches) and came to feel considerably more at home in the city. We did not regard these school experiences as particularly rewarding, nor did the children. At least part of the family's unconcern for the lack of academic depth in the schools was the fact that, once more, we came away loaded down with educational materials with which we (Mother) hoped to keep everyone up with their schoolmates back in Wisconsin. Both Scott and his cousin wrote papers and completed assignments which they mailed back to their high school teachers. This kept them busy for several hours almost every day, a time during which the younger ones had classes with Mother.

This experience was much less rich for our children. The reasons are obvious: the time was short, attention was diverted by the presence of a larger family and a group of college students, and we did not live in a close association with any Mexican families. We do not recall that it was in any way unpleasant or boring for them and when we ended the season with a long trip south and west they were delighted with everything they saw. Our reading still continued, although in a slightly different pattern. To complete one of Scott's high school assignments we sat under a *ramada* (brush sunshade) on the beach at San Blas and took turns reading parts in *As You Like It*. Everyone enjoyed it, and our children developed a continuing appreciation for Shakespeare which was only slightly diminished when we continued with a somewhat less amusing *Julius Caesar* while waiting for our car to recover from an accident in Culiacan. What we had learned in Popayan and Queretaro about the problems and pleasures of living abroad with the younger members of our family was reinforced and expanded three years later in 1961 when we gathered every one together once again and left home for a year and a half; a year in Spain and six months back in Popayan.

Regardless of the distance or time involved, it is difficult for teenagers at any place between junior high school and college to break off the relationships and careers which they have been developing. Not only are intimacies dissolved, often with members of the opposite sex, but hard-won positions on athletic teams or in political factions are lost, usually to rivals. These important elements of school life are relinquished reluctantly, even with the prospect of adventure ahead. No longer did the vague promise that we might buy a horse serve to ease the real grief the boys felt at leaving their close friends and the circle of activities in which they had won honorable positions. Departure was not exactly traumatic, but it took Mike at least six months before he shed his feeling of loss and began to take a real interest in what was happening around us. He was about to enter his third year in high school and had just succeeded in winning places on two athletic teams and becoming involved in social activities of various kinds. The girls had no such problems. Linda was thirteen and had just moved from a small country school into a larger junior high school where she had not yet made any intimate or important relationships; she was ready and willing to leave. Laurie, who was eight, never waited to find out where any of us were going before she eagerly volunteered to accompany us, it did not matter to her whether it was a trip to the grocery or a voyage to England, she was always willing to go.

We camped in Europe for six weeks before turning toward Spain, and everyone enjoyed traveling, picnicking, sight-seeing, and searching everywhere for a luggage rack for our Microbus, which we never did find. Spain generally was interesting and pleasant, but life in Malaga had its ups and downs for the family. The three older children all worked hard on extension courses from the University of Wisconsin, we all took language courses, and Laurie was enrolled in a small school, which she thought was wonderful. Because Father's research was largely archival during the early phases, it was not the sort of thing in which other members of the family could participate. It was also not especially conducive to the development of many social relationships in the community. The boys took tennis lessons from a Spanish professional and gradually made a few friends. Scott, who had finished his first year of college, enrolled at the University of Granada for a term, and Mike regained his constitutional ebullience when we went to Gibralter and began to look for a Volkswagen roadster. He also went off with a friend and spent New Year holidays in Morocco. It was not bad for them, but it did not result in many lasting friendships or any deep feeling of affection for Spain.

Again it was different for the girls. Laurie became immersed very quickly in the group of little girls who lived in adjacent houses and learned to speak Spanish like a native Andulucian. Linda was rather quickly noticed by a number of young Malagenos of high school and university age, who made various attempts to meet her by striking up acquaintances with her brothers. Invitations to parties were generally distained by our boys, who may have detected the real reasons for their popularity, but they were forced to put up with serenades by the local musical groups called *Tunas*,

which appeared at unpredictable hours, entertained the entire neighborhood, and expected to be invited into the house for wine or refreshments
after their performance. Linda loved it, her brothers thought it was much
ado about nothing, and we were not quite sure what to make of it. The
young admirers seemed to turn up everywhere, even when we went up to
Granada to bring Scott back from the University and to visit the Alhambra.
Our concern was eased, and Linda was able to cope with her sudden
popularity through the friendship she established with some Spanish girls of
her own age. They gave her learned instructions about the life of a young
lady living in Malaga and, in the process, established relationships with
each other which continued for many years. For Linda Spain was a
romantic and exciting place, and she returned by herself for another visit
several years later. It also prepared her for her return to Colombia.

The return route to Popayan led us to Portugal, then, after a very
pleasant voyage to Venezuela, a long drive through the mountains from
Caracas to Bogota and, eventually, to our colonial city in the Cauca Valley.
It was like coming home. Linda went off to live with the Velasco family,
Mike became a member of the Caicedo family, and the rest of us found
pleasant rooms in a pension. Scott was recovering from something which
he had contracted while living in Granada, but he planned and carried out
the survey of a lower middle-class neighborhood which had been almost
completely overlooked in our earlier studies. Linda and Laurie were
entered in a select parochial school where Linda made friends and Laurie
"majored in mass, embroidery, and recess." Whenever the good sisters at
the school were not quite certain about what to do with this little
energetic Andalucian-speaking *gringa*, they sent her to chapel with one
group or another. Laurie thought this was all fine and she left Colombia
with a complete repertory of Catholic hymns and prayers.

This was generally a productive and relaxing period for all of us.
There were many family reunions, picnics, visits to friends' *haciendas*,
horse-back trips into the mountains, and the gentle and genial routine of
life in Popayan. The boys did many things with their old friends and also
helped Father a great deal in the research. Each of them did independent
projects, as well as taking photographs and writing up interviews and
observations. They drew us closer to other families and each of the
children provided new and fresh views of the community and its people.
Mike went to school for a while at the Liceo with his Caicedo "brothers"
and Linda became a complete *Payanesa* with the Velascos. In company
with her "sisters," Clemencia, who was her age, and Tulia, who was older,
she went everywhere and participated in everything that took place, from
formal receptions for the president-elect (where she was photographed and
identified as "Linda Velasco") to riding at the family *haciendas*, and
swinging on the *columpio* (a popular May-pole swing). We did not realize
that she had reached a very special birthday when she became fifteen, but
the Velasco family gave her the complete Latin treatment, beginning with
a serenade at five o'clock in the morning and ending with a gala party and
many presents. This, according to the custom, launched her into full status

as a presentable young lady, and once again she was attended, escorted and wooed. It was enough to turn the head of almost any girl from a Midwestern family, and would surely have done so for Linda if she had not been "fortunate" enough to have two older brothers nearby to remind her that she was still a "kid sister." Nevertheless, it was an exciting and memorable experience for her, during which she perfected her Spanish, acquired various Latin graces, reached a new stage in maturation, and reinforced her deep affection for the Velasco family and for Popayan.

During this period our children felt so much at home that they were rarely aware of how much they were learning. The projects the boys worked on were special and separate matters which were usually done when they were not with their friends. For us, the pleasure and interest in watching our offspring as they interacted with their adopted families, and as they participated in games, parties, discussions, family projects and outings, was fascinating and enlightening. We could easily have become separated from at least three of them if we had not participated also in many of the same activities, and if we had not made a point of having frequent visits with them in our pension. Leaving Popayan at the end of the season, when we packed our Volkswagen Microbus and started back over the mountains for Caracas, was a very sad affair for all of us.

This second extended stay in Popayan affected our entire family deeply and gave each one of our offspring (no longer children) a personal and individual concept of the basic nature of the community and of Latin American culture. From this point forward events in Colombia, and in Latin America generally, were of deep concern to them. The depth of friendship they felt for many individuals, some of whom they had known for ten years, made it impossible for them to ever regard South America as a geographical abstraction, a far-off place on the map. The special attitudes which had been developed in them, and the various skills which they had acquired, were surely major factors in their later involvements with Latin America.

Subsequent field work in Latin America involved marked changes in the Whiteford personnel and quite different experiences from the earlier ones. Because they all contributed to the formation of our ultimate generalizations in one way or another, we will review them briefly and comment on their special features.

When we went to Oaxaca in 1966 our total company was completely new because we were involved in a National Science Foundation training program with a group of college students. Mike was one of them, and this was his first experience of formalized field research. Linda was in a college summer term and Scott was at Stanford, so Laurie, now in middle school, was our only uncommitted offspring. Her experience here was enlightening to us, and also to her. When we returned the from 1961-1962 Malaga-Popayan sojourn, Laurie was the most Latin member of the family and she spoke the most fluent and idiomatic Spanish. For a variety of reasons, which seemed to be beyond our control, she refused to have anything to do with Spanish during the next four years and she arrived in Oaxaca having forgotten everything. For the first month she made no effort to communicate with any of the native people and it was only after a chance encounter with some other North Americans opened her eyes and her mind to the depth of her experience that she began to come alive. Suddenly she began to listen intently to conversations and to reach into some inner depths for dimly remembered words and phrases. It cannot be said that she suddenly regained her former fluency overnight, but within two weeks she could carry on a conversation and was moving through the market and other interesting parts of the city with confidence.

In 1970 we were back in Popayan, with a slightly different family assortment. We were now into a phase of "secondary growth" because we had acquired two new daughters-in-law and one of them was with us in Colombia. This is not quite correct because Patty was really with Mike, and the two of them were engaged in their own independent research related to his doctoral program at Berkeley. Scott and his wife were working in Argentina and Linda was on a college program in Denmark. But Laurie was with us. She lived partly with us and partly with Mike and Patty when she was not out on some friends' *hacienda.* She arrived in Latin America this time with a considerable remembrance of Spanish and with a sense of confidence and interest which continued to grow. Toward the end of our stay she went alone to Bogota to stay with Roberto and Virginia Pineda and her fluency was such that some young people would not believe that she was not Colombian.

We have no satisfactory explanation for the erratic course of Laurie's linguistic prowess. In the early phase it confirmed the generally accepted facility which young children possess for the acquisition of a new language. The psychological block which she developed upon her return to Wisconsin seemed to result from immersion in a milieu where there was almost no interest in foreign countries and which tended to be critical of any of its young members who expressed anything except its own concerns and interests. There was no place in the country school which she attended to mention Spain or South America, and even less to speak Spanish. Instead of gaining her any prestige, as it did to some extent for her older siblings, her foreign experience was something which had to be concealed and, sub-consciously, forgotten. The influence of her peer group far outweighed the concerns of her family in this particular matter. It was not until she actually returned to Latin America that she was able to conceive of her previous experiences as having any great validity and value for her as a person. We believe it was a turning point which she has never forgotten.

We were not able to observe her further retention of the language because she was not with us when we returned to Popayan in 1974, she was away on a college field session in ecology. This season was not quite our final one in the company of members of our family, but it is worth including here because it represented our period of "tertiary growth." Not only were Mike and Patty in Colombia again to complete their research, but they had with them this time their fifteen-month-old son, Scotty. We had never been in the field with a grandchild before, or with any child so young. It may not have had much lasting effect upon him, but it had an effect in solidifying the family relationship during the period in the field. Although we lived apart and were working on different projects, we saw a great deal of each other and were often together with our old friends in the community. The effects of being in Popayan with children and a grandchild were not especially apparent, except to affirm our relationship with the society and to place us on an equal footing with our old friends, most of whom had several grandchildren. It also meant that we were able to look across as many as four generations with some understanding of the problems and satisfactions that we shared.

In this review of the Whiteford family's activities we have made a few generalizations, but it may be of some value in understanding something of the problems and advantages of taking children into the field if we make an attempt to list certain warnings and some bits of advice which we have distilled from our experiences.

1. *Age.* There is no "perfect" age at which children can best be taken into the field. Very young children, below the age of six or seven, have few objections and adapt easily. However, they usually need special health care, and their dependence absorbs time and energy from the research. Adolescents often experience great difficulty in leaving the home situation where they have become increasingly engrossed in establishing themselves in school, club, and team activities and where they may have developed special sentimental attachments to members of the opposite sex. They may well resent the interruption of their lives and actually resist adaptation to the foreign scene.

2. *Preparation.* Preparing the children for the foreign experience is very important, not only with regard to health protection, but with information and knowledge. This obviously varies with the ages of the off-spring involved, but even youngsters can be told about the countryside, the people they will meet, and some of the activities in which they may be involved. In our case the slides Father took and the gifts of dolls and clothing he brought back made Colombia real for our children long before they got there. They were prepared to find a beautiful and interesting country. Even for quite young children some language preparation can be very helpful, and for older offspring it is at the top of the list.

3. *Advance Reconnaissance.* An advance visit to the area in order to understand the logistics, lodgings, and regulations will help greatly to smooth the family's arrival and adjustment. We have done it both ways and the advantages of knowing the basic facts about where you are going are undeniable; not only do you get there much more easily, but the dispositions of everyone involved are less likely to be irritated by long waits, false moves, and general uncertainty.

4. *Prior Contacts.* Prior contacts can sometimes be counted on to make prearrangements. The value of knowing someone in the community to which you are taking your family is obvious: introductions and presentations are usually forthcoming, directions and guidance will save wasted hours and effort, etc. Even a contact which has been established only through communication is much better than none, and this is often the only kind of contact possible. Introductions through a mutual friend, a colleague, or a business acquaintance will establish a beginning point in the community, if nothing else. Official calls on various authorities or officeholders in the community will often elicit cooperation and assistance when other avenues are not open, and these too can serve to provide assurance for the family.

5. *Adaptation.* Families appear to get along best in the field when they are isolated from their fellow countrymen. As long as there are other North Americans available the temptation to socialize with them inhibits the use of the native language and delays the development of satisfying relationships with the local people. If no one else is available, the family will usually quickly, and always inevitably, make some kind of adaptation to the local scene. Isolation is really an advantage.

6. *Integration.* This involves participation and acceptance. The first step is a genuine effort to become involved in as many activities as possible within the limitations of age, sex, skills, strength, etc. Mother went to cooking school; Father took guitar lessons; and the children played on teams, marched in processions; and we all participated in an infinitude of social events, from poetry readings to children's masquerades. In spite of our own attempts at continuing education we usually enrolled the younger members of our family in schools, with the varying results described earlier. If nothing more, the enrollments served to make us appear to be more like regular or ordinary members of the community and the scholars found friends. We studied the patterns of hospitality and made an effort to entertain people in our home as much as possible; we also attempted to accept every invitation which was offered.

7. *Sharing.* It is helpful if the children have something which they can share with friends and acquaintances. In our case the shipment of comic books from their great aunt was truly a bonanza for everyone concerned. They also had their horse Amigo, who was shared by practically everyone in the neighborhood. In our early field trips Linda had her dolls and a few other playthings which she could share with her friends and the boys had their physical skills which they could share with their teammates. As time went on they shared a great many other things with their close friends: ideas, opinions, clothes, information, and friendship. In later seasons, when we had a car, they also shared transportation to some extent, but this never seemed to be very important.

8. *Treats.* Being able to provide the family with some exciting extras, or treats, makes life more exciting and stimulating for everyone. They

stimulate anticipation, something to look forward to, a condition which is always important, but especially when living in a foreign community. During our first season in Popayan our boys were buoyed up by the mere thought of getting a horse, and Amigo constituted something very special for them both throughout the year. In Spain, when things looked gloomy Mike could cheer himself up by contemplating the purchase of a Vespa, a project which was later abandoned to be replaced by the excitement of going to Gibralter in search of a Volkswagen convertible. Also, the boys took tennis lessons and Laurie learned Flamenco dancing. We did not make a great many promises to our family, but we tried to make the future look desirable with plans for a trip to Seville, preparation for Easter processions, a visit to the Guambiano Indian country, or a weekend in Cali. We were always planning something.

9. *Escape.* As every fieldworker knows, there are times when one has to withdraw and simply be alone, without the necessity of coping with the language, the customs, and the casual demands of the new life. This is true for children too. We provided some protection for them with our reading and story telling, we also took long walks with long conversations which included no one except our family. We almost never had to go out of town for the weekend, but we did sometimes hide by ourselves in the theaters and lose ourselves for a while in the English-language movies. Such retreats were not often needed, but their easy availability was almost certainly a source of security.

10. *Participation.* Involvement of the older children in the research can be productive as well as gratifying. Even when they were quite young (six years) the children seemed to have some ideas about the research and the reasons for being in a strange town far from home. We encouraged their curiosity and listened to them carefully in the evenings as they gave us detailed accounts of what they had done and seen during the day. It was good for family relationships and it also turned up many nuggets of information which otherwise would never have reached the notebooks. As the family became older and more independent the children took on projects of their own: Scott did his own study of a middle class *barrio* in Popayan and a report on the fishes living in the streams, and Mike mapped a section of Popayan in special detail. They never regarded themselves as tourists, they were always residents or researchers.

11. *Family Size.* The size of the family group and the ages of the children obviously affect the entire situation. A group of siblings have the advantage of being able to support each other, and perhaps divide paternal attention, while a single child may be forced to depend to a debilitating degree upon the attention and reinforcement of the parent(s). On the other hand, larger families generally require more care and a single child may find it easier to become accepted by a new group. The more the members of a family have participated and interacted together in a variety of projects the better prepared they will be to cope with the problems of situational change to a new environment.

12. *Re-entry.* Anyone who plans to be away from his home environment for six months or more should be prepared for "re-entry" problems. These problems are multiplied for a family. Re-establishment of a satisfactory position in the various peer groups, the understanding of changed relationships and even modified styles and customs, the loss of special status as a foreigner; these are some of the situations which are almost inevitable and for which an effort should be made to prepare one's children. This is probably done best by helping them to maintain some contact with the home base, and by emphasizing the positive aspects of returning to it.

In retrospect it is impossible for us to consider our experiences with children in the field as anything but a complete success. We were not always as well prepared as we might have been, our living and traveling conditions were sometimes on the Spartan side, and we had a few bouts of intestinal disorders, bug bites, and so on; but our young companions were almost always cheerful, enthusiastic, and willing to go anywhere at any time. We felt always that they were happier and more secure with us than anywhere else, regardless of where we happened to be. Their presence must have made us somewhat more cautious than we would have been without them, but as they grew older we undertook journeys we would not have taken alone: through the Atlas Mountains in a blizzard, across three ranges of the Andes during "La Violencia" in Colombia and Venezuela, and other places. We all felt that we could do things together that none of us could do alone.

A strong indication that our offspring do agree with this conclusion is the fact that Mike took his small son to Colombia at the age of a year and a half, and later took his two boys to Costa Rica (where he and Patty adopted a little girl); Scott and Weegee's son was born in Tehuacan and they will have their two small ones with them later this year in Mexico, and Linda and Doug are planning to take their two-year-old girl with them to Peru very shortly. If Latin America and Spain was a troubled or dismal experience for our children, they should certainly have the good sense not to repeat the mistakes of their parents.

REFERENCE

Whiteford, M. B. (1976). *The Forgotten Ones: Colombian Countrymen in an Urban Setting.* Gainesville, FL: University Presses of Florida.

CITY WALLS AND CAMPUS GROVES IN NORTHERN NIGERIA:

A PROFILE OF PARENTING IN THE FIELD

Gerald W. Kleis

Department of Sociology
Bayero University
Kano, Nigeria

INTRODUCTION

While we frequently fail to pay sufficient attention to the effects on research of our involvement as families in the field, as parents we are usually vitally concerned with the effects of the field experience on our children and on our functioning as parents. Parenting in a cross-cultural setting is especially challenging because the home society's physical and institutional support system is removed along with the widely shared understandings that provide clear normative bench marks for parent and child alike. In the field we are often our children's major culture brokers-- explaining the host culture, arranging opportunities to meet local children, listening to personal adjustment problems, and helping resolve misunderstandings with peers and teachers. Playing this mediating and interpretive role effectively demands social skills and an informed sensitivity to the nuances of the host society that ought to be standard equipment for all anthropologists. As anthropologists we may take cultural differences in stride, but for young children discontinuities between the home and the outside world may be bewildering and upsetting. As anthropologist-parents we should be especially alert to these discontinuities and better equipped than laymen to cushion their culture shock. This special alertness to cultural discontinuities can become a powerful research tool as well.

There may be however, severe tension between two of the roles we are called to play during fieldwork with children--that of socializing parent and that of dispassionate observer. Struggle as we may to be faithful cultural relativists and neutral mediators, we often find ourselves defenders and sustainers of our own cultural traditions when we have our children in the field. Since we are usually our child's primary source of his home culture, we feel a heavy responsibility to transmit it faithfully in all its depth and variety to him. Like most parents, we take pride in being reminded that our child resembles us, and like other migrants in far-off lands, we harbor the secret fear that he may turn out to be rather different from our expectations. As anthropologists, however, we may take the concern with cultural discontinuities one step further than other migrants. Parenting outside our home culture forces us to confront a host of fundamental issues and assumptions on a day-to-day basis that we seldom ask outside the realm of theoretical and philosophical speculation: What are the objectives of our own culture's socialization practices and what values do they embody? How sound are these values and how effective are our strategies for implementing them? What sort of person do I want my child to be or does he want to become? What are the effective limits of my responsibility or right to intervene in his life to achieve these objectives?

The issues and problems to be discussed here all concern the reciprocal relationships of parenting and research in a cross-cultural setting. They include the following: the relevance of all aspects of our own and others' social personhood to the participant observation that is the source of our cultural insight; the way children increase our involvement in, and understanding of, local social life and cultural meaning; the role of our families in illuminating new issues in ethnicity, my long-standing research interest; the extent of our right and ability to direct our child's acquisition of culture; and the relations between a child's adjustment process in the host society and his or her readjustment at home. After an introductory section about my family and its adjustment to Nigerian society, the text will be divided between the results of reflecting upon my own involvement as parent and researcher in the field and the insights that result from observing my children's participation in the host society.

All of these issues have been of special concern to my wife and myself during the course of my two years of research and university teaching here in northern Nigeria, where this account has been written. All this is, therefore, still very much a part of our lives, and I have had little opportunity to reflect on them with the detached objectivity of the returned, recuperated anthropologist. However, the immediacy of our experience gives special insight which often fades or loses its relevance after leaving the field.

PREPARATION AND ADAPTATION

I am a Euro-American from the Midwest who had worked as a Peace Corps volunteer (1963-65) in southeastern Nigeria prior to my doctoral research in Cameroon (1971-73). My wife, Susanna is of Banyang ethnic origin from northwestern Cameroon, an area with close historical and cultural links to Nigeria, especially the southeastern part where I had been in the Peace Corps. We arrived in Kano, Nigeria, in October 1981 with our two children--Nina, our five-year-old daughter, and Alan, our one-year-old son--and at the time of this writing have been in the field for nearly two years. Neither of our children had ever been outside of North America before. But because of our own African experiences, my wife and I were able to give our children some preparation for the field trip. Although there are a number of contrasts between northern Nigeria and the coastal zone of West Africa where we had both lived, there were also a number of familiar features, including shared patterns of English usage, similar educational systems, and a large southern migrant population.

Since our marriage, we have lived in ethnically heterogeneous campus settings in the United States where Africans and Africanists were regular guests. Our general lifestyle has provided our children, specifically Nina, because Alan was still an infant, with knowledge and interests that prepared them for the move. Members of Susanna's family have also visited us; her sister (a graduate student in Britain) paid us a month-long Christmas visit, and her mother stayed in the United States for nine months while recuperating from orthopedic surgery. During these visits, Nina was exposed to Cameroonian languages (Kenyang and Obang, both spoken in Susanna's family) and Pidgin English, which she would later hear and use in Nigeria. She listened eagerly to her mother's and grandmother's folktales and soon grew familiar with the recurring characters and moral themes. Nina had been raised on an improvised semi-West African diet, which included the wide range of foods available in university towns. Although our disciplining style had its African influences, it was more in keeping with my American standards, which Susanna's mother believed made us over-indulgent parents bound to produce willful children who would later turn their backs on adult authority.

As our plans for returning to Africa took a more definite shape, concern about our children's health and safety were uppermost in our minds. Although we had realistic expectations about African conditions, taking our children to Africa was a new experience. Susanna was especially concerned about the high child mortality rate because she recalled the deaths of her two young siblings. We gathered as much health care information as we could find and coached Nina on avoiding snakes, scorpions and unboiled water. After we moved to Kano some of these concerns seemed a bit exaggerated, while other threats, especially motor safety, were less clearly anticipated. As new arrivals we found that our strict health and safety standards were at variance with most Nigerians and expatriates, and it took several months before we were able to relax them.

Although Susanna welcomed our move as an opportunity to put our children in closer touch with their African heritage, she was often more concerned than I was with reinforcing their ties to American culture. She believed that in going to Nigeria they would sacrifice the advantages of the American school system and what she considered a highly stimulating learning environment, enriched by the mass media and an enlightened citizenry. Even if we succeeded in finding a good school for our children, she had serious doubts about how appropriate their education would be for eventual adaptation to life in the United States. These fears were reinforced by the experiences of a friend's daughter who, like our children, was of an African-American background. After spending two years in West Africa, she had had considerable difficulty reintegrating into American society. Susanna believed that the girl's culture shock was complicated by problems of acceptance arising from racial antagonism and having to relearn American norms and speech patterns. She had doubts about whether her own English was a proper model for her children, even though many Nigerians assume she is an American. She was concerned that our children would have, on the whole, less American influence on their socialization than in families in which both parents were American-born. To guard against the erosion of our children's American heritage, we carried books, cassette tapes and other cultural resources to Nigeria. After arriving we found that Nigerian television was well-supplied with programs from the United States, which gave them more exposure to American culture than anything we could have brought with us.

Susanna's concerns also stemmed from her own experiences with culture shock, and from her efforts to adapt to American society while not breaking faith with her home and heritage. At first, the United States was for her an unfamiliar world with an uncompromising emphasis on efficiency, promptness, universalistic values and achievement. In her home culture, where kinship and local origins are vital criteria for determining social status and sources of support, Western universalistic values run counter to expectations of preferential treatment from one's own people. Africans are also generally more concerned than Americans with their overall investment in human relations (being successful means "having people") and give greater attention to maintaining, mending and extending their social networks. As Susanna soon discovered, these concerns were often out of tune with Western lifestyles based on individualism and geared to the demands of the clock and the production line.

Striking a balance between these disparate values is often difficult. However, she now appreciates the greater role of western governments and voluntary agencies in dealing with problems that are beyond the ability of the family to handle, and is optimistic about mobilizing science, technology and the collective will to effect needed change. Although she has no illusions about the prevalence of injustice in America, she sees a basic commitment to social justice which usually outweighs concern about social origins. She believes that the lines of parental authority should be clearly drawn, as it is in most African societies, but admits that the greater freedom of American children promotes their development in a society where multiple career alternatives abound.

Susanna's own cross-cultural experiences arising during her eight and a half years in the U.S. helped brace her for the culture shock she met in the Nigeria of the 1980's. She was returning to a new part of her continent after a prolonged absence, with new insights, new attitudes and new perspectives. Since we had tried to keep abreast of social changes in

Africa while in the United States, we were intellectually, if not emotionally prepared for them. However, in the wake of the oil boom, the scale of development and pace of life in Kano, as in the rest of Nigeria, had undergone substantial transformation in the two decades since my brief visit in 1964. Traffic had intensified; buildings had mushroomed; and the country had been swept by a tidal wave of domestic and imported consumer goods. These changes have overwhelmed the south but are also keenly felt in the north, long regarded as a secure bastion of traditionalism. Since my earlier days in Nigeria, life had become more frenetic, more competitive, and--with higher crime and accident rates--much less secure. However, today Nigerians are better informed, more conscious and concerned about their place in the wider world, and--as the expanding network of communication draws the remotest areas into the arena of national life--local communities are fast losing their Redfieldian folk character.

There were also numerous other contrasts with the African scene we knew best, such as the long dry season, the *harmattan* (a cool dust-laden wind) from the Sahara in mid-winter, and the broad vistas with scattered trees and towering *inselbergs* (isolated mountains), all a far cry from the humid Southern Nigerian coastlands. The dominant population in Kano, and throughout the Hausa-speaking north, is Muslim; a fact immediately evident in the Sudanic architecture, modest elaborate dress, patterns of worship and social practices. Major Friday and smaller neighborhood mosques are numerous and prominent; public prayer is regularly observed. Women of child-bearing age are kept in strict seclusion, while children, the aged and the handicapped solicit alms from the faithful at busy intersections. In the southern, largely Christian areas where we had lived, architecture is less elaborate; women are highly visible in the economic sphere; and men and women dress casually in various combinations of Western and African attire. In the Islamic north, sobriety, self-control and restraint are dominant social values, while in the south spontaneity, straightforwardness and vigorous sociability are deemed hallmarks of a healthy, well-integrated personality.

The problem that occupied the greatest amount of our attention in the first year in Kano was attaining the best housing situation. The extent to which the presence of children increases one's needs and desires in such mundane matters is one of the more time-consuming and thus negative consequences of doing fieldwork with them.

We spent our first week in Kano as guests of my department chairman, a genial Scot bachelor who was a veteran of ten years of teaching and research in Africa. Needless to say, two active American-bred children were difficult to restrain in a house not properly child-proofed. After that we spent a few months in a university guest house on the Bayero campus, a veritable oasis of lush vegetation and flowering shrubs throughout the year. Our fellow tenants came from many countries and were either unmarried or unaccompained by their families. They appreciated the domestic touch that our family added. The children also enhanced our rapport with the African staff, breaking down walls of formality and providing a subject of common interest in a society where parenthood is highly esteemed.

For most of the following year and a half we lived in a building rented by the University for its staff. The building was part of a federal low-cost housing project near the southeast edge of metropolitan Kano. Our second-floor flat overlooked Gyedi-Gyedi Quarter, a densely settled area two blocks wide and one mile long, combining elite and lower-class housing. Although this quarter is relatively new and far from the traditional walled city *(birni),* the heart of old Kano, it is in many ways a microcosm of metropolitan Kano. The residents are predominantly Muslim Hausa, mainly from the traditional walled city. However, there is also a large, mainly Christian minority of southern origin, many of whom have lived most of their adult lives in the north and speak fluent Hausa.

Life in these Zoo Road Flats (thus named because they are situated on the road leading to the zoo) posed a number of problems. We missed the campus's quiet groves and our daily walks in them. In addition, it was necessary to commute five miles each way to work and even to do some daily shopping. Since our compound did not include servants' quarters, it was difficult to arrange for dependable domestic help. Because Susanna worked in the campus library, we shared a number of household duties, or tried periodically, and unsuccessfully, to hire teenage boys to relieve us of some of these tasks. Electricity and water supplies were frequently interrupted, and I often hauled water from ground-level standpipes to satisfy our family's heavy demand. These time-consuming tasks sapped energy that I needed to prepare daily lectures, read research essays, and mark periodic exams. I was left with disappointingly little time to do research.

We also felt confined in the small apartment. The children had little space to play indoors, which gave rise to tensions and quarrels between them and put heavy strains on our flagging patience. Although they played in the compound yard with their friends, we placed limits on them. The yard was dusty and, with the problems in the water supply, frequent playing meant hauling more water for baths and laundry. We justified keeping them indoors on disciplinary and educational grounds for home lessons, for stories, and for educational television programs. But this resulted in a continual tug-of-war between Nina and her mother.

There were positive aspects to living there, such as the sense of solidarity with our neighbors that shared hardship had created. During the weekly electric failures, when evening work and television were impossible, neighbors gathered together to commiserate and converse late into the night. The children either stuck by our sides, listening to adult conversation, or moved about the compound with their friends playing games in the moonlight. It was at these times that I was reminded of the nightly neighborhood gatherings which are a regular feature of life in remote unelectrified African villages.

After a year and a half on Zoo Road, our long awaited house on the new Bayero campus finally became available. Although no academic departments had yet shifted to the new location, approximately four miles west of the old campus, about thirty families had settled into their new quarters. About half of this number were old friends from Zoo Road, whose presence, together with the very regular water and power supply, made our new home seem a relative paradise.

In contrast to our old quarters, our new environment is distinctly rural, with Fulani herdsmen daily driving their cattle through our back yard. Occasionally, camel herders cross through our campus, while our children gaze wide-eyed at these plodding but stately beasts. The children, like the cattle and camels, are now able to roam freely over the wide spaces together with their old playgroups from Zoo Road. The relief from the previously crowded conditions has relaxed the relations with our children, and a new housekeeper has greatly lightened our workload. As we settle down in this new, exhilarating environment, I look forward to my next two years at Bayero with hope for making more progress in my research and for discharging my teaching duties with greater energy.

PARENT AND PROFESSIONAL

Although the demands of parenting and professional development may compete with one another, they are often complementary. The experience gained by parents in their adaptation to field conditions contributes to personal and professional growth and often provides unplanned opportunities for observing aspects of the host culture. For example, meeting our family's daily needs has led me to make numerous shopping trips into the local neighborhood, where I meet diverse people, explore new corners of the area, and practice Hausa. And deeper and more elaborate insights have come from the discussions about socialization practices and problems with our Nigerian friends, with whom we share parental concerns. However, continual attention to and reflection upon these issues is necessary to extract the maximum benefit from the time-consuming job of parenting in the field, and to prevent our parenting from having a negative influence on our professional performance.

Local African values and social realities both encourage and direct the interaction of my parental and professional selves. First, the ethnic diversity of Nigeria and the process of migration to such urban centers as Kano have provided us with many neighbors who, like us, are raising children in a foreign environment. In addition, parenthood is one of the most socially significant aspects of adult status here. "How are the children (yaya yara)?" is often the first question asked after preliminary greetings. Meeting friends in the company of one's children almost inevitably leads the friends to exchange pleasantries with the children before turning their attention to other matters.(1) An expressed concern for a person's children indicates the goodwill that is necessary for proper and meaningful interaction. Another important factor is that most

Nigerians expect that their neighbors and kin will help them socialize their children. Collective responsibility is a general value in African patterns of childrearing. In the multi-ethnic and urban setting of Kano, it is often difficult to collaborate with neighbors in overseeing and disciplining one another's children because of the differences in values and language. My sharing people's concerns about our respective children's socialization makes it all that much more natural and productive to investigate this important element of their social and cultural life. It also provides insight and information that I may apply to my own parenting.

All of this has thrown light on the broader issue of how the socialization process hinges on the crucial balance between the home and the wider society. In the course of my present fieldtrip, one Igbo (southern Nigerian) mother told me that it was difficult for her to monitor her son's activities and to get him to report home at a certain time, as is traditional in her homeland. "Now that he is in Kano," she said, "he wants to run around town and keep late hours, just like Hausa boys." This is also a familiar theme with my wife and I as we struggle with our children to enforce limits that are often stricter than those of our neighbors.

This common contradiction between the values of home and the outside world is perhaps more acute and especially meaningful when they are the result of major differences of ethnic (national or racial) identity. The sensitivities and insights arising from parenting in the field and my resultant attention to childhood socialization have proven especially useful in pursuing my long-established research interests in migrant adaptation and ethnicity. As a parent, I am now more conscious of the migrant's parental concerns as a dimension of the adaptation process than it was possible to be as a bachelor researcher in Cameroon a decade ago.

Interviewing parents about childrearing is a particularly productive approach for understanding the extent and general significance of inter-ethnic differences. In addition, questions about childrearing in the multiethnic setting are usually easier to raise than other sensitive issues associated with ethnicity. They seem more legitimate and appropriate as well when they come from a fellow migrant-parent. The questions I ask focus on issues of ethnicity arising out of my perspectives and interests as a parent: What is it like to raise your children in Kano? Is it different from raising them in your home area? What do you know about how Hausa raise their children? What do you think about these practices? What problems arise in raising your children here? Do you think that your children will be similar to those raised in the south? Why?

My informants also ask questions about our socialization practices, such as: Do men or women take the major responsibility for disciplining children in the United States? How much exposure do our children get to my own culture as compared to that of my wife? Are our children bilingual? Such questions are useful in giving me outside perspectives on our childrearing styles and on my informants' concerns. And this reciprocity of inquiry enhances my rapport with my informants.

The southern migrant parents whom I have interviewed in Kano have been candid and eager to share their opinions and observations on socializing children in the north. Igbos, who vividly remember the violent confrontations with the Hausa which took place in the north in the mid-1960's, are quick to assure me that their children must learn tolerance and respect for other ethnic groups to ensure peaceful coexistence. However, like the Igbo mother discussed above, they are equally quick to emphasize differences between their own socialization values and their perceptions of what these are in outgroups. The same mother went on to talk about her son and, with some amusement, said that he was the only member of the family who spoke Hausa. She said he was sociable but not very scholarly, unlike her daughter who did not speak Hausa but was a very good student. This was verified by her husband who showed me the girl's carefully kept homework file. They pointed out that while it was good to maintain friendly relations with the host society, one should not sacrifice those values which are seen as central to the Igbo self-image--diligence, studiousness, and ambition--which might be jeopardized by mixing with the carefree Hausa children.

Whether these alleged differences exist or are as extreme as migrants maintain, is less important than the fact that they are believed to exist and that they reflect deep-seated ethnocentrism. Such attitudes and sterotypes toward Hausa persist among Igbos (and other migrants) partly because interethnic contact tends to be so superficial. As the migrants (and other non-kin) are barred by the rules of purdah (the practice of secluding married women) from access to the interior of Hausa compounds, they have few opportunities to observe socialization practices first-hand. Being outside the Islamic community, they are separated from the symbols, sentiments, shared understandings and ritual-ceremonial life of the Hausa which may well exaggerate perceived differences in socialization and other areas of life.

A number of personal and professional factors in our backgrounds have made my wife and I especially sensitive to ethnocentrism and its pitfalls: my anthropological training, my wife's exposure to her pastor father's international social network, and the opportunities we have both enjoyed by living several years outside our home cultures. In our marriage we have had to give allowance for cultural differences and to incorporate aspects of both of our cultures into lifestyle and childrearing practices. While the former had forced us to be objective, the latter implies laying down standards for evaluating, and then emphasizing some aspects of our respective background and deemphasizing others. Finding culturally neutral standards for making these evaluations and avoiding the temptation to impose our own cultural values is--as we both recognize--difficult to achieve on a daily basis.

But such contradictions in cultural values and standards have special relevance to me as an anthropologist: anthropologists steadfastly affirm that cultural relativism is an indispensable canon of ethnographic research.

And however much I, as an anthropologist, may struggle to minimize ethnocentric bias in my work and other social relationships, I recognize that socializing children presupposes value judgements, usually enforced with scant time to weigh alternatives or analyze the cultural basis of one's choices. Parenthood often demands that we take a firm normative stand. Non-parent anthropologists are free of this constraint and may be more intellectually and emotionally neutral. The tenet of cultural relativism provides us with no maps for guiding young children through the bewildering maze of behavioral and normative choices. Hence, I find that the parent-anthropologist who suspends his objectivity in his home life may well need to strive harder to maintain it in his professional life.

I must confess that it has not always been easy for me to come to terms with my own cultural biases in order to gain a more objective perspective on local styles of parenting. As the father of a seven-year-old daughter, I sometimes feel a paternal concern for her Hausa counterparts that may well limit my ability to analyze parental values and children's roles. For example, Hausa mothers in purdah use their children, mainly girls, as intermediaries to carry on trade with customers in the streets and other women in seclusion. From my point of view this has the negative consequences of exposing the girls to dangerous traffic in the streets and to possible sexual abuse, as well as interfering with their schooling.(2)

For Hausa, however, this hawking of prepared foods and petty commodities known as *talla* provides domestic income and funds for a girl's dowry. It also gives the girl opportunities to attract a potential husband. Hausa prefer that a girl marry at the onset of puberty, fearing that delaying her entry into the honorable status of wife and mother may lead to indiscipline and promiscuity. Prenubile Hausa girls dress like little women and often wear jewelry, cosmetics and plaited hair. The institution of *talla* gives them an opportunity to display their charms publicly, to flirt with young men and to advertise their impending availability as brides.

The preoccupation with the sexuality and marriageability of young girls reflected in *talla* runs counter to both American and other Nigerian values, particularly as seen in the western-oriented schools. Southern Nigerian girls wear short dresses, adorn themselves with simple earrings, and generally have boyish short-cropped hair. This is an image promoted by mission schools to emphasize studiousness and discourage precocious concern with attracting the opposite sex. It is also in keeping with the Euro-American definition of prenubile girls as children, a definition that grants them more time for physical, social and intellectual maturation.

However, when I take account of the system of cultural values in which *talla* is embedded--where feminine virtue is equated with the secluded married status and where early childhood responsibility is empha-sized--I am able to explore my own cultural biases about childrearing and the assumptions which form a western definition of childhood. These assumptions include the following: a) Children are qualitatively different from adults. They live in their own enchanted worlds which are largely inaccessible to the adults who try to "communicate" with them. Adults admire children's freedom and enthusiasm. b) Living in their own imaginary worlds, children are naturally and excusably irresponsible and should not be saddled with burdensome work and responsibilities, but encouraged to develop through formal education and creative play. c) In their "Never-Never Land" children are innocent and unconscious of threatening situations and thus require constant vigilance and parental protection. This protection can obviously only be provided by adults, who are aware of the real world's dangers. Parents should provide this protection because they have a commitment to and concern for their children that more distant kin or non-kin lack.

As an anthropologist, I allow that there is nothing self-evidently true about the foregoing assumptions. But as a parent, it is often difficult to restrain the concerns and anxieties which arise when I see them regularly violated. Through such encounters, however, I have learned that although ethnocentric indignation may hamper fieldwork and analysis, it can at least counterbalance the sin of taking phenomena for granted. It may even lead one to a more dispassionate analysis of cultural differences.

Moreover, cultural relativism is never total freedom from ethnocentrism, but rather, a carefully honed sensitivity and understanding of cultural bias as a pervasive predisposition both in ourselves and in those we study. While in Cameroon I visited a Nigerian migrant's home and was chatting with an Ibibio mother who, in sudden annoyance at his misbehavior turned to her child and admonished him not to behave like a Cameroonian. As a bachelor researcher I took no special note of the behavior which provoked this reaction; I viewed her remark as a classic case of using the outgroup as a negative example in socializing children (Levine and Campbell 1972: 18-19). This would appear to have a double function of reinforcing the positive image of the ingroup for both parent and child, while discouraging undesirable behavior by identifying the child with a stigmatized outgroup. Being free of parental concerns, I was preoccupied with ethnicity as the dominant theme in this situation, and it was not until I had gained on-the-ground experience as a father that I could understand the motivation which leads other parents to resort to such stratagems. While I would not advocate this approach to handling disciplinary problems, I can readily empathize with the annoyed parent who draws on stock home remedies as readily available as ethnic stereotypes, without stopping to consider their possible consequences.

Ethnocentric indoctrination is closely linked to the transmission of ethnic identity and, in fact, one process virtually implies the other. These processes occur through the medium of language, and acquiring fluency in one's natal tongue is itself one of the clearest markers of ethnic identity. Such fluency is taken for granted in the home area, but often becomes a matter of concern when migrants' children become more facile in the host community's language than in their natal tongue. Here are two examples of this: Igbo children raised in Cameroon tend to prefer using Pidgin English to Igbo and many Igbo reared in Kano, Nigeria, are more familiar with central Igbo than with their parents' own dialects. Igbo parents take pride in their own and their children's fluency in the home language and regret a child's inability to converse freely in their local dialect. Such a child, they say, will be awkward in the home village and a poor reflection on the parents' ability to maintain home traditions and the child's identification with them.

These migrants' concerns parallel my own desire for our children to maintain contact with my culture and to speak American English. Although we rationalize this concern in terms of ensuring their future success in American society, which seems to be Susanna's dominant motive, I may well be striving to impose my own ethnic identity and subconscious conviction that my culture's folkways are objectively superior.   For whatever combination of reasons, both of us seem to give more effort than we can rationally justify to purging our children's speech of Nigerian patterns of usage and pronunciation. As with migrant Igbos, this concern grew as we approached our first home leave. We wondered if my parents would understand the children or be shocked at their accent; if they would fit into their American peer group; and how our American friends and relatives would evaluate us as parents based on our children's ability or inability to adapt.

The international academic environment in which we live is also something of an island separate from the wider society. While we enjoy and learn much through our contact with expatriate friends, we often tire of their frequent complaints about Nigeria--the alleged low quality of local goods, bureaucratic inefficiency, job absenteeism, corruption, and (as I once heard) Nigerians' neglect of their lawns and gardens! Because of our different backgrounds, my wife and I are not drawn into ethnic cliques in Nigeria and are relatively free from ingroup pressures to take sides on interethnic issues. For many expatriates, however, these cultural biases are taken as axiomatic and a vital part of their ethnic identity--yet another example of the universal syndrome of ethnocentrism which reinforces a group's self-image by downgrading the outgroup. To some degree our family has provided a refuge from the expatriate cynicism that often seems to be the worst obstacle to outgrowing ethnocentrism and to overcoming culture shock. But to some extent our children have hindered this development of cross-cultural understanding.

Parenthood in the field often multiplies the impact of cultural and environmental shock because a family usually has more adaptations to make than a single researcher or married pair. Western parents of young children, especially, demand higher standards of comfort, safety and sanitation; this promotes more occasions for complaining and frustration. Interruptions of electricity and water supply are more keenly felt by our family than a single researcher. Likewise, we feel that we are more alarmed by cross-cultural differences in driving styles, in highway etiquette and in road safety, as well as problems of access to emergency medical care. All of these concerns have, in varying degree, delayed our recovery from culture shock, reinforcing old fears that the environment may be threatening to our children. And yet, if reacting negatively to the host culture makes us re-examine our own assumptions, it may yield some benefits.

Boissevain has observed (1970:70) that, "...a family provides an island which is part of another way of life." He goes on to say that this gives the researcher a vantage point from which to view the culture objectively, and not become "completely absorbed in local events". This point underscores the fact that maintaining cultural relativism is not merely controlling one's own ethnic biases but avoiding wholesale adoption of those of the host culture. One could go on to add that this insular portion of one's life also provides a convenient reference point for understanding one's own cultural biases; it makes the anthropologist-parent more self-conscious about his child-rearing style than he would be at home.

As a final observation on the effects of family life on field research, families provide companionship, as noted by Boissevain (ibid.;70). This fosters the researcher's psychic well-being and may therefore facilitate his optimal professional performance. Sharing perspectives on the host society, reciprocal support and collective goals in the family may cushion culture shock by giving life meaning and bolstering morale for overcoming adaptive problems.

To sum up this section, my experiences as a parent in the field have led me to examine more closely the uses of cultural relativity and ethnocentrism for myself and for my culturally distinct neighbors, and for understanding one's choice of values and behavior patterns to inculcate in children. Variations in the content of the socialization process are the basis of human social differentiation. But what that means now for such culturally and racially "mixed" families as our own, and for the world of increasingly interconnected societies that has made families like ours possible, is a critical issue of our times.

CHILDREN IN THE CROSS-CULTURAL SETTING

Whereas reflecting upon my own performance as parent and professional in the field has led me to one set of observations and insights, examining my children's experiences and behavior has led to a different, although related set. Since Alan has been so very young throughout the past two years, his experiences have been far less informative than Nina's and therefore occupy a smaller portion of the following narrative. The topics to be discussed here include our general acceptability as a family in the local social setting, the contrast between Nigerian and my own American patterns of discipline and parent-child relations, Nina's efforts to adjust to her African peer groups, and the possibility of differences between the experiences of an anthropologist's children and those of the children of other expatriates.

Our family's adaptation to the field has been made easier by the fact that the great majority of the people whom we have met have received us gracefully, and often with a good deal of interest. The fact that we are a culturally and racially "mixed" family seems to be viewed positively, and we have encountered no negative reactions. On the contrary, this has often put us and our children at an advantage in relating to Nigerians and expatriates alike. The only objection we encountered--if it can be called that--to our family's composition is its size. The concern about another's children that is expressed in normal greetings often extends to asking us "when are you going to have some more children?" In this society, where children are a collective concern and a couple's child-bearing functions are not the exclusive preserve of the nuclear family, this becomes an acceptable if not inevitable question.

In Africa our patterns of disciplining our children have become stricter than they were in America, partly as a result of our felt need to insure their health and safety. From time to time, they are reminded to keep their shoes on, stay out of the tall grass, and, above all, stay out of the streets. But we are also influenced by our need to fit into this society and to avoid negative reactions from Africans who are unaccustomed to Western children; thus, we have come to emphasize that our children exercise self-restraint and deference to adults.

We often remind Nina that she should defer her own gratifications, should yield to parental priorities, should listen more, should not disturb adult conversation, and should avoid the frequent American practice of calling adults by their first names, unless she prefaces the address with a respectful "Auntie" or "Uncle." She has also learned to use the widespread African convention of teknonymy, referring to and addressing adults with reference to their children, e.g., "Papa (of) Obi," or "Mama (of) Anna." This ingenious compromise equally avoids presumptuous overfamiliarity as well as the social distance implicit in the Mr./Mrs. form. Susanna does not encourage Nina to use the latter because she finds it overly formal and virtually a denial of relationship, quite inconsistent with the African genius for maximizing opportunities for generating meaningful human ties. Affirming these ties through forms of address which emphasize fictive kinship or links to peers and friends, on the other hand, implies human concern. This is consistent with the adult practice of greeting someone by inquiring about his or her children.

Our children's present need to adapt to Nigerian society, together with our desire to equip them with the social and academic skills needed to eventually reintegrate into American society, requires a flexible parenting style that somehow balances African with American expectations. This has made for some ambivalance in the definition of parent and child roles. Often we must make the choice between playing the stern, distant authority figure--more typically African--and the empathetic, communicative companion--a current middle class American ideal. For our children it is equally difficult to reconcile the divergent role expectations of both worlds. While the American child is generally allowed and encouraged to be a spontaneous, adventurous, imaginative explorer, his African counterpart is more often expected to be a respectful, responsible household deputy.

For those of us raised in the Euro-American tradition there seems to be an inconsistency between the African emphasis on early childhood responsibility and a child's status which is distinctly more subordinate than that of his Western counterpart. One explanation for this phenomenon is offered by Schildkrout (1980:481): "It seems that parental authority over children is greatest in those societies where children's economic contribution is most valued within a familial production unit." While children in these societies do have greater responsibility, firm parental authority insures that they carry out duties assigned to them by adults and not follow their own inclinations. According to Hake (1972:39):

> Because these religions (Islam and Christianity) stress the importance of children being obedient and respectful to their elders, most Nigerian parents and guardians demand unquestioning submission to their wills...The child, according to traditional and religious beliefs, is born imperfectly and if given his own way, he will do many foolish and harmful things not only to himself but to other people as well. Thus the Northern Nigerian parent believes it is his duty to curb the evil nature of his children.

Although this account falls short of providing a broad-based socio-cultural analysis of parental authority, it does suggest the relationship between firm authority and the perceived urgency to channel children's activities in productive directions. In contrast to Schildkrout, Hake attributes causal priority to religion and defines the objective of socialization primarily in moral rather than economic terms.

If we turn this argument around and attempt to view Western society from a hypothetical African visitor's perspective, an opposite paradox emerges. Why should Euro-Americans emphasize the distinctiveness of childhood as a developmental phase, downplaying responsibility, yet foster more egalitarian relations between children and adults? One probable explanation is the corollary of Schildkrout's observation: where children's economic contribution is less significant, parental authority is more relaxed. In addition, where children tend to follow their parents' occupations (as in many African families) they are seen as qualitatively similar to adults; in Africa the emphasis is on quantitative differences between children and adults. Age equals experience and authority. But in Western society, where occupational training is postponed and children tend not to follow in their parents' footsteps, the qualitative differences between parent and child are emphasized, while authority is downplayed to allow them to develop the flexibility and initiative needed to "make it" away from home.

One probable consequence of the Western emphasis on the "separate but equal" status of children is the generation gap and our preoccupation with bridging it. We find it difficult to communicate with children because they have their own activities, their own interests, their own fantasies which make them citizens of another world. Yet our democratic inclinations demand that we consider their opinions and give them access to our world. For most Africans this is hardly a problem because inter-generational communication is of little concern when children are immature, and as many have observed, this improves markedly with age--especially when one's children become parents themselves.

As an American father I feel an earnest need to communicate with my children, offer friendship and support their quest for self-actualization. To this extent I feel out of step with many African parents who seem to value conformity, to take the status differences between child and adult for granted and to worry less about the generation gap. Although coming to Africa has led us to emphasize discipline, we are also mindful of the dangers of excessive authoritarianism and alienating our children's loyalty and affection--an issue which seems to concern Africans less because they take their children's devotion for granted as a filial duty.

For Nina, understanding and adapting to new and often conflicting cultural expectations has sometimes been difficult. Although there have been some adjustments to changes in her home environment, this has, at least, remained more consistent than the outside milieu. Fortunately, she did not have to make much of a transition in school during her first year because she attended a school organized and taught by a British woman. The school met in the teacher's campus home; it was well-supplied with books and modern teaching aids. Although there was some need for cultural and language adjustment, since the children were nearly all British, the discipline and expectations were similar to those in the United States. During this year there were no obvious changes in her speech or patterns of social behavior, and her reading skills markedly improved.

When her teacher returned to Britain at year's end, Nina enthusiastically looked forward to starting Bayero Staff School. Although we had warned her that discipline would be a good deal stricter, this did not appear to give her much concern. She had long admired the bright purple school uniforms of her Staff School friends and when her mother sewed her own--complete with badge and matching head tie--she was ecstatic. Her first few weeks in the new school were fraught with culture shock. Her previous schools had not prepared her for her first encounter with the stern language and physical punishment which are part and parcel of the West African school experience. Her American accent and distinctive appearance had both advantages and disadvantages. Although many children took an active interest in her and became fast friends, others taunted her and excluded her from their play group. These hostile children called her an "Indian" and it soon became clear that there was frequent rivalry between the handful of South Asian children (Indians, Pakistanis, Sir

Lankans and Bangladeshis) and some African children. She responded by denying the Indian label and becoming "more African" by acculturating to local play and language styles. By the end of the first two months she seemed well-integrated into her peer group and her complaints about being teased virtually disappeared.

Nina learned a number of songs and games from her Nigerian friends. One of the most popular playground pastimes she enjoys is clapping-skipping-singing games played by girls in face-to-face pairs to the tunes of Hausa or English songs. She has also learned a number of Arabic prayers in her Islamic Religious Knowledge class--a standard feature of the northern Nigerian primary school curriculum.*(3)* She surprised us when she began to recite these spontaneously about the house. When she shows off her knowledge to our Muslim friends, they are duly impressed. Although non-Muslim children are not required to take religious classes, and are free to go elsewhere, when it became clear that she preferred to remain and to learn with her friends we raised no objection. We told her headmaster that we saw it as a positive factor in promoting her social integration and enhancing our own rapport with the Islamic community. Smiling approvingly, he responded, "Yes, and certainly all knowledge is useful."

Before Nina was enrolled in the Bayero Staff School she had little contact with her Hausa peers, and in the school she is able to interact freely with children of different ethnic backgrounds in English, the language of instruction. As with many expatriate children, Nina soon developed bilingual facility and shifted between American and Nigerian styles of English. At home we insist that she speak "American," quickly pointing out any lapses. With her American friends, she speaks nearly pure midwestern U.S. English. However, while she is playing with Nigerian friends and unaware of her eavesdropping parents, she shifts effortlessly to West African English. Consequently her knowledge of Hausa is limited to the few select words and phrases she has learned from friends and in her language class, which is given from time to time. However, she is eager to learn Hausa, takes pride in what she already knows, and given her intense sociability and penchant for imitation, will learn much more in the months ahead.

Discussing school experiences with Nina for the present paper was a personal reminder of the universal concerns and anxieties of children--the hunger of peer recognition and approval, the sting of insults and rejection, the lingering dread of the playground bully--all of which may be intensified in a new cultural environment. For Nina, living in America and moving to Africa has meant learning, and then relearning all the norms and lore of her peer group. Reflecting on her adaptation has sharpened my awareness of the profound influence which our children's peer culture--like all culture--has on their behavior and of their astounding human flexibility in adapting to new cultural environments.

Alan, our two-year-old, is more difficult to evaluate in terms of linguistic and social development. As he spends the overwhelming part of his day indoors and his range of friends has been limited, he is largely cushioned from local influences. We have noticed, however, that he is beginning to copy the speech patterns of his Igbo (southern Nigerian) baby sitter.

At this point, given their early ages, it is difficult to measure the possible effects of my being an anthropologist on my children. Certainly my career partly explains our being in Africa, but how does our family situation differ from that of non-anthropologist expatriates living here? Can I isolate the influence of whatever zeal I might harbor to deputize my children as junior participant-observers, from the effects of their mother's cultural background which automatically makes them participants? Although Nina recognizes that I am some sort of teacher—a role familiar to her as a schoolgirl—she is not yet old enough to understand my professional interests. She still resents the fact that I cannot read to her if there are exams to mark, or that we don't go to buy *kosai* (fried bean cakes) when I have a lecture to give. Although my academic pursuits often draw me away from the family circle, I try to set aside some time in the evening for the children. Occasionally, it is even possible to conveniently combine my professional and the children's interests. From time to time I read them Hausa folktales in which small and clever animals—spider, rabbit and jackal outwit large and powerful beasts—lion, leopard and elephant.

In general my observations on our attempts to reconcile African and American values concerning parent-child relations, and on Nina's own adjustment to Africa return to my original questions about how and to what extent a person can guide his children's socialization in a pattern of his own choosing that is also cross-culturally valid. As the examples here demonstrate, even if he could marshal the evidence to make and justify a particular course of action, the limits imposed by the world outside the family are enormous. As Americans, we worry greatly about our own responsibility to aid our child's self-actualization. But for an anthropologist, the tensions created among our own expectations, the values of others in an ethnically heterogeneous setting, and our actual social experiences of parenting in the field are a rich source of data.

CONCLUSION

Given the importance of the foregoing issues to us as anthropologists and as parents, we are hard pressed to explain our colleagues' relative silence on parenthood in the field. I suspect, however, that if we could conduct a survey it would reveal that most anthropological research has been carried out without accompanying children.*(4)* In the early years of the discipline, children were largely excluded from fieldwork because of considerations for their health, comfort and safety. Today much early-career and long-duration research is carried out by single scholars or those without children (often postponed for the duration of one's graduate program). Subsequent research may be too brief to yield much observational data, the scholar may be absorbed in his primary research problem, or the children are conveniently parked with the home-based spouse or grandparents.

There are also a host of personal and professional motives which deflect our attention away from these issues or make us reluctant to discuss them. If we find that bringing children into the field is burdensome, this seems to cast doubt on our professional competence. If they facilitate our integration into the host society, we might prefer to credit our own expertise. Talking about our families at all in a public forum does not come easily for most of us and discussing them in detail may reveal too much of ourselves for comfort. We seek security by cautiously keeping our academic posture, holding our professional personae close to our faces.

The fact that these papers have been written and presented seems a hopeful sign. Perhaps our discipline is now old enough, and we are beginning to feel sufficiently at ease with each other to examine our own participation.

ACKNOWLEDGEMENTS

I would like to acknowledge my debt to wife, Susanna Kleis, whose opinions and reflections form a substantial portion of this chapter. I am also grateful to Diane M. Turner and Barbara Butler for their stimulating and insightful suggestions.

REFERENCES

Beals, A. R. (1970). Gopalpur, 1958-60. In G. Spindler (Ed.), *Being an Anthropologist*, (pp. 32-57). New York: Holt, Rinehart and Winston.

Boissevain, J. (1970). Fieldwork in Malta. In G. Spindler (Ed.), *Being an Anthropologist*, (pp. 58-64). New York: Holt, Rinehart and Winston.

Hake, J. M. (1972). *Child-Rearing Practices in Northern Nigeria*. Ibadan, Nigeria: Ibadan University Press.

Hiskett, M. (1975). Islamic Education in the Traditional and State Systems of Northern Nigeria. In G. Brown and M. Hiskett (Eds.), *Conflict and Harmony in Education in Tropical Africa*, (pp. 134-151). London: Allen and Unwin.

Hostetler, J. A., and Huntington, G. E. (1970). The Hutterites: Fieldwork in a North American Communal Society. In G. Spindler (Ed.), *Being an Anthropologist*, (pp. 194-219). New York: Holt, Rinehart and Winston.

Levine, R. A. and Campbell, D. T. (1972). *Ethnocentrism: Theories of Conflict, Ethnic Attitudes and Group Behavior*. New York: John Wiley and Sons.

Schildkrout, W. (1980). Children's Work Reconsidered. *International Social Science Journal*, (32):479-489.

Spindler, G. (1970). *Being an Anthropologist: Fieldwork in Eleven Cultures*. New York: Holt, Rinehart and Winston.

NOTES

(1) The Beals' reverse culture shock on their return flight from India when they encountered their American fellow passengers' indifference to their children rings true for parents who have worked in Africa (Beals, 1970, p. 55).

(2) It should be added that many Hausa are highly critical of *talla* and argue that a proper understanding of Islam endorses the education of women.   *Talla* is by no means universal among Hausa girls (it is found mainly in non-elite families) and will likely decline due to the current trends toward wider availability and acceptance of female education.

(3) Despite this concession to the dominant religion, the curriculum of the Staff and Local Government Area schools is overwhelmingly secular and, from the viewpoint of many religious teachers, too Western-oriented (Hiskett, 1975, p. 144).   There are, however, many Islamic schools which operate either as alternatives or as supplements to the secular systems.

(4) Six of the twelve contributions to the volume, *Being an Anthropologist* (Spindler, 1970) mention taking children into the field.   Only two of these, Boissevain's and Hostetler and Huntington's, discuss the interrelationship of parenthood and research in any degree of detail.   Both authors found that being parents conferred full adult status and credit their children with contributing insights while extending their range of contacts with informants.

AUTHOR INDEX

American customs
  appreciation of, 47
Anthropological field research
  advantages and disadvantages of,
    133-136
  and attempts to minimize ethno-
    centric bias, 146
  and childlike status, 108
  effects on children, 81
  effects on family, 93-94, 119, 152
  effects on language acquisition,
    131-132
  and enculturation of fieldworker's
    children, 102-104
  influence of researcher, 74, 93-94,
    109-110
  reasons for including children, 117-
    118, 124-125; 133-136
  and researcher's fears for children,
    78-81, 104; special nature of, 32
  traditional emphases, 75
  and sense of powerlessness, 109
Caste system
  animosities toward, 45
Child rearing
  and absence of sibling rivalry, 46
  and childbearing in India, 43
  and children's will, 60
  and conflict with professional roles
    of parents, 32
  cultural biases about, 146
  among the Hutterites, 53-69
  among the Igbo, 147-148
  and interviewing parents, 144
  and love of children, 48
  and sex categorization of children,
    43
  and use of affection
  and use of punishment, 60
Children
  and anthropological fieldwork
    positive and negative con-
      sequences of, 8-15, 148
    securing parents' adult status, 27
  and anthropologist parents
    in Australia, 6, 9
    in Brazil, 4
    in Cameroon, 139, 147-148

in Canada, 6
in Colombia, 12
in the Dominican Republic, 11
in Ecuador, 73-94
in Fiji, 25, 99-113
in Guatemala, 11
among the Hutterites, 9, 53-69
in India, 10, 31-49
in Japan, 10
in Lebanon, 6
among the Menomini, 10
in Mexico, 4-5
among the Navajo, 12
in Nigeria, 6, 138-154
in the Pacific Islands, 8
in Rhodesia, 6
in Serbia, 12
in the Sudan, 13
in Taiwan, 11
in Uganda, 6-7
in the United States, 10-12, 16
and family socialization, 57
and folkcures for illness, 42
negative views of, 34
and parental conflicts in the
  field, 54
Class status
  and socialization values, 77
Colombians
  characteristics of, 123
  contrast with Mexican city life,
    127
  intimate relations with, 124
  the Popayans, 118-128, 132-136
  school experiences of, 128-129
Cultural discontinuities: 138
Cultural incongruity
  and discipline of children, 83
Cultural relativity
  and ethnographic research, 19, 145,
    147, 149
  and objectivity, 111-112
  and questions of compliance, 19
Ecuadorian
  bases of adult status, 88-89
  belief in Indian inferiority, 86
  Hispanics and separation from
    Indians, 87